W9-AUO-163

Industrial
Revolution
Almanac

Industrial
Revolution
Almanac

James L. Outman
Elisabeth M. Outman
Matthew May, Editor

THOMSON
GALE

Detroit • New York • San Diego • San Francisco • Cleveland • New Haven, Conn. • Waterville, Maine • London • Munich

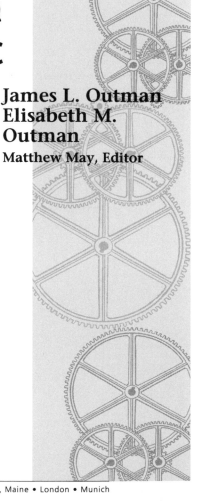

Industrial Revolution: Almanac

James L. Outman and Elisabeth M. Outman

Project Editor
Matthew May

Permissions
Lori Hines

Imaging and Multimedia
Robert Duncan, Lezlie Light

Product Design
Pamela A. E. Galbreath, Michelle DiMercurio

Composition
Evi Seoud

Manufacturing
Rita Wimberley

LIBRARY OF CONGRESS CATALOGING-IN-PUBLICATION DATA

Outman, James L., 1946–

Industrial Revolution. Almanac / James L. Outman and Elisabeth M. Outman.

    v. cm.

  Includes bibliographical references and index.

    ISBN 0-7876-6513-4 (hardcover : alk. paper)

    1. Industrial revolution—Juvenile literature. [1. Industrial revolution.] I. Outman, Elisabeth M., 1951– II. Title.

HD2329 .O978 2003
330.9'034—dc21

2002155422

Printed in the United States of America
10 9 8 7 6 5 4 3 2 1

Contents

Reader's Guide

The Industrial Revolution, which began in England in the middle of the eighteenth century and spread across the globe by the beginning of World War II, shaped a new world. The introduction of new technology into manufacturing processes at the heart of the revolution turned simple agricultural societies into complex industrial ones. Consequently, the way we worked, where we lived, and how we communicated with one another were altered. Governments, even the physical environment of the planet, were forever changed. The Industrial Revolution was in every sense a revolution.

Industrial Revolution: Almanac, in eight chapters, provides an overview of this era, from its roots in the philosophies of the Renaissance to the first technological advances, from the first migrations of workers to urban areas to the rise of giant corporations. Each chapter of the *Almanac* features informative sidebar boxes highlighting glossary terms and issues discussed in the text and concludes with a list of further readings. Also included are nearly sixty illustrations, a timeline, a glossary, and an index providing easy access to subjects discussed throughout *Industrial Revolution: Almanac.*

Related reference sources

Industrial Revolution: Biographies profiles twenty-five significant figures of the Industrial Revolution. The essays cover such people as economic philosophers Karl Marx and Adam Smith; innovators like Henry Bessemer, Henry Ford, Robert Fulton, and Eli Whitney; financial wizards Andrew Carnegie and J. P. Morgan; and crusading journalists such as Upton Sinclair and Ida Tarbell. The volume includes more than fifty photographs, sources for further reading, a timeline, and an index.

Industrial Revolution: Primary Sources presents twenty-seven full or excerpted written works, speeches, and testimony from the period. The volume includes excerpts from *An Inquiry into the Nature and Causes of the Wealth of Nations* by Adam Smith, *The Communist Manifesto* of Karl Marx, *Twenty Years at Hull-House* by Jane Addams, and the United States Supreme Court decision in *Northern Securities Co.* v. *United States* enforcing federal regulation of corporations. Each entry includes an introduction, things to remember while reading the excerpt, a glossary of difficult terms from the document, information on what happened after the work was published, and other interesting facts. Forty photographs, sources for further reading, a timeline, and an index supplement the volume.

Acknowledgments

The authors extend their thanks to U•X•L senior editor Diane Sawinski, U•X•L editor Matthew May, and U•X•L publisher Tom Romig for their assistance throughout the production of this series. Thanks, too, to Judy Galens for lending her editorial talents in the form of proofreading. The editor wishes to thank Marco Di Vita of the Graphix Group for always working with flexibility, speed, and, above all, quality.

Comments and suggestions

We welcome your comments on *Industrial Revolution: Almanac* and suggestions for other topics in history to consider. Please write: Editors, *Industrial Revolution: Almanac*, U•X•L, 27500 Drake Road, Farmington Hills, Michigan, 48331-3535; call toll-free: 800-877-4253; fax to 248-699-8097; or send e-mail via www.gale.com.

Industrial Revolution Timeline

1650–51 The British Parliament passes the Navigation Acts, designed to give preference to English merchant ships over the Dutch.

1631 David Ramsay receives a patent from the British government for a pump that is driven by heated water that is converted into steam.

1674 Jethro Tull is born. Tull is credited with developing the first seed drill.

1690 English philosopher John Locke writes that governments derive their power from the people.

1712 Thomas Newcomen builds his first steam engine in England.

1764 James Hargreaves invents a new version of the traditional spinning machine.

1765 The first iron rails are introduced in England by Richard Reynolds.

1776 Adam Smith's *An Inquiry into the Nature and Causes of the Wealth of Nations* is published.

1781 James Watt invents a rotary motion device for his steam engine.

1793 Eli Whitney develops and introduces the cotton gin.

June 14, 1798 Eli Whitney signs a contract with the U.S. government to produce 10,000 muskets in 28 months.

1779 Samuel Crompton introduces the spinning machine, combining the efforts of earlier machines in the production of cotton products.

1802 Richard Trevithick develops the steam locomotive.

August 17, 1807 Robert Fulton launches his steamship *Clermont*. Two years later he obtains a patent from the U.S. government for his steamship.

1823 Richard Guest's *Compendious History of the Cotton Manufacture* is published.

1824 Englishman Robert Owen purchases the town of New Harmony, Indiana, and attempts to implement his cooperative business ideas in an entire community.

September 27, 1825 George Stephenson operates his locomotive *Locomotion* along a 20-mile rail in England, the first time a steam locomotive hauls cars on a public railway.

1832 The British Parliament passes the Reform Bill of 1832, radically changing the system of representation in Parliament.

1833 Member of Parliament Michael Sadler issues a report to Parliament detailing working conditions of children in British factories.

1833 The British Parliament passes the Factory Act of 1833, setting standards for the employment of children in textile factories.

1834 Cyrus McCormick takes out a patent on the first mechanical reaper.

May 1, 1844 Samuel F. B. Morse sends the first telegraph message from Washington, D.C., to Baltimore, Maryland. Five years later he is granted a patent for his invention.

1848 *The Communist Manifesto,* written by Karl Marx and his friend Frederich Engels, is published.

1856 Henry Bessemer establishes the Bessemer process, in which steel could be made in more quantities for less money.

1869 George Westinghouse takes out a patent on his invention of the air brake and forms Westinghouse Air Brake Company.

1869 Uriah Stephens and fellow garment workers in Philadelphia, Pennsylvania, found the Noble Order of the Knights of Labor.

May 10, 1869 A golden spike is driven into the railroad tracks at Promontory, Utah, completing the first rail line to cross the United States.

1870 John D. Rockefeller and associates organize Standard Oil Company.

1879 Thomas Alva Edison lights street lights along a half-mile stretch in Menlo Park, New Jersey.

1881 Samuel Gompers helps establish the Federation of Organized Trades and Labor Unions of the United States and Canada.

1886 A bomb explodes during a labor union rally at Haymarket Square in Chicago, Illinois, killing seven.

1889 German engineer Gottlieb Daimler develops an engine that resembles the motors in modern-day automobiles.

1890 The U.S. Congress passes the Sherman Antitrust Act.

1890 Mary Harris Jones, better known as Mother Jones, is hired as a paid organizer by the United Mine Workers.

1890 *How the Other Half Lives* by Jacob Riis is published.

1892 Steel workers at Andrew Carnegie's Homestead Mill plant go on strike; violence breaks out and eighteen strikers and guards are killed.

1894 Workers of the Pullman railroad car company strike to demand fair wages. Other railroad workers go on strike in support, shutting down U.S. railroads. U.S. president Grover Cleveland sends in 12,000 troops to restore railroad traffic, and most of the strikers return to their jobs at their original wages.

1901 J. P. Morgan purchases Carnegie Company, Limited, the nation's leading steel company, for $480 million.

February 18, 1904 The Theodore Roosevelt administration files a lawsuit against Northern Securities, claiming it is an illegal trust and in violation of the Sherman Antitrust Act.

1904 Ida Tarbell's collection of articles on John D. Rockefeller is published as a book entitled *The History of the Standard Oil Company.*

1905 The term smog is first used in London, England, to describe the unhealthy nature of the air due to the smoky output of factories.

1906 Upton Sinclair's *The Jungle* is published.

October 1908 Henry Ford introduces the Model T.

1911 American engineer Frederick Taylor publishes *The Principles of Scientific Management,* a collection of essays on the organization of industrial companies.

March 25, 1911 A fire at the Triangle Shirtwaist Company in New York, New York, kills 146 female workers.

1914 Henry Ford begins paying his workers $5 a day.

1919 Henry Ford resigns as president of the Ford Motor Company.

1929 The stock market plummets and sends the United States and most of the industrialized world into the Great Depression. By 1932, 25 percent of American workers will be jobless.

1935 The Congress of Industrial Organizations is founded, a federation of labor unions.

1935 The National Labor Relations Act is passed, giving workers the right to organize unions and strike in order to influence their employers to create better working conditions.

1939 World War II breaks out in Europe. Within two years the American economy is invigorated.

1945 Nuclear bombs are dropped on Japan to bring an end to World War II. The world enters a new, nuclear, age.

Words to Know

A

Absolute monarch: A ruler who is not controlled by law.

Anarchism: A social philosophy that advocates voluntary associations among people as a form of self-government, as opposed to central governments dominated by a monarch or other central figure.

Apprentice: A person learning the basics of a skilled trade, such as masonry (working with brick or stone) or weaving.

Aristocrat: Someone who controls land and the people who live on it. Aristocrats generally inherited their positions from their fathers (occasionally from their mothers).

Assembly line: A system of manufacturing goods in which many workers, often arranged in different stations along a line, carry out the same precise task over and over on multiple products, as opposed to a single worker carrying out many tasks on one product.

Automation: A process designed so that one event follows another without active intervention; usually such processes involve machines that carry out tasks by design, rather than with human intervention.

C

Capitalism: A system of organizing a society's economy in which ownership of machines and factories is private, rather than public.

Communism: A form of government in which all the people own property, including both land and capital, in common.

Corporation: A business organization that is given the right to act as if it were a person in certain legal matters, such as buying or selling things or entering into binding agreements (contracts).

Cottage industry: The economic system in which skilled craftspeople manufactured goods, such as cloth, from their homes rather than in factories. This scenario was typical of the period before the Industrial Revolution.

D

Democracy: A political system in which a majority of the people determine the government and its policies, as opposed to governments determined, for example, by inheritance (such as those run by kings and aristocrats).

E

Economy of scale: The reduction in cost of a product resulting from mass production.

F

Factories: Buildings used for manufacturing products.

Feudalism: A social and political system prevalent in Europe from about 400 to 1500, in which aristocrats, or lords, controlled the land and in which so-called common people (known as serfs) were legally bound to work on the land under the direction of the aristocrat and with the benefit of his protection.

G

Guilds: Associations of skilled craftsmen that set rules and standards for their work. Guild members generally advanced from apprentice (beginner) to journeyman (ordinary worker) to master, the highest level.

I

Industrialization: The process of introducing machines to supplement or replace human labor.

Interchangeable parts: Identical components of a product that are produced separately from the product itself and then assembled.

L

Labor union: A voluntary association of workers who join together to apply pressure on their employer for improved pay, shorter hours, or other advantages.

Laissez-faire: A French expression meaning "free to do," referring to the belief that governments should let economic activity take place without interference.

Loom: A machine, sometimes called a frame, used to weave fabric.

M

Mass production: Making large numbers of identical products, often using a system like an assembly line in a factory, rather than making products one at a time.

Medieval period: Another name for the Middle Ages (500 to 1400), the period from about the end of the Roman Empire to the beginning of the Renaissance.

Mercantilism: An economic system in which government manages national economies by regulating trade, agriculture, and manufacturing with the aim of accumulating wealth. It was a system criticized by England's Adam Smith, who argued that people acting in their self-interest would result in the greatest good for the greatest number of people.

Microchips: A tiny complex of connected electronic components produced on a small slice of material. Microchips are the basic building block of computers.

Monopoly: A business large enough to be able to control the price of a product without regard to competition.

Muckraker: A journalist who focuses on uncovering corruption, abuse, or other wrong-doing. The term is most often applied to a group of journalists writing about business practices in the late 1890s and early 1900s.

N

Natural laws: The rules, thought to be taken from nature, by which the universe operates.

P

Patent: A permit given to an inventor allowing exclusive rights to make, use, or sell an invention.

Pension: A monthly payment made to employees who retire from a company after reaching a certain age or after working a certain number of years for that company.

Proletariat: Lowest economic or social class of a community.

R

Reaper: A machine for gathering grain that is ready to harvest.

Renaissance: A period in European history from about 1400 to 1700 in which classical (ancient Roman and Greek) ideas about art, literature, and other intellectual pursuits began to replace long-held religious beliefs.

Robber baron: The owner and manager of a very large business that was judged to be a monopoly.

S

Service economy: An economic system in which most people are engaged in helping or serving other people, rather than raising food or manufacturing products.

Socialism: A political and economic system in which the people control both the government and also major elements of the economy, such as owning (or tightly regulating) factories.

Social work: Efforts to alleviate a variety of problems often encountered by poorer people such as unemployment, poverty, and lack of housing.

Spinning: Twisting the short fibers of wool or cotton into a continuous yarn.

Strike: The refusal to work by members of a labor union who aim to close down a factory or other facility as a means of putting pressure on the employer to grant higher pay or other improvements in work conditions.

Strikebreakers: Workers who take the places of employees who are on strike. They are hired by company owners in an effort to defeat strikers.

T

Tariff: A tax on imports.

Textile industry: The manufacture of cloth, typically for clothing but also for other purposes, such as bedsheets and sails.

W

Weaving: Making yarn into cloth by crisscrossing threads of yarn on a loom.

Industrial Revolution
Almanac

Introduction

Starting in the mid-1700s in England, a series of inventions sparked the biggest change in human life since tools first had been used in the growing of crops thousands of years earlier. These inventions caused profound changes in the ordinary lives of people and in the way society is organized. The entire process—technical innovation and social change taken together—is called the Industrial Revolution.

These changes, which are still being felt at the beginning of the twenty-first century, came in two stages. The first stage, sometimes called the first Industrial Revolution, lasted from about 1750 until about 1850 and took place largely in England. It was dominated by two developments in technology: the steam engine driven by coal and machines used to make textiles, or cloth.

The second stage, sometimes called the second Industrial Revolution, lasted from about 1850 until about 1940 and occurred primarily in the United States as well as in continental Europe. It was dominated by two new sources of power: the internal combustion engine and electricity.

Life in Europe was once dominated by peasants, such as the Russian serfs depicted here, living on the land, sowing and reaping crops as they had for centuries. *Reproduced by permission of the Corbis Corporation.*

In addition to the introduction of new sources of power and machinery, the Industrial Revolution resulted in new ways of thinking about work. The process of making things began to be viewed in terms of a system: machines and people functioning together in workplaces, typically in factories as parts of a factory system. Previously, goods had been manufactured by individual craftspeople working at home. The system approach was introduced gradually, starting in the late 1700s and progressing steadily into the twenty-first century. It is difficult to overemphasize how important this change has been. It has affected the way people view their work and the way they view one another, in the workplace, in society, and in government.

Some observers have suggested that the introduction of computers and the Internet in the last half of the twentieth century will prove to be yet a third stage of the Industrial Revolution, in which a machine takes over parts of human mental activity, just as machines earlier took over parts of human physical activity.

The nature of technical change

Technology was a critical element in the Industrial Revolution, though by no means the only element. The fundamental technical developments associated with the Industrial Revolution occurred in four areas:

- **Mechanical power.** Mechanical power was derived first from the steam engine, which burned coal to heat water to create the steam that powered the engine, and later from engines that burned oil (internal combustion engines) or ran on electricity (often generated by burning coal).

- **Manufacturing.** Manufacturing resulted in the shift from handmade to machine-made, and from homemade to factory-made, goods.

- **Transportation.** Horses, mules, and oxen were replaced by railroads and steamships driven by steam engines, and by cars, trucks, and eventually airplanes powered by oil.

- **Communications.** Messages carried by people were replaced by instantaneous communication over long distances via telegraph, telephone, and, much later, the Internet.

Alongside the Industrial Revolution was an agricultural revolution, which brought similar changes to agricultural practices—the introduction of technology to manual farming, new procedures that greatly increased the output of both farmers and their land—and resulted in new attitudes toward the relationship between "natural" and "scientific" farming. The combination of new systems and new technology was first introduced on English farms around 1700 and has over the years greatly increased the productivity of farmers and the land. The agricultural revolution has also changed humankind's relationship to animals and food and, to some extent, to the basic process of eating.

Social changes

Changes in technology helped drive major changes in the way people lived and worked and, later, in the way government was organized and controlled.

The Industrial Revolution changed the relationship of workers to their jobs and to the products they made. Previously, skilled workers ran small family businesses, spinning thread and weaving cloth at home under contracts with merchants. In the late 1700s these so-called cottage industries began to be replaced by much larger enterprises, housed in factories, in which machinery supplemented or replaced human skills and energy. People were hired to operate the machines and were paid wages based on how many hours they worked, rather than on their output. Workers, unlike craftspeople, had no influence on the nature of the products that were being made. The factory system, one of the most important results of the Industrial Revolution, increased worker productivity but also dramatically changed the nature of work.

The factory system also introduced changes in the structure of society. Until the Industrial Revolution, wealth, prestige, and political power lay in the hands of the aristocracy, people who controlled large tracts of land and those living on that land. By the late 1800s many aristocrats had been replaced by a relative handful of extremely wealthy owners of business enterprises. In the United States, where there had never been an established aristocracy, the new power structure gave rise to the "robber barons," as wealthy industrialists were known. They included such men as Andrew Carnegie (steel), John D. Rockefeller (oil), and J. P. Morgan (banking), all of whom used their positions to stifle competition and manipulate prices to their enormous advantage. Such actions prompted the government to move to control the power and influence of the most dominant business owners.

At the level of the individual factory, workers came to be viewed as parts of the larger machine. Factory employees were paid barely enough to stay alive, and it was common for children as young as six to work many hours a day, six days a week. The idea that humans were part of the machinery did not always sit well with the workers, and the resulting tension helped set the stage for new challenges to fundamental ideas of private property and the rights of individuals in the context of a larger society.

Another part of the story involves how business was organized. At first, individual entrepreneurs (people who start and own businesses) bought machines and hired people to work them. Later, groups of individuals pooled their funds

to purchase expensive machines and build factories, and to share their profits. These enterprises were called "corporations," a word that implies that the business has some of the characteristics and rights of a person. Eventually, the interests of this artificial person, the corporation, came to dominate the interests of any one person working there. While individual managers might question the morality of certain actions or policies, the corporation has no emotions or feelings, just a set of numbers that tells its shareholders whether it is making a profit.

The combined results of the Industrial Revolution and the agricultural revolution meant that over a period of two hundred years, vastly more people came to live in cities, where the majority of the factories were being built, as opposed to the countryside, where increased farm productivity lessened the need for agricultural workers. And as the total population of industrialized countries grew enormously, society changed drastically: a society coming to be dominated by

In modern-day America, few people (such as the Amish) still use horse-drawn carriages. The substitution of the power of a horse for the horsepower of a car was one of the significant changes brought about by the Industrial Revolution. *Reproduced by permission of Getty Images.*

The Idea of Progress

For many people in the twenty-first century, time seems to progress along a straight line. We can look back, thanks to history books, and see a previous time (say, 1800) that was "then" and envision a future time (for example, 2100) that will be different. A whole category of books called science fiction is about the future, rather than about the present or the past.

But several hundred years ago, time was not envisioned as a straight line. Instead, it was seen as a circle, largely based on the seasons. People living on farms planted in the spring, watched crops grow in summer, harvested in the autumn, and rested in the winter until the cycle began all over again. Each year was much like the one before and the one after. Life did not change from year to year, not even from generation to generation. Of course, new individuals would fulfill certain roles in society: a king or another aristocrat might die and be succeeded by his son (for a long time, women were not allowed to own property and rarely held positions of importance), but the basic social roles of the king, the aristocrat, the farm laborer, and the craftsperson were the same year after year. Any changes that might come about—such as those effected by the Magna Carta (1215), a document that gave more influence to the British aristocrats at the expense of their king—seemed remote from the lives of most people.

This cyclical aspect of life affects the way people think. If there has been no real change for generations, people tend not to think about bringing about change, except perhaps on the individual level (a farmer's son might become a craftsman in town, for instance). The idea of progress thickly settled cities was quite different from one that had been dominated by people living on farms or in small towns.

Political changes

The dislocations brought about by the movement of people to cities and the rise of factories as a source of wealth came together to diminish the power and influence of the old aristocracy, including kings and queens, that had arisen in Europe in the Middle Ages (roughly 500 to 1400). Instead, business owners and, later, workers assumed domination over government. At first, factory owners fought for a greater voice in and influence over government affairs. Later, beginning in the mid-1800s, voices were raised on behalf of the rights of workers. The does not exist; it does not describe anyone's practical experience.

Cultural and political developments starting with the Renaissance (a period of intellectual and artistic rebirth from about 1400 to 1700) and leading up to the Industrial Revolution changed people's way of thinking, just as everyday life started changing dramatically. One key element was a new invention, the steam engine, which came about in part because in Britain, ancient forests of oak had all been chopped down for firewood, and a new means of heating homes was needed. Coal was found to be a substitute, but mining coal required pumps to keep the mines free from the groundwater that seeped into them. Thus a mechanized pump was the motivation for the first practicable steam engine built by Thomas Newcomen in 1712.

Now time began to be viewed differently, as a straight line, in which the machinery available in one year might be different, and better, the next year, or in five years. One machine inspired an improved version, or the application of the same principle to some other activity. These modifications brought changes to people's lives, the first in hundreds of years. Farmers found themselves living in towns or cities. Craftspeople saw factories producing cloth and other goods. Merchants became factory owners. And these changes in the way people lived led to changes in the way they governed themselves. People could imagine a future that might look very different from the present, and they started pushing for improvements in all aspects of their lives. Humankind's perception of time itself had undergone a revolution.

dramatic changes affecting workers raised a number of questions: Does ownership of a machine or factory give the owner the right to abuse his workers? To what extent should government interfere in the voluntary relationship between a business owner and his employees? Should workers have the right to join together to assert influence over their conditions of employment? If workers have that right, what about factory owners?

The struggle between business owners and workers for political influence and power continues, even as the landowning aristocracy of the Middle Ages is largely a thing of the past except perhaps in the British House of Lords, part of Britain's Parliament, or governing body. Modern notions of democracy are firmly rooted in the social changes resulting from the Industrial Revolution.

Origins of the Industrial Revolution

1

Some revolutions have famous starting dates. On April 19, 1775, a band of North American colonists fired on British soldiers on Lexington Green in Massachusetts—the "shot heard 'round the world" that launched the American Revolution. The next year, on July 4, 1776, these colonists declared their independence. On July 14, 1789, a mob stormed the Bastille prison in Paris, France, sparking the French Revolution. In November 1917, Russian Communists seized power from the monarchy in Moscow to ignite the Russian Revolution.

But the Industrial Revolution did not start with a formal declaration, or with mobs storming a fortress of the old order, or with dramatic speeches and slogans that would move the hearts and minds of men and women for generations afterward.

Instead, the Industrial Revolution took place one small step at a time over a period of more than two hundred years. A pattern developed in which one individual designed a new machine (such as the steam engine or the spinning jenny, a machine used to make cloth), another individual started a business using the machine in a factory, and a fami-

Words to Know

Apprentice: A person learning the basics of a skilled trade, such as masonry (working with brick or stone) or weaving.

Aristocrat: Someone who controls land and the people who live on it. Aristocrats generally inherited their positions from their fathers (occasionally from their mothers).

Cottage industry: The economic system in which skilled craftspeople manufactured goods, such as cloth, from their homes rather than in factories. This scenario was typical of the period before the Industrial Revolution.

Democracy: A political system in which a majority of the people determine the government and its policies, as opposed to governments determined, for example, by inheritance (such as those run by kings and aristocrats).

Empiricism: The belief that knowledge derives from examining subjects.

Feudalism: A social and political system prevalent in Europe from about 400 to 1500, in which aristocrats, or lords, controlled the land and so-called common people (known as serfs) were legally bound to work on the land under the direction of the aristocrat and with the benefit of his protection.

Guilds: Associations of skilled craftspeople that set rules and standards for their work. Guild members generally advanced from apprentice (beginner) to journeyman (ordinary worker) to master, the highest level.

Laissez-faire: A French expression meaning "free to do," referring to the belief that governments should let economic activity take place without interference.

Medieval period: Another name for the Middle Ages (500 to 1400), the period from about the end of the Roman Empire to the beginning of the Renaissance.

Mercantilism: An economic system in which government manages national economies by regulating trade, agriculture, and manufacturing with the aim of accumulating wealth. It was a system criticized by England's Adam Smith, who argued that people acting in their self-interest would result in the greatest good for the greatest number of people.

Natural laws: The rules, thought to be taken from nature, by which the universe operates.

Renaissance: A period in European history from about 1400 to 1700 in which classical (ancient Roman and Greek) ideas about art, literature, and other intellectual pursuits began to replace long-held religious beliefs.

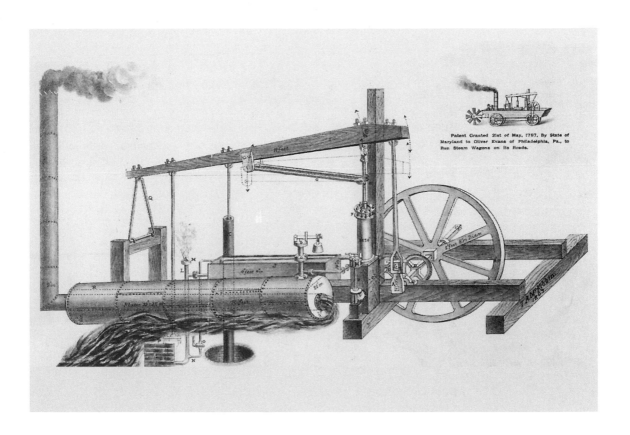

Patent Granted 21st of May, 1787. By State of Maryland to Oliver Evans of Philadelphia, Pa., to Run Steam Wagons on Its Roads.

ly moved to a town from the countryside to work in the new factory. Multiplied thousands of times, this series of events was the Industrial Revolution.

In this way, the Industrial Revolution came to touch the lives of nearly everyone, although initially most people did not realize they were living through a "revolution." That phrase came into popular use in the late 1800s after it was introduced by British sociologist Arnold Toynbee (1852–1883) at least a century after the process had begun.

Historians often say the Industrial Revolution started around 1750 or 1760. One symbolic moment for the start of the Industrial Revolution was the morning in 1754 when a Scottish teenager named James Watt (1736–1819) left his home in the small town of Greenock. Jamie Watt was eighteen years old, and he planned to make scientific instruments for a living. He set off for the nearby city of Glasgow to find someone to teach him the finer points of the trade.

An early steam engine wagon. *Reproduced by permission of the Library of Congress.*

It is a modest beginning for a revolution. But in the course of the next fourteen years, Watt tapped into a rapidly growing body of scientific knowledge and designed a new type of steam engine that would revolutionize the world by substituting the energy trapped in coal for muscle power.

It is an oversimplification, though, to say that Watt's design for a more efficient steam engine was the sole cause of the Industrial Revolution. The process was infinitely more complex. His engine, however, was the key invention that got the action started.

Great Britain in 1754 was on the edge of the greatest change in human behavior since prehistoric man fashioned a tool from a stick and stone. The world had been changing rapidly and dramatically for the past 350 years, changes that, taken together, eventually transformed society.

Setting the stage

The Industrial Revolution did not spring up overnight. Instead, it was a logical next step after several hundred years of developments in Europe that gradually replaced the medieval period (also known as the Middle Ages, from 500 to 1400) with the so-called modern era. These changes included dramatic new ways of thinking about the role of human beings in the world, their religion, and their relationships with one another. Without these preparatory changes, it is almost impossible to imagine the Industrial Revolution taking place. In parts of the world that did not undergo these changes, the Industrial Revolution never took root.

The Renaissance

Beginning around 1400, western Europe entered a period of radical alteration after hundreds of years during which little change had taken place. This period of change is called the Renaissance, meaning "rebirth." The Renaissance involved artists, scientists, and political thinkers—initially in Italy, then throughout Europe—who began looking at the world in a new way. Many features of the Renaissance centered on rediscoveries of the cultures of ancient Greece and the Roman Empire, hence the name Renaissance.

For almost one thousand years after the fall of the Roman Empire in 476, religion had been at center stage in almost all aspects of life. With the Roman Empire gone as a center of power, the Roman Catholic Church was the most vibrant and dominant institution in western Europe. Its teachings about virtually all subjects—not only religion but also politics and science—went largely unchallenged. The explanation for natural occurrences was generally religious; according to the Church, events happened because it was God's will. Warriors became princes or kings only with the Church's blessing. Gradually a social and political structure evolved in Europe called feudalism, in which armed warriors (the first aristocrats, prominent landowners called "lords") exercised political power with the blessing of the Church. Most people were farmers, called serfs, who did not own their own land (they worked on land owned by aristocrats). They had no property or legal rights and were required by law to work the land of the aristocrat, their "landlord." Religious teachings, which in Europe meant the teachings of the Catholic Church in the thousand years leading up to about 1400, went largely unquestioned.

Around 1400, a new attitude began to take hold. It started with renewed interest in the writings of Greek and Roman thinkers of ancient history. These writings were never lost in the sense of having disappeared; they were stored as manuscripts in monasteries right through the fall of the Roman Empire and for the duration of the medieval period, starting around the year 500. But in the fifteenth century, they came into renewed prominence as European thinkers began to consider alternative explanations for the natural world.

The term "Renaissance" is often applied to art of this period, particularly the paintings and sculptures of such figures as Leonardo da Vinci (1452–1519) and Michelangelo (1475–1564). But it also includes a broad range of other thinkers and philosophers whose names remain famous. Nicolaus Copernicus (1473–1543) in Poland and Galileo Galilei (1564–1642) in Italy were astronomers who asserted that the Earth revolved around the Sun. Galileo was put under house arrest by Church authorities, who insisted that the Earth (and thus humankind) was the center of the universe. Leonardo da Vinci was not only a famous painter and sculptor but also a designer of ingenious machines. Niccolò Machiavelli (pronounced mack-ee-ah-VELL-ee; 1469–1527)

Niccolò Machiavelli was one of the most significant thinkers of the Renaissance. *Reproduced by permission of Getty Images.*

was an Italian writer who described how a successful political leader should behave in order to hold on to his office. At around the same time, in Portugal, Prince Henry the Navigator (1394–1460) sponsored expeditions around Africa, looking for a sea route to Asia in order to buy spices (used in part to prevent meat from rotting in the absence of refrigeration).

The Renaissance marked the beginning of three important revolutions that played key roles in history. One was the scientific revolution; the second was a revolution in religious and political thought; and the third was a revolution in navigation that opened sea trade between Europe and Asia and opened North America to European colonization.

The scientific revolution

The scientific revolution started with the idea that the world around us behaves in a predictable way, and that nature follows laws that can be figured out by close observation. This way of thinking replaced the medieval belief that God is responsible for whatever happens in the natural world, and that God's ways are unknowable or mysterious. Under that way of thinking, the best way to understand the world was to study the nature of God.

During the Renaissance, scholars took a different attitude. They began trying to understand nature by means of close observation. Many scientists believed that God had designed the natural laws that govern nature, but that once these laws were in place, the natural world followed them in a predictable way.

The idea of natural laws was very powerful. At first, people applied the concept to the behavior of physical objects: Why does a rock fall to the ground when it is dropped? Why does the Sun seem to rise in the morning and set at night? What happens to water when it is heated and disappears as steam?

Once the scientific revolution got started, there was no stopping it, even when it challenged religious teachings. Every aspect of the world was subjected to intense scrutiny by scientists. The scientific method involved observing the behavior of objects and recording those observations in detail.

Although it is tempting to think of a scientific revolution as occurring rapidly and dramatically, in fact scientists are still engaged in the process six hundred years later. Gradually, by accumulating thousands of detailed observations and measurements, early scientists learned that most occurrences do in fact follow patterns. One way of thinking about the Industrial Revolution is to see it as a process of applying natural laws to manufacturing goods.

Two figures associated with the scientific revolution were particularly important to the future of the Industrial Revolution. One was the French scientist René Descartes (pronounced ra-NAY day-CART; 1596–1650); the other was the English scientist Isaac Newton (1642–1727).

Descartes's pioneering approach to solving problems in science requires breaking a problem down into its smallest parts. In considering the unknown, Descartes insisted that scientists must examine every idea and theory and throw out any explanations that they cannot prove for certain to be true, or that rely on many complicated explanations. Eventually, he said, a scientist will come down to one basic truth that can be proved, probably mathematically, and use that basic element to build upon. This approach of breaking a problem down into its smallest parts and building up from there was later used in organizing work in factories.

Isaac Newton was also a mathematician and a physicist, a scientist who studies the physical properties of objects. He pioneered the use of detailed measurements in trying to understand the natural laws of physics. The idea that physical objects consistently obey such laws gave rise to a way of thinking about the world. Scientists began focusing on understanding natural laws by taking careful measurements and conducting experiments to test their theories.

Isaac Newton, depicted presiding over a meeting of the Royal Society.
Reproduced by permission of the Corbis Corporation.

In the Industrial Revolution, some of these newly discovered natural laws were applied to new machines. For example, when water is heated to 212 degrees Fahrenheit (100 degrees Celsius), it becomes steam. A given amount of water, converted to steam, occupies over 1,300 times as much space as water in its liquid form. The power of this expansion was put to use in the steam engine (see Chapter 2). Over time, with the benefit of scientific discovery, human attitudes toward events changed, from feeling powerless to affect events to feeling that events could be controlled, at least on a small scale, with study and effort.

Widespread literacy

The revolution in scientific thought was gaining momentum just about the time that a German named Johannes Gutenberg (c. 1400–1468) developed the modern printing press. The story of Gutenberg usually mentions his most famous product: Bibles. Previously, Bibles had been painstakingly copied by hand by monks. These valuable manuscripts were chained to tables in monasteries, and lay people (those who were not priests or other members of the clergy) did not have access to them. Gutenberg made it possible for many people to own their own Bible, to read it for themselves, and to interpret it as they liked: another challenge to the exclusive authority of the Church.

Gutenberg's technology—and further innovations that soon followed—had another implication: it made books much more commonplace. Another early printer, Aldo Mannucci (also spelled Manuzio and in Latin Aldus Manutius; 1449–1515), in the city-state of Venice, manufactured books in a smaller size that could be held while reading (like modern books) or carried in a saddlebag. Books were no longer huge volumes copied by hand and occupying a whole table, but instead were small and portable enough to carry elsewhere as a means of spreading knowledge.

René Descartes was a leading intellectual during the Renaissance. *Reproduced by permission of the Library of Congress.*

The profusion of books that followed Gutenberg's innovation was soon followed by a marked increase in literacy. The ability to read was no longer confined to monks, priests, and other religious figures. With new scientific observations being made constantly, books became a key way of circulating this new knowledge. University students who once would have been limited to studying theology (the study of religious faith) in preparation for a life as a monk or priest in the Church had new career opportunities in science.

The Reformation

Just as the German-invented printing press was expanding the number of individuals able to read, another development in Germany was ending the religious monopoly of the Roman Catholic Church in Europe.

In 1517 a German priest named Martin Luther (1483–1546), in the German town of Wittenberg, challenged some teachings of the Church (at the time, the Catholic Church was the only Church) by tacking his famous ninety-five theses to a church door. Luther challenged the Church's teachings in religion much as the scientific revolution challenged Church teachings in science. His challenge soon gained adherents in a movement called the Reformation (so named because it was intended to reform, or change, the Church).

People who agreed with Luther's protest against Church teachings became known as Protestants.

Luther's desire to reform the practices of the Roman Catholic Church soon led to arguments that in turn led to military battles in Europe over which church—the Roman Catholic Church or one of the new Protestant churches— would be the official religion of a country. (At the time, people in Europe did not have a choice about which religion to follow: their ruler decided for them.)

These religious conflicts had an impact on the Industrial Revolution, which was still more than two hundred years into the future, in three ways. First, the challenge to the Church's authority in strictly religious affairs was tied to the challenge to the Church's authority in science, making the scientific revolution more likely to succeed. Second, the new Protestant sects allowed followers to charge interest (a fee paid to borrow money that is generally a percentage of the amount borrowed) on money that was loaned. Previously, Catholic teaching forbade charging interest on loans, which discouraged people from lending money since it meant taking a risk (the loan might not be repaid) with no counterbalancing advantage (money earned as interest on the loan). As the Industrial Revolution advanced, lending money (as well as investing money) was critical, since it enabled borrowers to buy expensive machinery to set up factories.

Third, the challenge to the Church's authority in religion paved the way for challenges to political authority, which for centuries had been linked to the Church. Traditionally, the pope, as head of the Church, was thought to be infallible because he was God's mouthpiece on Earth. Thus when he blessed monarchs, he had given them a sort of moral authority as well as military power. But if a king's moral authority comes from God, interpreted by the pope, and the pope's authority is now subject to question, then does it not logically follow that the king's authority is also subject to question? This general line of thought, developed over many decades by a variety of writers, eventually led to the idea that the authority of political rulers does not come from "above"—that is, from God as interpreted by the Church—but instead comes from "below," from the people who are ruled by the king. This idea opened the way for some people, notably the newly wealthy industrialists, to gain significant political as well as economic power (so-called common people remained fairly powerless). Whereas in earlier ages, political power flowed from the monarch and the sword (with the blessing of the Church), in the new industrial world it flowed from wealth, with or without the blessing of the governed.

One key idea that grew out of new attitudes toward political power was the notion that individuals have certain rights the government cannot take away. The Industrial Revolution depended on people accumulating money and investing it in new businesses that required large investments to get started—money needed to purchase machinery to run a factory, for example. It proved crucial that people trusted that a government would not swoop in and seize their property; otherwise, people with money would have been tempted to leave it in vaults in the form of gold or silver bullion (bulk forms of these metals), as they had during the medieval period. In England, especially, the idea of limits on government power had taken root and grown ever since King John signed the Magna Carta in 1215, a document that limited his powers as king and gave aristocrats a voice in government. For the English, the idea of sharing power between the ruler and the ruled had become deeply ingrained.

The English philosopher John Locke (1632–1704) wrote in the second of his *Two Treatises on Government*, published in 1690, that governments derive their power from the people. Locke's ideas were the inspiration for statesman Thomas Jefferson when he wrote the American Declaration of Independence in 1776 and are largely taken for granted in twenty-first-century America. But in Locke's time, these ideas were considered revolutionary. Locke echoed scientists of his day by insisting that there was a set of natural laws that governed social relations among people, similar to the laws that governed nature. Among these laws, he said, was the right to own property. Property could not be seized by the government without good reason, Locke insisted.

Navigation

The story behind the discovery of North and South America is familiar to most people: Christopher Columbus

(1451–1506), an Italian financed by the monarchs of Spain, was looking for a shortcut to Asia when he discovered the New World, meaning the continents of North and South America. This discovery had many implications, including the expansion of commerce. Businessmen in Europe saw Asia—and eventually the New World—as a new source of raw materials as well as a new market for finished goods.

The voyage of Columbus is not usually thought of as being part of the Industrial Revolution, but it did add to new ideas about the world. It helped expand the horizons of economic activity, leading to practices that would be commonplace three hundred years later, such as importing cotton from North America or India to England to make cloth in new factories.

The Enlightenment

The set of grand theories of science, religion, and politics that marked the era we call the Renaissance culminated in the late 1600s and 1700s in a period called the Age of Enlightenment. In particular, the Enlightenment refers to the period when political philosophers began applying some of the principles of the Renaissance and Reformation to government. The writers of the Enlightenment wanted to apply science and reason to society, overturning ancient ideas about the rights of kings and aristocrats as well as the dominant role of religion in organizing human affairs. The influence of the Catholic Church was central to French society, and thus it was a particular target of some political philosophers in the seventeenth and eighteenth centuries. Freedom of religion became an important issue in England as well, where the head of the Church was also the reigning monarch. Prominent names associated with the Enlightenment include French writers Jean-Jacques Rousseau (1712–1778) and Voltaire (whose given name was François-Marie Arouet; 1694–1778) and English writers including Locke and David Hume (1711–1776). Together, the writers of the Enlightenment justified significant political changes that occurred in both England and France, the two most prominent European powers at the time, and helped establish an environment in which the Industrial Revolution could take place.

One of the most important ideas to emerge from the Enlightenment was the notion of predictable government.

David Hume

A Scottish historian and philosopher, David Hume (1711–1776) believed that science could proceed only on the basis of facts that could be seen and tested, a philosophy called empiricism. He also believed that this scientific method could be applied to human affairs. In this respect, Hume believed that experience alone can teach us anything; belief, including religious belief, cannot yield anything certain. Hume was one of many philosophers who contributed to the mind-set that eventually contributed to the growth of the Industrial Revolution, a way of thinking that was generally unfettered by religious restraints.

Rather than being subject to the whims of a hereditary monarch or aristocrat, the Enlightenment thinkers advocated government based on reason and consent of the governed: in short, democracy, a political system in which a majority of the people vote to determine the government and its policies. A critical ingredient of the Industrial Revolution was the willingness of wealthy individuals to invest money in building factories. An unpredictable political environment would have put this money at risk, in danger of being seized by the king, for example.

The Renaissance and Enlightenment, taken as a whole, marked the change from a society centered on religion to a society centered on human beings. In the medieval period, only a few individuals at the top of society had the ability to influence events. The great majority of people worked as farmers, often on land they did not own. During the Renaissance, more and more people began living in cities and towns. The discovery of sea routes to Asia and North America in the 1400s and 1500s created new economic opportunities not linked to ownership of land. The trade made possible by these routes generated significant new fortunes in Europe that eventually would be invested in machinery and factories, making possible the process we call the Industrial Revolution.

England in 1750

England is the country where the Industrial Revolution began, and it is worthwhile to consider the particular aspects of English society that led to this development.

By 1750 England had already changed significantly from medieval society, but it was not entirely modern. Most people still lived in the country in small villages and seldom traveled far from home. Most "commoners," or people who lived on land held in common, had little influence over government.

England had enjoyed a half century of domestic peace after a civil war in the 1600s that divided the country between Protestants and Catholics. Abroad, England fought repeated wars with France and gradually established superiority. After the Seven Years War (1756–63; called the French and Indian War in the United States), England had gained control of the eastern half of North America and was well on its way to establishing domination over India.

Although England was at peace at home, significant changes were on the horizon. In 1696 there were about five million people living in England (fewer people than lived in New York City at the turn of the twenty-first century), and the population was growing slowly. By 1750 the population had increased by only 20 percent, to about six million. But in the next fifty years, the population grew by 50 percent again, to more than nine million.

The enclosure movement

In the early 1700s, three-fourths of England's population lived in the country. Much of the English countryside was a patchwork of tiny plots called freeholds that were worked by individuals. No one "owned" the land; it was held in common, or shared, and long traditions dictated who worked on which patch. One farmer might work several plots of land separated from one another by similar plots worked by another farmer.

Beginning in about 1500, a gradual process called enclosure (sometimes spelled inclosure) had resulted in the transfer of common lands to individual property owners. The enclosure movement was a process by which wealthy individuals, often aristocrats, petitioned the Parliament (the legislature, or governing body) in London to grant them exclusive title (ownership) to land previously held in common, that is, land with no specific owner. The petitions to Parliament were accompanied by significant sums of money. The petitions usually applied to a parish, a local area served by one church. Several individuals often got together to submit a petition for a parish; they then divided the common lands into larger plots, which were devoted to grazing sheep prized for their wool.

The enclosure process had started in northwestern England around 1500, and it gained momentum after 1760, especially in southern England, to the extent that the period between 1760 and 1850 is sometimes called the second enclosure movement. The second movement coincided almost exactly with the rise of the new factory system that marked the start of the Industrial Revolution. Poor people could not afford to contribute to the fees paid in exchange for title. After title to the land was granted, the new owners typically built fences (sometimes in the form of hedges) around their property and started grazing sheep, which generated a steady supply of wool for England's textile (cloth) manufacturers.

Those who did not buy land lost both a place to live and a place to grow food. These displaced people moved into towns and cities. The enclosure movement resulted in a major shift of population. In 1696 only about one-fourth of the population lived in English cities; by 1760 one-half of the people of England lived in cities. These new city dwellers, most of them poor, provided the pool of labor for the factories about to come into existence.

Even at the beginning of the process, enclosure was sharply criticized as theft of communal land by aristocrats at the expense of poor rural dwellers. In 1516 the English writer Sir Thomas More (1478–1535), in his book *Utopia*, said that enclosure allowed "one covetous [grasping] and insatiable [never satisfied] cormorant [greedy person] and very plague of his native country ... [to] compass about and enclose many thousand acres of ground together within one pale or hedge, [while] the husbandmen [farmers] be thrust out of their own."

The agricultural revolution

The enclosure movement coincided with, and encouraged, an agricultural revolution, a term that describes farming practices that emerged in England around 1700. Farming was a conservative occupation in 1700; farmers were cautious about adopting changes. Nevertheless, new attitudes about science began to be applied to farming, as well as to other occupations, resulting in both machinery and new practices that eventually overturned centuries-old ways of working. These changes took place around the same time as the Industrial Revolution and helped support some aspects of English society in ways that benefited industrialization.

As with any significant social and economic change, it is difficult to credit one individual with responsibility for it. On the other hand, certain names have become strongly associated with important changes, especially that of Jethro Tull (1674–1741). Tull was trained as a lawyer, but he instead took up farming with his father, a member of the gentry (prosperous farmers who were not aristocrats). Tull is credited with developing the seed drill, a horse-drawn device that planted seeds in straight lines and then covered them over. Previously, farmers had followed the centuries-old practice of scattering seeds by hand (sowing), meaning that plants grew in a random pattern. Tull's approach resulted in straight rows that could be weeded by a horse-drawn hoe.

Tull's invention was hardly a cure-all, and in fact English farmers were slow to adopt it (although English colonists in North America were more enthusiastic). But his technique did increase the amount of crops that could be harvested from a field.

Technology was just one aspect of the agricultural revolution. British farmers in the eighteenth century also started using a new system of crop rotation. Instead of leaving fields fallow (empty) one year out of four in order to re-plenish the soil's nutrients, farmers began rotating crops. In year one, they planted turnips (which could be used to feed animals). In year two, the field would be used to grow barley. In year three, clover, which nourishes the soil, would be raised. In year four, wheat would be planted. In this way, a field could be planted each year, instead of just three out of four, and sown-under plants could help keep the soil fertile. This new method resulted in greater output from the land and increased income for farmers.

Private ownership of land resulting from the enclosure movement also led to such improvements as the installation of drainage systems, which added to agricultural productivity.

The agricultural revolution—use of machinery, crop rotation, and land improvements—had several important implications related to the Industrial Revolution. The same amount of land could now raise more crops and support more people. Fewer farmers were needed to achieve the same results, due partly to new machinery. Some of the farmers displaced from the land became available to work as employees in the factories that were being built. And the new techniques worked better on larger fields, and therefore encouraged expansion of the enclosure movement.

Mercantilism

English economic life in 1750 was rapidly evolving from an ancient way of doing things. During the 1500s and 1600s, England, France, and Spain had each been striving to achieve superiority over the other two nations. In addition to building up armies and navies and gaining colonies in North America and Asia, the English government tried to establish economic superiority through a government policy called mercantilism, a system in which a government regulates trade and business in a way designed to promote the interests of its own country at the expense of its rivals.

Mercantilism came about during, and just after, the age of exploration in which European sailors opened sea routes to Asia and North America. Merchants and manufacturers were eager to secure government protection and support for their economic interests, and often succeeded. For example, although England had been an important exporter of wool for hundreds of years, the government banned the export of wool between 1660 and 1820, in order to benefit domestic textile makers. Clothiers no longer had to compete with foreigners for a supply of wool, and foreign manufacturers were hurt by their sudden inability to buy English wool. (In this process, those in England who raised sheep in order to sell their wool tended to suffer from the lack of competition. In this respect, they lost out to the manufacturers in competition for the government's favor.) France also frequently placed restrictions on exporting wool. Similar restrictions were placed on food, especially wheat (called corn in England). Restrictive regulations also applied to exporting tools and the immigration of skilled workers to other countries.

Governments often prohibited imports as well, in order to protect industries at home from foreign competition (and to avoid the export of the gold and silver used to pay for the imports). England banned imports of silk in order to protect its silk industry from French and Italian competitors. France barred imports of printed cotton cloth from 1686 to 1759 to protect French manufacturers from the competition offered by cloth imported from India and China.

In 1650 and 1651 England passed the first of a series of laws called the Navigation Acts that were designed to give preference to English merchant ships over the Dutch. They required that imports to England be carried in English ships. They also regulated shipping between England and its colonies, including its North American colonies. These laws were a major irritant to those living in England's American colonies, since the absence of competition in shipping tended to make imports more expensive.

Other European governments also tried to regulate the balance of foreign trade to preserve as much wealth as possible. In the mid-1600s, governments were concerned about the quantities of gold and silver that were being exported as payment for imports. Since gold was a way to finance armies and navies, governments wanted to preserve as much gold as possible and therefore adopted policies to encourage exports and discourage imports. The aim of these policies, such as taxes placed on imports, was to assure that the value of goods sold abroad was greater than the value of goods bought from abroad—called a positive balance of trade.

Thanks in part to the expansion of European colonies following the discovery of North America and the islands of the Caribbean (the "West Indies"), and also to the growth in shipping between Europe and Asia (the "East Indies"), foreign trade was growing rapidly. Between 1715 and 1789, foreign trade grew by around 400 percent.

The guild system

Restrictive rules dating to the medieval period also governed the behavior of merchants and workers. Merchants and workers in various skilled trades that required expertise and training (such as printing, or weaving) joined organizations called guilds. (Some labor unions, especially those representing highly skilled workers, are still named guilds today.) Merchant guilds wrote rules and regulations for conducting their particular trade. The guilds regulated prices, weights and measures, and other conditions of business. The rules were designed partly to assure high standards, but also to prevent price competition.

Trade guilds were a system that supplied training to young men (women were generally not involved in skilled work during this period) and also protected established workers from competition. Boys progressed through three stages. As teenagers, they would become apprentices for several years, learning a skill in a particular trade such as weaving. Once the skill had been learned, they became journeymen and then masters, at which point they might set up a shop of their own and employ journeymen or apprentices.

The guild system was still in operation at the beginning of the Industrial Revolution around 1750. The introduction of machinery powered by steam engines seriously challenged this system in some trades, but not in others.

Many skilled workers worked from their homes, as part of what was called a cottage industry. Manufacturing cloth in particular was largely done by workers at home. Making fabric is a two-stage process: the basic material, fibers like wool or cotton, are twisted tightly to make thread in a process called spinning. Then the thread is woven, on a device called a loom, to make the cloth. It takes several people spinning thread to keep pace with one weaver. Making cloth was often a family enterprise: the children and women of the household spun the thread from wool (and, later, from cotton), while the husband operated the loom that wove the thread into cloth.

Merchants typically dropped off the wool or cotton at a weaver's house and came back later to pick up the finished cloth. Cloth merchants had little or no control over how quickly a family produced cloth from the wool or cotton. This system made it difficult for the merchants to promise delivery of finished cloth to their customers (a clothing maker, for example) at a particular time. On the other hand, the cottage industry system benefited workers, leaving them in control of their lives—how many hours a day they worked, how much their children helped, and so forth.

Spinning and weaving were among the first industries to be affected by the Industrial Revolution. Innovations to the machinery used to make cloth and the rise of the factory system combined to radically change the textile industry (see Chapter 4).

Colonialism

In the 1700s England was expanding its overseas empire, both in North America and in India. This expansion came about primarily as a result of England's rivalries with France, but it happened to contribute to the success of the Industrial Revolution by creating, in the colonies, both a source of raw materials and a source of customers for manufactured goods.

At the same time, England was experiencing a rapid increase in its population due to such factors as freedom of religion. Some people did leave the country for new lives in the English colonies, but their numbers were too low to make a dent in England's overall population. At the time, the increase in population seemed enormous, and some writers worried that England would not be able to feed its population if it kept growing at that rate in the future. But the increases in England's population did supply vast numbers of both workers and consumers, contributing to the vast changes of the Industrial Revolution.

New economic philosophy

Starting in the mid-1700s, thinkers in both England and France began to object to the theory of mercantilism. In France, these thinkers were known as the Physiocrats. In Britain, two Scottish thinkers in particular, David Hume and Adam Smith (1723–1790), opposed government control over the economy.

In 1776 Smith published *The Wealth of Nations,* which became a best-seller when it was released and continues to be studied today. In it, Smith argues in favor of competition, rather than regulation, as the best means of maximizing a nation's wealth. Smith maintains that no government can fully understand or control economic activity, and that the best way to assure a nation's wealth is to let business proceed without government restrictions or regulations. This same approach was advocated by the French Physiocrats, who used the phrase *laissez-faire* (pronounced lay-zay-FAIR, a French term meaning "free to do") to describe this philosophy.

In the English colonies of North America, laws designed to enhance the wealth of England at the expense of others became very unpopular. The colonists considered themselves to be English, and they did not see why their government should pursue policies that would enrich Englishmen living in England but not Englishmen living in North America. These economic policies thus contributed to the sentiment for independence, sentiment that broke into open revolution in 1775, just one year before Smith published his famous treatise arguing against mercantilism.

Peace at home, war abroad

After years of strife and civil war in the 1600s, England enjoyed domestic peace in the 1700s, even as it fought a series of wars abroad. From 1740 to 1748 England fought against France, Prussia (a region of modern-day Germany), and Spain in the War of the Austrian Succession. In 1756 the Seven Years War (referred to as the French and Indian War in North America) ended in a British victory over France, giving Britain control of French North America (essentially Canada) and India. The end result for England was that it controlled a wide range of colonies from which it gained raw materials as well as customers for finished goods made in England. Extensive trade with the colonies made many merchants wealthy. They were later able to invest their wealth in new industrial companies that required large sums of money to acquire new technology, such as the steam engine.

In many ways, changes in society in England in the period between 1700 and 1760 set the stage for the Industrial Revolution. Although some of these changes were also seen in other European countries, no other country had the same combination and extent of expanding trade, expanding population, and growing urbanization (people moving from farms into towns) that were present in England.

For More Information

Books

Allen, Robert C. *Enclosure and the Yeoman*. New York: Oxford University Press, 1992.

Berlin, Isaiah, ed. *The Age of Enlightenment: The Eighteenth Century Philosophers.* New York: New American Library, 1984.

Burns, Edward M., and Philip R. Ralph. *World Civilizations.* New York: Norton, 1969.

Campbell, R. H., and A. S. Skinner. *Adam Smith.* New York: St. Martin's Press, 1982.

Chadwick, Owen. *The Reformation.* London: Penguin Books, 1990.

Chaunu, Pierre, ed. *The Reformation.* New York: St. Martin's Press, 1990.

Gomes, Leonard. *Foreign Trade and the National Economy: Mercantilist and Classical Perspectives.* New York: St. Martin's Press, 1987.

Johnson, Paul. *The Renaissance: A Short History.* New York: Modern Library, 2000.

Kramnick, Isaac. *The Portable Enlightenment Reader.* New York: Penguin Books, 1995.

McClelland, Peter D. *Sowing Modernity: America's First Agricultural Revolution.* Ithaca, NY: Cornell University Press, 1997.

Mingay, G. E. *Enclosure and the Small Farmer in the Age of the Industrial Revolution.* London: Macmillan, 1968.

More, Thomas. *Utopia.* Reprint edition. New York: Viking Press, 1965.

Renaissance. Danbury, CT: Grolier Educational, 2002.

Richetti, John J. *Philosophical Writing: Locke, Berkeley, Hume.* Cambridge, MA: Harvard University Press, 1983.

Spellman, W. M. *John Locke.* St. Martin's Press, 1997.

Periodicals

Campbell, Roy. "Scotland's Neglected Enlightenment." *History Today,* May 1990, p. 22.

Edkard, E. Woodrow, Jr. "The Free Market Incentive: Self Interest versus Greed." *Business Economics,* September 1980, p. 32.

Kaufman, Henry. "What Would Adam Smith Say Now? He Would Like Much of What He Sees, but He Would Also Be Worried." *Business Economics.* October 2001, p. 7.

"Voices in the Population Debate." *Scholastic Update,* March 2, 1984, p. 14.

Web Sites

The Adam Smith Institute. http://www.adamsmith.org (accessed on February 6, 2003).

Internet Modern History Sourcebook: The Enlightenment. http://www.fordham.edu/halsall/mod/modsbook10.html (accessed on February 6, 2003).

Toynbee, Arnold. "Lectures on the Industrial Revolution in England." *McMaster University Archive for the History of Economic Thought.* http://www.socsci.mcmaster.ca/econ/ugcm/3ll3/toynbee/indrev (accessed on February 6, 2003).

The Revolution Begins: Steam Engines, Railroads, and Steamboats

2

The Industrial Revolution started in the 1700s with the development of machines that substituted for human or animal muscle power. The newly invented machines, powered by burning wood or coal, or by the flowing water of a stream or river, could accomplish the same amount of work that previously required several people or several animals flexing their muscles. Not only could the machines do the work of several living beings, machines could do it at a much faster speed. Imagine substituting a horse for the motor of a car; one or two horses could easily pull the weight of a car with its passengers, but no horse could run down the highway at sixty miles an hour, hour after hour, as a car can.

There were two separate, but related, aspects to the development of new machines in the Industrial Revolution. One was the use of sources of energy besides muscles. In particular, inventors found ways to capture and utilize the natural characteristic of water to expand when it is heated and becomes steam. The other aspect was the invention of machinery that could emulate work done for centuries by skilled workers, especially in the manufacture of fabric. Eventually

About Energy

The science of physics is, in part, the study of energy. It is a complex subject that people study over a lifetime, but some of the basic principles lie at the heart of the Industrial Revolution.

Physicists define energy as the ability to do work, by which they mean the capability to move an object. Energy has three fundamental characteristics that are useful to know in understanding the Industrial Revolution: (1) it can take different forms, including light, heat, and motion itself; (2) it can be stored for long periods of time in different forms, of which coal and wood are two examples; and (3) the total amount of energy in the universe is constant.

The phrase "use energy" really refers to *moving* or *converting* energy from one form to another form, from one place to another, or both—from a storage container (such as a lump of coal) into heat felt across the room, for example, or into light

seen miles away, for example. Energy can also be transferred from storage into motion (in this form, energy is called "momentum), which is the essence of industrial machinery. In all these processes, energy never disappears entirely. Physicists sometimes refer to this as "the rule of conservation of energy."

The natural source of energy on Earth is the Sun. Its energy is transferred to the Earth in the form of light. In this sense, energy equals light and vice versa.

Plants absorb this light (energy) through their leaves, and in a biological process called photosynthesis they convert minerals in the earth into living cells. In effect, the cells of plants are little storage containers for the energy that arrived from the Sun.

When humans or animals eat plants, the stored energy is again transferred and stored in animal cells. When a human or animal flexes its muscles to pull a

these two aspects came together, in the form of steam-driven machines to spin thread or weave cloth. The new energy sources also enabled the development of reliable, high-speed transportation, in the form of trains and steam ships.

In less than a century, these technological developments had an enormous impact on the nature of work, the way society was organized, and the ways in which wealth was generated and shared.

Steam power

In order to understand the development of steam-powered machines, it is useful to examine the nature of water.

cart along the road or raise a hand in class, for example, the energy is converted yet again—into the motion of the cart or hand.

Over millions of years, dead plants decayed and were crushed by the weight of the earth. In effect, they became collections of carbon atoms, sometimes combined with other elements. The resulting substance is coal, which looks like black rocks but could be thought of as being ancient trees in ultra-compact form. The energy absorbed from the Sun by trees and plants millions of years ago is still stored in the form of molecules of coal, which is in effect a type of storage container for the same energy that started out as sunlight and got stored in plant cells countless millions of years ago.

Burning coal is a way of transferring this stored (one could say "saved") energy yet again, by converting it into still another form: heat. In a coal-burning steam engine, the energy stored in coal is trans-ferred, in the form of heat, to water. When enough energy (or heat) has been absorbed, the water suddenly turns into steam (a process that could be described as water molecules moving apart from one another).

The steam engine then transfers the energy of expanding water molecules in order to move some other object. This last step results in the work of the steam engine, whether it be moving a vehicle or pumping water.

In the process of transferring ancient stored energy (and remembering that energy can take the form of light, heat, or motion) from its ancient container (coal), some energy escapes as heat into the atmosphere, where there is no natural way of reconverting the heat to another form of energy. This process is, at base, the cause of concern about global warming: mankind has released so much ancient energy that the Earth is reaching the limits of its capacity to absorb it.

Water comprises molecules (a molecule is the smallest particle in a chemical compound, and is composed of two or more atoms joined together) made of two types of atoms: hydrogen and oxygen. Each molecule of pure water contains two atoms of hydrogen and one of water; scientists write this as H_2O.

When these molecules are between 32 degrees Fahrenheit (0 degrees Celsius) and 212 degrees Fahrenheit (100 degrees Celsius), they are in a liquid state called water, the most common substance on Earth. When the molecules are heated to above 212 degrees Fahrenheit (100 degrees Celsius), they fly apart from one another and become a gas called steam. At that instant, the volume (space) occupied by

Some Components of Steam Engines

In discussing steam engines, there are a few terms common to all such engines that are useful to know in understanding how they work:

- Boiler: A container of water that is to be heated to create steam. Boilers usually are shaped like giant metal bottles (although the first ones looked more like round pots) with pipes to let in new water and other pipes to let out the steam. These pipes are opened or shut by one-way doors called valves.

- Cylinder: A round pipe, closed at one end and, usually, with a small hole at the other end. Cylinders can be of almost any diameter and height, although the practicality of using them usually limits both dimensions.

- Piston: A round, solid piece of metal designed to move up and down (or back and forth) inside the cylinder. The piston fits so snugly inside the cylinder that neither steam nor water can squeeze between the sides of the piston and the walls of the cylinder. However, a very thin coating of oil usually lines the surface of the piston to avoid friction between the two pieces of metal. Friction could cause the metal to expand slightly, preventing the piston from moving inside the cylinder.

- Rod: A piece of metal, usually round, attached to the top of the piston. The rod extends outside of the cylinder and transfers the movement of the piston to some other object (a wheel, for example, or a pump handle).

molecules of H_2O instantly expands many times over (1,325 times over, to be precise). The same number of molecules that, in liquid form, would fit in a one-gallon plastic bottle measuring about five and a half inches square on the bottom and a little more than eight inches high suddenly need a container that would measure five and a half inches square by more than eleven thousand inches high. Normally, of course, the molecules simply escape into the atmosphere, as can be seen when a teakettle is boiling on a stove.

Not only do molecules of steam occupy more space than they did when they were in liquid form, they expand very rapidly and with tremendous force. If a sealed metal container of water is heated, the container will explode if the resulting steam is not given someplace to escape to—one reason why experiments using heat and steam can be very dangerous.

- Valve: A sort of one-way door that lets liquid or gas pass through in one direction only. The design of valves makes them shut a passage (such as a pipe) automatically if a liquid or gas tries to reverse direction.

In a theoretical steam engine, a coal fire underneath the boiler heats the water, creating steam. The steam escapes through a valve into the cylinder, just underneath the piston, which is initially sitting near one end of the cylinder. As the steam continues to enter the cylinder, it pushes on the piston, forcing it toward the other end of the cylinder, and thereby pushing the rod attached to the top of the piston. Steam is quite powerful: the rod may be attached to a very heavy weight, which the force of expanding steam can also move.

When the steam underneath the piston is suddenly cooled, perhaps with a squirt of water, and no more steam is allowed to enter, the piston is pulled down by the force of the vacuum, or empty space, created by the condensation of the steam back into water.

Then the process begins again: steam is let into the cylinder and pushes the piston back up to the top. An arrangement of levers and gears attached to the bouncing rod allows the steam engine to do useful work, such as pumping out a flooded mineshaft or moving a train locomotive.

When steam is cooled, it has the opposite reaction: it contracts back into water, occupying much less space. If steam housed in a large container is quickly cooled so that it converts to water, the contraction creates a vacuum, or empty space, inside the container. Other molecules rush to fill this vacuum, even from outside the container. If a vacuum were created inside an aluminum can of soda, for example, the molecules of the surrounding atmosphere would crush the can in an effort to fill the empty space. Alternatively, a vacuum can be controlled to create a strong suction that can bring a substance, such as water, into the container. A strong cylinder with a pipe leading to the outside can raise water from a well, for example.

These two basic principles lie at the heart of the steam engine. Beginning in Europe in the early 1600s (at about the time the Pilgrims were establishing new settlements in North America), a series of inventors began designing devices to control these reactions. The result was the steam engine, which started out as a kind of pump and evolved into a powerful engine for transportation and manufacturing. Indeed, the steam engine could be said to have powered the Industrial Revolution.

Early experiments with steam

The characteristics of water and steam have been known since ancient times. More than two thousand years ago, around 50 B.C.E., the ancient Greek mathematician and engineer Hero (sometimes called Heron) lived in Alexandria (now in Egypt). His surviving writings describe a device he called the "aeolipile," (pronounced a-LIP-ah-lee), or "windball." It was a sphere in which water was heated to create steam. Steam escaped from two L-shaped pipes sticking out of either side; the rush of escaping steam sent the sphere spinning.

During the Renaissance, the period of great scientific, literary, and artistic achievement in Europe between about 1400 and 1700, scientists and engineers began thinking about how to take advantage of the characteristics of heat and water.

In 1615 the engineer and architect Salomon de Caus (1576–1626), who worked for both King Louis XIII of France and the Prince of Wales in England, published a work in which he described a machine designed to lift water by using the power of expanding steam. A drawing of the device shows a hollow copper sphere with a horizontal pipe sticking out from the top and extending to almost the bottom. Another small pipe, with a valve like a faucet (like those found in bathrooms) leads into the sphere from the side. As the water in the sphere is heated, the hottest molecules rise to the top and turn into steam, which expands. The expanding gas pushes down on the surface of the water inside the sphere, forcing water up through the vertical pipe. After the water is pushed out, the source of steam is shut off and more water is let into the sphere from a second pipe by opening the faucet, and the process can begin again.

In 1631 David Ramsay (sometimes written as Ramsaye) of Scotland received a government patent (the exclusive right, for a period of time, to use an invention) for a device that could "raise water from low paths by fire." Although details of Ramsay's invention are obscure, he evidently referred to a pump that was driven by water heated and converted into steam. Several European inventors of the early 1600s also wrote about devices that used steam for the purpose of raising water, including from the bottom of mines.

In the very earliest "steam engines," the steam and the water that was meant to be pushed higher occupied the same container. Some of the water was turned into steam and pushed the rest of the liquid down. The water had no place to go but upwards through a vertical pipe that entered the container from the top and extended almost to the bottom. As the steam pushed down on the surface of the water, the water rose through this vertical pipe, where it sometimes spurted out as if from a fountain. Indeed, some of the earliest examples of the technology could be seen in decorative fountains, rather than in engines that perform work.

The next advance lay in using the power of suction to bring water from the bottom of a pipe (in a well, or the bottom of a mine, for example) into the chamber. A container was filled with steam, which was rapidly cooled (at first by pouring cold water on the outside of the container, and later by squirting cool water into the steam-filled chamber). As the steam condensed back into water, occupying much less volume, a vacuum was created. This vacuum was used to suck water up a pipe and into the chamber. In the case of a steam-driven pump, for example, this water could then be transferred from the chamber into some other container, and the process could be repeated.

Edward Somerset, second Marquis of Worcester

A key inventor in the history of the steam engine was Edward Somerset, the second Marquis of Worcester (pronounced WOO-ster). He published a work in 1663 describing devices he claimed to have developed, including a sort of double-chambered steam engine.

Based on his description (Somerset did not supply a drawing), it appears that water was boiled (converted into steam) in one chamber, and that the steam was then al-

Charles II and the Pace of English Invention

The English king Charles II (1630–1685) played an indirect role in launching the Industrial Revolution.

Sometimes called the "Merry Monarch" for his easy-going nature, Charles had to fight for his crown during the English civil war (1648–1660), which was fought over the question of whether England would be a Catholic nation or a Protestant one.

Entirely apart from the religious and political issues that swirled around Charles II after he was restored to the throne of England, the monarch seemed to enjoy exploring science and mechanics, which were both flowering at the time. The king set up a laboratory and employed people to carry on experiments in the areas of mechanics and chemistry, as well as matters involving navigation at sea.

Some writers believe that the king's interest in such matters helps explain why England leaped ahead of other European countries in the areas of science and technology in the late 1600s and early 1700s.

lowed to escape into a second chamber, creating a vacuum. The vacuum sucked water through another pipe that led from a source of water, such as a well. While this was taking place, an identical chamber next to the first was filling with steam so that it, too, could be chilled and create a vacuum. As the steam poured into the chamber, it pushed down on the surface of the water, forcing it up an exit pipe, as described above. The source of steam for both chambers was a "boiler," a container of water off to the side of the chambers and sitting over a fire or furnace.

Somerset's machine thus used characteristics of water and steam to provide power. The expansion of steam pushed the water in a chamber up a pipe to a higher level, and the contraction of the steam (when the container was cooled) created a vacuum, which sucked water up from a lower level (which could have been a mineshaft or a well or just a stream). Although no examples of Somerset's machines are known to exist, one was installed in Raglan Castle, in southeastern Wales (part of Britain), and the outlines have survived.

Somerset's design had one disadvantage: it wasted a lot of fuel, either wood or coal, used to make steam. The reason was that when steam was admitted to a container nearly full of water, some of the heat was absorbed by the water, turning the steam back into water. Steam could still be forced into the chamber fast enough to push down on the surface of the water, and thereby force it up through the central exit pipe. But the absorption of heat by water intended to be pushed out was wasteful of the wood or coal used to create steam in the first place.

This underlying problem was solved with introduction of the piston (see box on page 36). The piston, a solid, round piece of metal that slid up and down inside the round chamber, meant that steam coming in at the top of the water-filled chamber could push down on the piston, instead of on the surface of the water. The piston was forced down, and it pushed on the surface of the water. But the piston also introduced a new design possibility: a rod (a solid, round piece of metal) could be attached to the piston, and as the piston went down, the rod would move down. When the steam pushing down on the piston was cooled, the piston would go back to the top, drawn by the vacuum created by the cooled steam.

By using a series of levers and gears, the up-and-down motion of the rod attached to the piston could be used to move other parts of a machine.

Coal mines and development of the steam engine in England

In the 1600s, England faced a particular problem: its once vast forests of oak trees had been chopped down over many centuries to be used as logs to heat homes, as well as used for timbers in making sailing ships. Fortunately for England, it had an alternative for home heating: extensive deposits of coal buried underground, particularly in the northwestern part of the country. Getting coal out of the ground required digging vertical shafts (holes) and networks of horizontal tunnels, and coal mining led to another problem: flooding.

Water seeping through the earth from the surface penetrated the tunnels and gathered at the bottom of the mineshafts, threatening to flood the horizontal tunnels that followed the coal "seam." To avoid drowning miners, horses were used to haul buckets to the top. But as mines were dug deeper and the network of tunnels expanded, flooding started to outstrip the ability of a horse-driven bucket brigade to keep the mines relatively dry. (At one mine, even 500 horses could barely keep pace with the water seeping into the bottom of the mine.)

A different, more efficient means of removing the water was needed, and a pump like Somerset's that used coal

Coal was a vital natural resource in the developments that took place during the Industrial Revolution. *Reproduced by permission of Photo Researchers, Inc.*

to create the steam seemed like an ideal answer.

Thomas Savery (c. 1650–1715) was a British military engineer who is usually credited with the next breakthrough in steam engine development. Savery applied for many patents for inventions between 1694 and 1710, including an application dated 1698 titled "a new Invention for Raising Water and Occasioning Motion to all Sorts of Mill Work by the Impellant Force of Fire, which will be of great use and Advantage for DRAINING Mines, Serveing Towns with Water, and for the working of all Sorts of Mills where they have not the Benefit of Water nor Constant Windes."

Savery's application was interesting not only for the device, but also for the fact that he included what he hoped would turn out to be reasons for its financial success: people could build machines away from energy sources such as rivers, streams, or windmills; they could drain mines, especially coal mines; and they could supply power to mills and factories. Doing this, however, raised a new requirement: transporting fuel to the new engine, a consideration that played an important role later in the Industrial Revolution.

Savery's device used the same principles that made Somerset's steam pump work. Water was heated in a large container (the boiler) built over a furnace. Steam from the container was directed into two cylinders. Leading out of the chambers were pipes that extended nearly to the bottom, and through which water could be ejected, just as in Somerset's device. At the same time, another set of pipes led from the chambers downward, into a mine, where suction power was designed to suck up the water. After steam from the boiler fills one of the cylinders, the supply of steam is shut off and the chamber is quickly cooled, causing the steam inside to contract and create a vacuum. The vacuum sucks water from the bottom of the well, filling the chamber. This intake pipe is then closed, by a valve, and steam is again let into the chamber, forcing the water up through the exit pipe. The process alternates between the two containers; while one is in suction mode, the other is filling with steam. Then they reverse roles.

The machine had some drawbacks, however. It required a skilled operator to open and close the various valves that let in steam and water. It was limited in the depth from which it could pump water. These limitations led to the success of the next major figure in steam engine history, Thomas Newcomen.

Thomas Newcomen's engine

The first business success in the development of the steam engine came to Thomas Newcomen (1663–1729) of England. Historians have wondered whether Newcomen borrowed his basic ideas from Savery or whether Newcomen's steam engine was entirely his own invention. Either way, it was Newcomen who made a successful business of manufacturing steam engines, and in the first half of the 1700s, the Newcomen engine started dotting the English countryside, pumping water out of mines.

In Newcomen's design, a piston moved up and down in a cylinder, as described earlier. The piston was attached to a strong bar acting like a lever. As the piston rose and fell, the bar also rose and fell, just like with the operation of a hand pump, except in this case the steam engine was providing the up-and-down movement. Steam flooding into the chamber pushed the piston up; cold water was squirted into the chamber, causing the steam to condense back into water and creating a vacuum that drew the piston down. The downward motion created a vacuum on the top, and this sucked the water up from below and into the chamber above the piston. Another squirt of steam from the boiler pushed the piston up, expelling the water through a separate pipe. This cycle repeated endlessly: the expansion power of steam pushing the piston up, the contraction of cooled steam creating a vacuum and pulling the piston down, creating another vacuum that sucked in the water from the bottom of a coal

Other Contributors to the Steam Engine

Many inventors contributed to the development of the steam engine. Among these are:

- The Dutch scientist Christiaan Huygens (1629–1695), who, working in France, left drawings of devices that closely resemble the first steam engines. His drawings showed how exploding gunpowder, instead of steam, could move a piston inside a cylinder.

- Jean de Hautefeuille (1647–1724) of France, who described the idea of pistons to push water, or air, out of a cylinder.

- Denis Papin (1647–1712) of France, who built on Huygens's idea of gunpowder and suggested using steam instead.

- Samuel Morland (1625–1695), a British clergyman, scientist, and master mechanic to King Charles II, who conducted early experiments on how pressure is created when steam is contained in a limited space. It was a key discovery along the road to development of the steam engine.

mine. The cycle could repeat as long as coal heated water and created steam.

Newcomen built his first engine in 1712. It worked at the rate of twelve strokes (vertical movements) per minute. Each stroke could remove about ten gallons of water from the bottom of a mine. Eventually, machines built on Newcomen's design grew very large, in order to increase the amount of water removed. One such machine, built in Russia in 1775, had a piston 66 inches (168 centimeters) across and moved vertically 102 inches (259 centimeters).

It was expensive to build and install one of Newcomen's pumping devices. This fact led to one of the social changes brought about by the Industrial Revolution. It required either a rich individual to put up funds, or the pooling of funds by individuals who had extra savings, to build a machine. This money was called "capital," and the people investing their savings to build steam engines were the first capitalists. Their role was to provide the capital (money), not the work.

The cost of building a steam-driven pump proved to be worthwhile. Over time, it was much less expensive to operate a Newcomen machine than it was to pay for workers and horses to haul water from the bottom of a mine, even if the horses had been able to keep pace with the water collecting at the bottom.

The idea that a machine could cost less to operate while doing the same amount of work (in this case, bringing water to the surface) introduced another element that would mark the Industrial Revolution: productivity. In the case of a Newcomen engine, two men running a steam engine could accomplish the same work (measured in the amount of water pumped) in forty-eight hours as previously was accomplished by twenty men and fifty horses working day and night for a week.

Newcomen's engine also led to changes in the manufacture of iron, a strong metal. Iron was preferable to brass, a weaker metal that previously had been used to make pumps. A mutual dependency developed among coal, iron, and steam-engine manufacturers. As the steam-driven Newcomen engines required coal for energy, mining that coal required larger Newcomen engines to keep the mines from being flooded. Making larger Newcomen engines required manufacturing iron, a process that required coal.

For England, it was a lucky coincidence that iron mines and coal deposits were located near one another. It was one reason that England took an early lead in the Industrial Revolution.

James Watt repairs a model

After Newcomen introduced his first steam engine, there was one big step forward in this technology before the Industrial Revolution really got rolling. That advance was introduced by James Watt (1736–1819) of Scotland.

Watt worked for the University of Glasgow, in Scotland, making scientific instruments. He associated with a group of young scientists, including Dr. John Robison. In 1759 Robison raised the idea that a Newcomen steam engine could be used to move carriage wheels, as well as pump water. Watt later recalled that he had read Robison's paper and was intrigued by the idea.

During the school year 1763–64 Watt was asked to repair a working model of a Newcomen engine that was owned by the university. The model engine, quite miniature (its piston was just two inches in diameter), did not work properly. The engine started, ran for a few strokes, and then stopped.

Watt soon concluded that the Newcomen engine had two fundamental problems. One, it wasted much of the steam it generated because some of it escaped into the atmosphere before it could get into the cylinder to drive the piston.

James Watt improved on Thomas Newcomen's steam engine. *Reproduced by permission of the Library of Congress.*

A related problem lay in the way the steam was condensed back into water. In Newcomen's steam engine, water was sprayed inside the cylinder to cause the steam to condense and create the vacuum that pulled the piston back down. This process also cooled the cylinder, which could potentially condense the next batch of steam before the piston had been pushed all the way up.

Watt observed another inefficiency. When cold water was sprayed inside the cylinder, it condensed most—but not all—of the steam. This meant that the remaining bit of steam was resisting the vacuum in pulling the piston back down.

Watt realized that there was a basic problem with the design of Newcomen's engine. On the one hand, it was important to cool the cylinder sufficiently to condense all the steam; on the other hand, if the cylinder were cooled too much, it would take time and energy to heat it back up when the steam was introduced for the next cycle.

Thinking about the model steam engine on a walk through a park in Glasgow one Sunday afternoon, Watt had an inspiration. The next day, he started work on a model incorporating his idea: to use a separate container to condense the steam instead of condensing it in the cylinder where the piston was moving. His notion was to pump the air out of this second container—called a condenser—so that the steam would rush into the vacuum of the condenser, where it could be cooled and condensed without chilling the cylinder where the piston was moving. Watt also wrapped insulation around the cylinder so that it would stay as hot as possible. In this way, the next time steam was inserted, no heat would be lost when it came into contact with the walls of the cylinder.

Watt added two other innovations to Newcomen's engine. First, where Newcomen had used ordinary air to push the piston against the vacuum created by condensing the steam, Watt had the idea of using steam to push the piston in both directions. When he let the steam out of one end of the cylinder, he let steam into the other end so that steam pushed the piston in both directions, up and down. In this sense, Watt's engine was the first true "steam engine" since it used steam throughout, instead of a combination of steam and air, as in Newcomen's design.

Watt's other improvement involved the way in which steam was admitted to the cylinder. Originally, steam was injected until the piston moved all the way to the top of the cylinder. Later, Watt tried injecting steam only until the piston was one-fourth of the way through its stroke. The natural tendency of steam to expand provided the rest of the "push" against the piston. The result was an engine that needed less coal to generate steam, yet delivered the same energy in moving the piston.

 Engine or Machine?

Machine and engine are two words that are often used interchangeably, but there is a subtle difference. An engine converts a source of energy, such as coal or oil, into movement. A machine uses the power generated by the engine to manipulate or make something. Machines can weave thread into sheets of cloth or stamp metal into different shapes, for example.

Machines can use different sources of energy, including human or animal muscles, running water, or steam, to provide the movement required for making objects. Engines are sources of power that do not depend on muscles or running water from rivers or streams.

Coal

Coal has been used for heating for hundreds of years. Archaeologists have found evidence that the ancient Romans used it; in China, its use dates back over two thousand years.

In England, the use of coal started increasing by the early 1700s, partly to replace depleted forests of oak trees as a source of heat for homes.

Coal has qualities that make it an ideal fuel. Compared to wood, coal burns at a higher temperature and produces more heat from the same volume of material. And while burning wood depletes forests, the supply of coal buried in the earth is so large that shortages have not yet been encountered after more than two hundred years of extensive use.

The Lunar Society

James Watt and Matthew Boulton were members of a distinguished group of scientist-inventors called the Lunar Society, which met in Birmingham, England. The American statesman and inventor Benjamin Franklin was also associated with the society while he lived in England in the 1760s and early 1770s.

The society consisted of a small group of men who met each month on the Monday closest to the full moon. After an evening of dining and discussion, they made their way home by the light of the moon; hence the group's name.

Besides Watt and Boulton, other members included William Small, a doctor who once taught at the College of William and Mary in Virginia, and one of whose students was future American president Thomas Jefferson; Erasmus Darwin, a physician, inventor, and poet; Joseph Priestly, a chemist and Unitarian preacher; and Josiah Wedgwood, founder of a pottery company that still exists, as well as an amateur scientist interested in chemistry, minerals, clays, and glazes.

Members of the Lunar Society collected fossils and minerals, and they once set about trying to classify (organizing by species) all of the plants in Britain. They also conducted frequent experiments in laboratories, seeking to learn about nature through empiricism, or the practice of learning by closely observing the properties of objects rather than forming theories about them in advance. Other topics of interest included electricity and the nature of "airs" such as oxygen, hydrogen, and carbon dioxide.

The so-called Lunars for the most part supported the American Revolution and formation of a republic in North America to replace the monarch. Later, in 1789, many of them also supported the French Revolution, in which that country's king was removed from power.

The Lunar Society represented the unique combination of science, business, and independent thought in religion and politics that became hallmarks of the early Industrial Revolution in England.

On the other hand, coal has long been controversial. During the reign of King Edward I (1272–1307), burning coal was banned in England because some coal contains significant amounts of sulfur, which gives off an unpleasant odor as it burns. The sulfur in coal also combines with rain to create "acid raid," which can corrode buildings. Coal also produces great amounts of soot, a black, powdery substance comprised

Types of Coal

Coal is a combustible material found in nature that is primarily made up of the element carbon. There are four main types of coal, each with different characteristics.

- Lignite is a soft, brownish-colored coal. It is textured somewhat like wood and has a higher moisture content than other forms of coal; it therefore produces less heat per ton than other coal.

- Subbituminous coal is black with little texture. It contains less water than lignite and produces more heat per ton, but it deteriorates if exposed to the weather and tends to crumble when transported.

- Bituminous coal is black and shiny. It has little moisture and produces more heat from a given volume than any other form. In the United States, bituminous coal is found throughout the Northeast and Midwest.

- Anthracite is very high in carbon and therefore burns efficiently and with little soot. It is harder to start burning, but it burns longer than other coals, giving a steady, clean flame. When coal was used to heat houses, anthracite was often the preferred form.

of pure carbon. In areas where large amounts of coal are burned, soot can cover everything in sight and darken whole cities and towns.

Despite its drawbacks, coal as an energy source played a key role in the Industrial Revolution and influenced it in indirect ways as well.

As factories were being established, investors saw an advantage to locating the new coal-burning steam engines close to the source of coal. Railroads were not well established until the early 1800s, so placing coal-burning machines near the coal made economic sense. In Britain, deposits of iron ore were often situated near deposits of coal, making it inevitable that Britain's factory belt would be built in the northern part of England, near the sources of coal and iron.

Life in the mines

There were—and still are—many dangers associated with coal mining. Coal is usually found in horizontal strips, called seams, that run deep beneath the surface of the Earth. Deep shafts are dug, then horizontal tunnels are hollowed out and coal is dug from the seam. These horizontal tunnels were often so low that adults had difficulty crossing them, but children did not. For this reason, little children often were sent into coal mines to help chip away the coal or push carts (which ran on rails, like little trains) filled with coal back to the vertical shafts, where they were pulled to the surface. (The sight of young boys, their faces smudged with coal dust, trudging from mines after twelve hours of work, was a powerful image for politicians who insisted on legislation to reform the industry.)

Another danger was that explosives were used to blast the coal free from the seam, and sometimes these explosions caused sections of the tunnel to come crashing down, either crushing miners or blocking their access to the surface. Also, depending on the type of coal being mined, highly flammable gases sometimes seep from coal seams. Coal miners learned that canaries would be overcome by these gases before humans would be, so birds in cages were often carried into mines as early warning signals for the presence of gas, which could either suffocate miners or explode with deadly force.

Steam locomotives

Transportation is a critical part of manufacturing. Raw materials, including coal for steam engines, need to be brought to a factory, and finished goods need to be distributed to customers. The Industrial Revolution fundamentally changed the nature of transportation and travel, much as it changed the nature of manufacturing. Steam engines, themselves major users of coal, played a critical role in the evolution of transportation.

Railroads were critical in advancing the Industrial Revolution. Without them, it would not have been economical to transport coal to factories where steam-powered machines burned coal for fuel. Railroads also made it faster and cheaper to transport raw materials and manufactured goods to distant markets.

Moving coal from the mine

Like the steam engine, railroads owe their invention to the coal mine. The first prototype railroads were carts on wooden wheels that ran along wooden tracks inside the coal mine. The carts on rails helped miners haul large amounts of heavy coal to the surface. No particular individual or exact time and place is credited with this invention, but illustrations of German coal mines as early as 1530 show little trolley cars loaded with coal and hauled by horses. In the early models, the cars, wheels, and rails all were made of wood.

Industrial Travel

In 1755 young James Watt set off from Glasgow, Scotland, to London, England, to become a maker of scientific instruments. He traveled by horse, and the trip took twelve days. About a century later, a passenger riding a railroad powered by a steam engine could make the trip in about twelve hours.

Rails greatly reduced friction, compared to wheels on the earth. Using rails, a single horse could haul a wagon holding about 4,500 pounds (2,043 kilograms) of coal; the same horse pulling a wagon over a road could haul only about 1,600 pounds (726 kilograms) of coal. The horse hauled the wagons uphill; going downhill, the horse was detached and gravity took over. A man sitting on the car tried to maintain control by applying a brake to one pair of wheels by sitting on a lever. Accidents were common.

By 1602 this system of hauling coal from the mines was installed in mines around Newcastle-upon-Tyne, England. Over the next 150 years, an extensive network of wood-based "rail roads" was working in this area. In 1765—while Watt was working on the improved steam engine—a typical coal mine railway was composed of rails made from discarded masts taken from sailing ships. The rails were about 5 inches (13 centimeters) wide and 7 inches (8 centimeters) high; they were anywhere from 3 to 5 feet (90 to 150 centimeters) apart.

Gradually, these primitive wooden rails were extended from the mouth of the coal mine to a canal, where the coal was transported via barges. During the late 1700s extensive canals were built in England; floating barges could hold enormous weights and could be pulled by horses on a towpath alongside the canal. But these little artificial rivers were

Early History of Coal in the United States

Deposits of coal were discovered in North America as early as 1673, in what is now Illinois, by a French expedition led by Louis Jolliet (sometimes spelled Joliet; 1645–1700) and Père Marquette (1637–1675). The earliest coal mining took place in Virginia in the early 1700s. Between 1750 and 1800 many coal deposits were discovered in the areas of the Appalachian Mountains in what is now West Virginia, Kentucky, Pennsylvania, Ohio, and Maryland. There was limited mining of coal in the late 1700s; the coal industry got its big boost from the introduction of the steam locomotive and railroads after 1830.

Railroads provided both a need for coal—to run steam locomotives—and the means to haul it from the mines to the sites of early factories and cities where it could be used for heating homes. The next push for increased coal production in the United States came in the second half of the 1800s, when the steel industry substituted coke, a byproduct of coal, for charcoal in the manufacture of iron and steel. The presence of extensive coal deposits in Pennsylvania and West Virginia led directly to the building of the steel industry around Pittsburgh, Pennsylvania.

Still later, with the advent of electric power, coal was used extensively in generating electricity, a role that it continues to play in the twenty-first century.

difficult and expensive to build. They posed special difficulties in transporting goods over hills and mountains. Eventually, railroad builders ignored the canals and built the railroads all the way to the eventual destination.

In 1758 the British Parliament passed a bill establishing the Middleton Railway, which claims the distinction of being the oldest railway in the world. The Middleton Railway gave rise to another first: the first commercially successful use of steam locomotives. But these did not begin operating on the Middleton until 1812, fifty-four years after it was founded.

From wood to iron

Wood was not an ideal material for building railways. Both the wooden wheels and wooden rails wore out rapidly. After 1760 the wheels were often made of iron, but these wore out the wooden rails even faster. For a while, railways

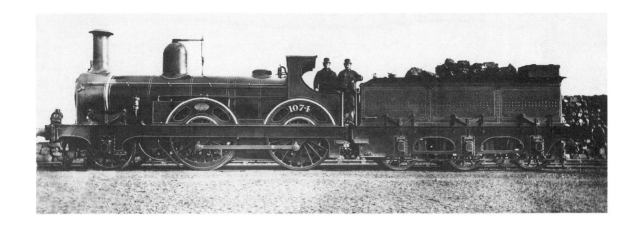

that served coal mines were fitted with strips of iron on top of the wooden rails, but these strips soon came loose.

The first iron rails were introduced in 1765 in Coalbrookdale, England, by an iron manufacturer named Richard Reynolds. The all-iron rails were an instant success for two reasons: they did not wear out, and because of reduced friction on the wheels of the coal carts, a horse could haul more than twice as much coal.

As more railroads were built, engineers devised other improvements. In 1797 English engineer Benjamin Outram (1764–1805), for example, devised a new shape for the rails, which included a flange, or rim. The flange gave the flat rail an L shape; the vertical piece helped keep the wheels from sliding off the rails. In 1801 Benjamin Wyatt of Bangor, England, thought of putting the flanges on the wheels instead of the rails. He designed a wheel with a groove that fit over a flat iron rail.

Until this time, the carts loaded with coal were being hauled by horses. The innovation that completed the picture of a modern railroad came from Richard Trevithick (1771–1833) on Christmas Eve, 1801, when he first demonstrated his concept of a locomotive (an engine that moves under its own power), which was essentially a steam engine mounted on wheels.

Trevithick increased the engine's steam pressure so that the steam, rushing into the cylinder, pushed the piston to the other end of the cylinder with greater force. And by

Two men stand on the Victoria Express steam locomotive. *Reproduced by permission of the Corbis Corporation.*

injecting steam into both ends of the cylinder, Trevithick eliminated the need to condense the steam; it could simply be vented into the air. This technique applied the power of steam (as opposed to the power of suction) to both ends of the cylinder and made the engine both faster and more powerful. In the engine that Trevithick mounted on wheels (his locomotive), the steam was released from the same chimney that released smoke from the fire heating the boiler. Every time this happened, the flow of air feeding the fire increased, causing the fire to burn hotter and therefore to turn water to steam faster.

Trevithick built his first locomotive at Coalbrookdale in 1802. An iron manufacturer in South Wales, Samuel Homfray, saw it and asked Trevithick to build one to use on a railway nine miles long that hauled coal to his ironworks at Dowlais. Trevithick's locomotive made the first trip, hauling a loaded train, on February 13, 1804, on the Penydarren railway in South Wales. The maiden trip had mixed results. The train hauled the coal, but the weight of the locomotive (7 tons; 6.3 metric tons) caused many of the rails to break. After just two more trips Homfray took the engine off its wheels. Instead, he used cables to pull the loaded cars along the tracks. For a while, this arrangement struck many people as being a safer way of using a steam engine to haul cars along tracks.

Trevithick was widely admired as an engineer, but he never achieved financial success. In 1808 he built a little circular railway in London, called Catch-Me-Who-Can, and offered rides for one shilling. It was a sort of amusement park ride, and he thought people would be thrilled to travel the astounding (at the time) speed of fifteen miles an hour. It turned out to be too much of a thrill—the public stayed away out of fear that the ride was dangerous. Eventually Trevithick took a job working in a silver mine in Peru, and after further business setbacks, he died penniless in London in 1833. Although Trevithick never profited from his designs, he is recognized as a key inventor in the history of railroads.

Three years after Trevithick showed Catch-Me-Who-Can in London, the English inventor John Blenkinsop (1783–1831) built two engines based on Trevithick's locomotive—but Blenkinsop's were lighter, in order not to break the rails. They were a big success. Trains hauled by locomotives of Blenkinsop's design began operating, at 5.5 miles an hour, in August 1812. The next year, another English inventor, William Hedley (1779–1843), built a locomotive mounted on eight wheels instead of four. This design spread out the load, allowing the iron rails to support the weight without breaking. Hedley's design was named "Puffing Billy," and several such locomotives were put into operation over the next fifteen years. They were still in use as late as 1862.

For the next decade, further refinements were made in the design of locomotives. One English engineer in particular, George Stephenson (1781–1848), became interested in the subject of locomotives and built one for the Killingworth Railway in 1814. In 1821 Stephenson was appointed chief engineer of the Stockton and Darlington Railway, even before construction had begun. He hired his son Robert, then age eighteen, as an assistant.

George Stephenson made an important change in Stockton and Darlington Railway's original plans: he insisted that iron rails be used, rather than iron strips on top of wood, which tended to loosen. Stephenson also persuaded the company to use locomotives, rather than horses or stationary steam engines.

On September 27, 1825, the Stockton and Darlington Railway introduced a locomotive—named Locomotion and designed by George Stephenson—to haul coal for the twenty miles between Brusselton and Etherley. It was a momentous occasion: the first time a steam locomotive had hauled cars on a public railway anywhere in the world.

George Stephenson and his son Robert continued to lead the effort to use locomotives to haul freight and passengers. And as the technology improved, it led to more widespread uses that eventually had a major impact on society, in England, the United States, and eventually around the world. Steam locomotives significantly increased the speed of travel. And by cutting the time it took to cross a country, they made it feasible for manufacturers to sell goods to a much wider market. Faster travel also changed perceptions of time and space. To a young man in Glasgow, London went from being a city that was twelve days' ride away when James Watt was a young man to a city that could be reached in twelve hours toward the end of Watt's life. Riding in a railroad carriage gradually became more like sitting in a comfortable living room on wheels, a far cry from sitting on a horse's back for hours on end or in a horse-drawn carriage bouncing down rough roads.

Steamboats

The nineteenth century marked the end of a long era of wind-powered ocean travel when the sail was replaced by the steam engine. The notion of using a steam engine to propel a boat or ship arose at about the same time James Watt developed his improved steam engine. Engineers soon thought of using this new form of power to propel boats on water, as well as wagons in coal mines and carriages on roads.

Water transport was critical long before the industrial era. Boats on rivers or barges on canals could carry great weight with relatively little effort, and sailing ships had long been used for global commerce. But while horses could tow a canal barge in any weather, a boat on a larger body of water, such as a river, lake, or ocean, usually needed wind to move, and wind was unreliable. Ships in the eighteenth century sometimes floated in harbors for days or even weeks waiting for enough wind to let them maneuver into open water.

As early as 1707 the French-born inventor Denis Papin experimented with using a paddle wheel to propel a boat. In 1736 an Englishman, Jonathan Hulls (1699–1758), secured a patent for a tugboat powered by a paddle wheel in its stern (rear) driven by a Newcomen steam engine. Watt's improved steam engine promised a great improvement when it was patented in 1769, and it touched off many efforts to apply this new invention to transportation.

An early success using steam to propel a ship was achieved in France, where the Marquis de Joffroy d'Abbans in 1783 used a steam engine to move a boat with a paddle wheel. In 1788, in England, Scottish banker Patrick Miller (1731–1815) designed a boat with paddles between an outer and inner hull and that was driven by a steam engine. Miller put his design to work on a boat that ran along Scotland's Forth and Clyde Canal. Also in Scotland, William Symington (1763–1831) launched the *Charlotte Dundas* in 1802 using a steam-powered paddle wheel in the stern to propel it on the Forth and Clyde Canal.

In the United States, water transport was especially important as the newly settled country had few good roads but many navigable rivers. In Virginia, an American inventor named James Rumsey (1743–1792) in 1787 exhibited a boat that took in water at the bow (front of the ship) and forced it out through a pipe in the stern: an early form of a jet engine.

In the summer of 1790, another American inventor, John Fitch (1743–1798) of Connecticut, used steam engines to power a boat that used canoe paddles on each side to propel it forward at a speed of six to eight miles per hour. The boat transported passengers between Philadelphia, Pennsylvania, and Bordentown, New Jersey. Passengers looked on the craft as an amusement more than as a serious, reliable form of transportation. After one summer, Fitch shut down the service.

The missing element in the early efforts to apply steam-engine technology to water transport was success in business, rather than technology. Potential customers were not accustomed to technical innovation, and they did not use the new craft often enough to cover the costs. By 1791 the underlying technological challenge had been met; the boats of that period were very similar to the boat that eventually succeeded almost twenty years later. In this respect, the story of the steamboat contains an important lesson of the Industrial Revolution: technology without business success could not change the world.

Thus, the person most closely associated with the successful introduction of steamboats—the American Robert Fulton (1765–1815)—might better be considered a successful business entrepreneur, rather than as the inventor of the steamboat.

Fulton was an artist and prolific inventor who launched a steamboat named the *Clermont* on the Hudson River in 1807. Simultaneously he launched a successful business ferrying passengers and freight between Albany, New York, and New York City. How he managed this feat is as much a story of politics and business as of technology.

Fulton had left his home in Philadelphia for England in 1786, at age seventeen, to pursue a career as a painter. Seven years later, after achieving modest success as an artist, he devoted his energies to technology. He designed a steam-powered machine for cutting marble—for which he achieved a silver medal for ingenuity from the Society for the Encouragement of Arts, Commerce, and Manufactures in London—and then devoted his attention to canal building. At the time, canals were attracting major investment in England as a means of improving inland transportation.

Fulton designed a machine to dig canals, as well as a new method of hauling ships up inclined planes to get over hills and mountains. In 1796 he also published a book, *A Treatise on the Improvement of Canal Navigation*. In 1797 Fulton moved to France, where he designed a working submarine, which he called the *Nautilus*. He demonstrated the *Nautilus* to the French navy in 1801, piloting it for seventeen minutes in twenty-five feet of water. Although Fulton's submarine could submerge, maneuver under water, and surface, the French navy was not interested.

But more important for Fulton, while in France he met the new American ambassador, Robert Livingston (1746–1813), a prominent signer of the Declaration of Independence. Before leaving for France, Livingston had persuaded the New York State legislature to grant him an exclusive license to operate steamboats in New York State. But Livingston had no working steamboat. He saw in his fellow American, Robert Fulton, someone who might be able to provide him with one.

In October 1802 the two men signed a formal agreement under which Fulton would develop a steam-powered boat, and Livingston would pay the costs. If the experiment worked, they would become business partners.

Fulton spent the next two-and-a-half years in Paris working on the project. His first boat sank in the Seine River after a storm tossed the boat violently and caused the steam engine to fall through the bottom and into the river. In the summer of 1804, Fulton demonstrated a working model. A Paris newspaper (quoted by Fulton's biographer, H. W. Dickinson) described the boat's first trial this way:

> On [August 6, 1803] a trial was made of a new invention, of which the complete and brilliant success should have important consequences for the commerce and internal navigation of France. During the past two or three months there has

been seen at the end of the quay Chaillot a boat of curious appearance, equipped with two large wheels mounted on an axle like a cart, while behind these wheels was a kind of large stove with a pipe, as if there was some kind of a small fire engine [steam engine] intended to operate the wheels of the boat.... At six o'clock in the evening, assisted by three persons only, [the builder] put his boat in motion with two other boats in tow behind it, and for an hour and a half he afforded the curious spectacle of a boat moved by wheels like a cart, these wheels being provided with paddles or flat plates and being moved by a fire engine.

In following it along the quay the speed against the current of the Seine appeared to us about that of a rapid pedestrian, that is about 2400 toises [a French measurement equivalent to about 2.2 miles] per hour; while in going down stream it was more rapid.... It was maneuvered with facility, turned to the right and left, came to anchor, started again, and passed by the swimming school.... This mechanism applied to our rivers, the Seine, the Loire, and the Rhone, would be fraught with the most advantageous consequences to our internal navigation. The tows of barges which now require four months to come from Nantes to Paris would arrive promptly in from 10 to 15 days. The author of this brilliant invention is M. Fulton, an American and a celebrated mechanician [mechanic].

Robert Fulton is widely credited as the inventor of the steamboat, but his most significant contribution was developing a practical way of applying a steam engine to water transport.
Reproduced by permission of the Library of Congress.

Satisfied with his basic design, Fulton ordered a larger steam engine from Boulton and Watt, the English company formed by the steam engine's developer, James Watt. But English authorities refused to permit Boulton and Watt to export a steam engine to France: the two countries were at war, and France was threatening to invade England. Consequently, in the spring of 1804, Fulton returned to England to buy a steam engine that he planned to use in building a full-scale boat in New York.

In England Fulton contracted with the British navy to develop his plans for a torpedo, essentially a floating bomb designed to sink French warships poised to invade England from across the English Channel. It was a controversial idea, not enthusiastically supported by the British navy. Nevertheless, Fulton spent the second half of 1804 and most of 1805 developing a torpedo. In the end, a demonstration Fulton staged did not succeed, and he abandoned the torpedo project to return to New York with his Boulton and Watt steam engine.

In New York, in December 1806, Fulton began building a full-scale model of a steamship to use in his partnership with Livingston. Shortly after noon on Monday, August 17, 1807, the ship—named the *Clermont,* after Livingston's estate near Albany, New York—was launched, four-and-a-half years after Fulton and Livingston signed their agreement in Paris.

In a letter to a friend, as quoted in Dickinson's biography, Fulton described the *Clermont*'s maiden voyage:

> My steamboat voyage to Albany and back has turned out rather more favorably than I had calculated. The distance from New York to Albany is one hundred and fifty miles. I ran it up in thirty-two hours and down in thirty. I had a light breeze against me the whole way both going and coming and the voyage has been performed wholly by the power of the steam-engine. I overtook many sloops and schooners beating to windward and parted with them as if they had been at anchor.

> The power of propelling boats by steam is now fully proved....

> It will give a cheap and quick conveyance to the merchants on the Mississippi, Missouri, and other great rivers which are now laying open their treasures to the enterprise of our countrymen; and although the prospect of personal emolument [wealth] has been some inducement [motivation] to me, yet I feel infinitely more pleasure in reflecting on the immense advantages that my country will draw from the invention.

Important as Fulton's technological achievement was—the *Clermont* was the first feasible steamboat in the world—it was the business proposition first presented to Fulton by Robert Livingston that succeeded in making the boat a part of history. The story of their business is less about technology than about politics, and about how Livingston was able to influence the government to favor his company and its newly invented steamboat.

It took at least another decade before a steamship ventured beyond inland rivers and crossed the Atlantic. In 1819 the American ship *Savannah* claimed to be the first steamship to cross the ocean, although the *Savannah* had sails and relied on the wind for a good deal of the journey. Ships propelled exclusively by steam did not make the ocean crossing until 1838, by which time the propeller had replaced the paddle wheel as the means of propulsion.

For More Information

Books

Ashton, T. S. *The Industrial Revolution, 1760–1830.* Westport, CT: Greenwood Press, 1986.

Bunch, Bryan H., and Alexander Hellemans. *The Timetables of Technology: A Chronology of the Most Important People and Events in the History of Technology.* New York: Simon and Schuster, 1993.

Crowther, J. G. *Scientists of the Industrial Revolution: Joseph Black, James Watt, Joseph Priestley, Henry Cavendish.* London: Cresset Press, 1962.

Deane, Phyllis. *The First Industrial Revolution.* 2d ed. New York: Cambridge University Press, 1979.

Mantoux, Paul. *The Industrial Revolution in the Eighteenth Century: An Outline of the Beginnings of the Modern Factory System in England.* Rev. ed. New York: Macmillan, 1961.

Toynbee, Arnold. *Lectures on the Industrial Revolution in England, 1884; reprinted: The Industrial Revolution.* Boston: Beacon Press, 1956.

Periodicals

Petroski, Henry. "Harnessing Steam." *American Scientist,* January/February 1996, p. 15.

"Steam Engines: Puffed Up." *Economist,* December 25, 1999, p. 99.

Web Sites

Carnegie, Andrew. *James Watt.* Reproduced on *University of Rochester History Resources: Steam Engine Library.* http://www.history.rochester.edu/steam/carnegie/ch8.html (accessed on February 7, 2003).

Dickinson, H. W. "Robert Fulton, Engineer and Artist: His Life and Works." *University of Rochester History Resources: Steam Engine Library.* http://www.history.rochester.edu/steam/dickinson/index.html (accessed on February 7, 2003).

Hart, Robert. "Reminiscences of James Watt." *University of Rochester History Resources: Steam Engine Library.* http://www.history.rochester.edu/steam/hart (accessed on February 7, 2003).

Internet Modern History Sourcebook: The Industrial Revolution. http://www.fordham.edu/halsall/mod/modsbook14.html (accessed on February 7, 2003).

New Machines and the Factory System

3

It seems like an idealistic scene: In a quaint English cottage, a mother sits spinning cotton or wool, twisting the short fibers into yarn. Perhaps the older children are sitting at smaller spinning wheels. Upstairs, the father sits at his loom, weaving the yarn spun by his family downstairs into cloth. Not far away, a farmer tends a flock of sheep that provided the raw wool to the family, whose name might well be Weaver. An unmarried older daughter still working at home spinning yarn is literally a spinster.

This picture of cottage industry stood on the brink of extinction in 1760. Within a generation, most of the spinning and weaving in England had moved out of homes and into factories. Men and women, even children, still participated, but as employees, not as semi-independent skilled workers. A set of machines that could imitate the work of spinners and weavers had almost completely taken over the textile industry in England. These machines would soon stand as models for other industries in which machines could do the work of individual craftspeople.

Words to Know

Cottage industry: A system in which skilled craftspeople manufacture goods, such as cloth, from their homes rather than in factories. This scenario was typical of the period before the Industrial Revolution

Cotton gin: A machine used to comb the seeds from cotton balls.

Industrialization: The process of introducing machines to supplement or replace human labor.

Loom: A machine, sometimes called a frame, used to weave fabric.

Spinning: Twisting the short fibers of wool or cotton into a continuous yarn.

Textile industry: The manufacture of cloth, typically for clothing but also for other purposes, such as bedsheets and sails.

Weaving: Making yarn into cloth by crisscrossing threads of yarn on a loom.

These machines brought enormous change to the way people lived and worked. A large and growing population of people began living in large towns or cities, employed in new factories and facing little or no prospect of improving or controlling their lives. At the same time, factory owners were making huge fortunes independent of the land. They soon insisted that their new economic power be reflected in their political influence. Both the powerful factory owners and the powerless factory workers created by the Industrial Revolution threatened the established political order based on ancient patterns of land ownership.

Soon the new textile machines were installed in the United States, where a textile industry developed in New England. In the American South, large plantations started growing more cotton to be processed into cloth, thanks to the invention of the cotton gin, which made it fast and easy to get rid of the seeds in raw cotton that had previously made cotton difficult to turn into yarn. The new textile machines had an unexpected consequence: they breathed new life into slavery, since cotton growers were convinced that slave labor was essential to operating a large plantation.

The introduction of new machines, housed in factories, resulted in major changes not only to English society,

but also in other countries. Two hundred years later, as the textile industry opened factories in Asia and boosted many national economies there, the same social issues associated with industrialization—exploitation of children and low wages paid to workers—surfaced again.

Two men are depicted working a model of the first cotton gin at a marketplace. *Reproduced by permission of the Library of Congress.*

Textiles: The second "engine" of the Industrial Revolution

The steam engine was one driving force behind the Industrial Revolution (see Chapter 2); the textile industry was the other. Starting in 1738, a series of inventions introduced major changes in the way fibers were spun into yarn and yarn was woven into cloth. The machines not only changed the mechanics of making cloth; they also changed the relationship between the people who did the spinning and weaving and the merchants who supplied the natural fibers and bought the cloth. What had been home-based, family-based businesses gave way to factory-based businesses on a much larger scale.

Over time, this combination of labor-saving inventions and changing business relations brought about changes in society that spread to other industries and changed the face of politics.

Changes affecting the textile industry

Making cloth traditionally comprised three steps: Raising sheep or plants (cotton or flax) to produce the raw materials used in fabric; twisting the fibers into yarn, a process called spinning; and weaving or knitting yarn into cloth. In the 1700s, changes in England affected all three steps.

The enclosure movement (see Chapter 1) allowed wealthy individuals to take title to many small plots of land and to turn them into large estates suitable for grazing large herds of sheep. This movement resulted in an increased supply of wool. At the same time, in English colonies in North America and India, large plantations were established in climates ideal for growing cotton, the chief alternative to wool. Traditionally, merchants had bought raw wool or cotton from farmers and delivered these materials to skilled workers who made a living by spinning the fibers into yarn and weaving the yarn into fabric. Spinning and weaving often took place within a single family. The mother and children were engaged in spinning the yarn, while the father operated a loom to weave the spun yarn into cloth. It usually took several family members spinning yarn to keep pace with the weaving. (A skilled weaver could use as much yarn as four or more spinners could produce.) This system of manufacturing cloth at home was called a cottage industry, for the obvious reason that it took place in cottages, or houses.

The system had certain advantages for the families engaged in making fabric. When they felt like stopping work for the day, there was nothing to prevent them. They worked at a pace that suited their need for money, rest, food, or sleep. They set their own hours and pace of work. They could make their own decisions, within limits, about what kind of cloth to weave and how much to weave. They could take their time and produce high-quality work, or they could work faster to earn more money, even if it meant producing lower-quality fabric. And although they were paid money, weaving families could also measure their output in yards of cloth produced in a month or a year.

Textile merchants were not always happy with inconsistent quality and schedules as their customers were counting on receiving material in order to make clothing, sails for ships, bed sheets, tents, and other items.

The disparity between how much yarn a spinner could produce and how much a weaver used to make cloth created an opportunity for innovation. In the case of cotton, it took four or more people spinning yarn to keep up with one weaver operating a loom; in the case of wool, it took up to ten spinners to keep up. It was clear that a machine that promised to speed the process of spinning would help increase weavers' output.

In the second half of the eighteenth century, there was a market for more cloth. England's population was growing rapidly—from six million people in 1750 to about nine million in 1800—which meant a strong demand for cloth used in clothing of all sorts, sheets, towels, and curtains.

Just in time to serve the rapidly growing population, a series of inventions revolutionized both spinning and weaving. The new equipment required less time to spin yarn and weave fabric; therefore one person operating one of the new machines could produce several times as much yarn or fabric than previously possible.

Making cloth

To understand how the new inventions changed the industry, it is useful to understand the basic process by which yarn and fabric are created.

First, the curly fibers of sheep's wool or cotton are combed into short, straight strands (a process called carding). Next, these strands are twisted tightly with overlapping ends to create long strands of yarn—the process called spinning. For generations, spinning had been done by a hand-operated spinning wheel. The operator sat on a bench or chair and pushed a large wheel (around three feet, or one meter, in diameter) that turned gears connected to a spindle that was turning (or spinning) quite rapidly. With one hand, the operator (spinster) kept the large wheel turning, in order to keep the spindle going quickly. With the other hand, the operator fed strands of wool or cotton fiber onto the spindle, which twisted the fibers tightly and produced yarn. The basic spinning wheel was evidently developed in India as early as 700 B.C.E. In the 1400s, a modification was introduced that fed the newly spun yarn through a hole onto another turning piece, a bobbin, where the yarn was wrapped.

To make yarn strong and uniform in thickness, spinners had to be careful to feed just the right amount of cotton or wool fiber; mistakes made yarn pull apart, or become too thick, in which case the process had to be reversed and done again. Most spinning was done by women, and the sight of a woman sitting at a spinning wheel was a familiar one in the early 1700s. By 1800, new machines had been developed (see below) that almost entirely eliminated the traditional spinning wheel.

The next stage in making cloth was weaving the yarn into cloth. This process, usually done by men, used a loom, which looked a bit like the edges of a box without sides (which is the reason looms were sometimes called frames). Parallel strands of strong yarn were stretched vertically between two bars on either end; this yarn was called the warp. Sitting in front of the warp, the weaver used foot pedals to lift every other string of the warp, creating a space between the alternate yarns called the shed. The weaver, sometimes with an assistant, passed a shuttle, a tapered piece of wood on which yarn had been wound, through the shed from one side to the other, creating the web of over-and-under yarn that constitutes woven material. The horizontal yarn is called the weft; the weft could use weaker yarns, since the warp yarns hold the fabric together. After one strand of the weft was added, the weaver used the pedals to operate a sort of comb that pushed the horizontal weft yarns tightly together. The pedals also shifted the warp so that every other yarn changed places, after which the shuttle was passed back to the other side. Sometimes weavers lifted only selected yarns of the warp, resulting in patterns woven into the cloth.

This back and forth movement, under alternating parallel yarns, was repeated dozens of times for every inch of fabric woven. The width of hand-operated looms (and consequently the width of cloth produced) was dictated by how far the weaver's arms could stretch out (about six feet, or two meters, for most adults) to catch the shuttle on one side and throw it back to the other.

Technical innovation: Faster, more consistent spinning

Using traditional methods, weavers normally used as much yarn as three or four spinners could produce. Spinning was often slowed when too many fibers were fed into the spindle, making the yarn too thick and leaving a spot where the fibers were not twisted tightly enough to resist being pulled apart. Finding a faster, more efficient way of spinning yarn was seen in the early 1700s as a worthwhile subject for innovation, and it was here that the process of mechanization of the textile industry began.

The first of these innovations was the roller-spinning machine, patented in 1738 by two Englishmen, Lewis Paul and John Wyatt. (A patent is a permit given to an inventor allowing him exclusive rights to make, use, or sell his invention.) Using this machine, the spinster fed fibers into two sets of rollers, which in turn fed them into the spindle. Instead of a woman rotating a large wheel to keep the spindles spinning, as well as making the rollers turn, the roller spinning machine used donkeys for the purpose. The invention was not a commercial success, however, largely because it was prone to breaking down. But it was the forerunner of another machine that did change the face of textiles.

In 1764, an English carpenter and weaver named James Hargreaves (c. 1720–1778) invented a new version of the traditional spinning machine, which he called the spin-

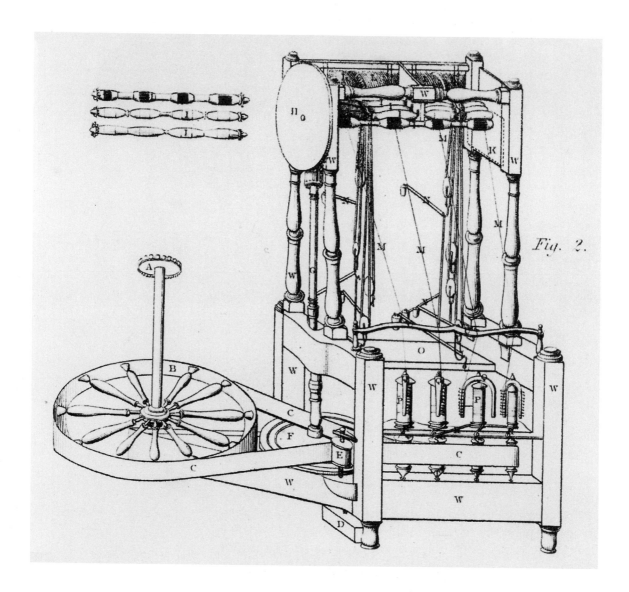

Fig. 2.

Diagram of a spinning machine. *Reproduced by permission of the Library of Congress.*

ning jenny. According to folklore, Hargreaves had a daughter named Jenny (some versions of the story say it was his wife who was named Jenny) who tipped over a spinning wheel one day, at which point Hargreaves noticed that the machine kept turning. This realization sparked the idea of attaching multiple spindles to one large wheel, producing several strands of yarn at once. Hargreaves started working on his idea in 1754, and it took fourteen years to produce the first version of a spinning jenny, which had eight spindles. To feed the cotton fibers, Hargreaves developed a moving bar, operated by a foot

pedal, to draw out the cotton fiber and feed it onto the spindles. Soon, versions of the spinning jenny supported up to 120 spindles. Hargreaves sold a few models of his invention to earn money, and soon copies had been made. Some spinsters realized that the greater productivity of the jenny could cost them their jobs (since one operator could now produce as much yarn as eight or more workers using traditional spinning wheels). They broke into Hargreaves's home and wrecked some machines. Eventually, though, about twenty thousand spinning jennies were made (many of them copies of Hargreaves's original, for which Hargreaves received no money). The spinning jenny set the stage for further innovation.

Yarn from a spinning jenny, like yarn spun with traditional spinning wheels, had a drawback: it was not strong. Both the spinning wheel and the spinning jenny failed to feed fibers into the spindles consistently. Sometimes larger bunches would go through, resulting in yarn that was not of uniform thickness and spots where the fibers were not twisted tightly

Richard Arkwright.
Reproduced by permission of the Library of Congress.

enough to resist being pulled apart. Consequently, yarn from a spinning jenny or traditional spinning wheel was only used for the horizontal yarns (the weft), while the warp needed stronger, more expensive yarn spun from flax to hold the fabric together. Five years after Hargreaves introduced his spinning jenny, English inventor Richard Arkwright (1732–1792) patented another spinning machine that addressed the problem of inconsistent thickness and strength.

Arkwright, together with a clockmaker named John Kay, developed a machine that could separate the fibers of cotton or wool and feed them into the spindles more consistently. Arkwright's machine, called the water frame (because it used a waterwheel pushed by water in a river or stream to keep the spindles spinning), passed combed cotton or wool fibers through four pairs of rollers, each pair moving faster than the last. The last rollers had grooves that enabled fibers to be fed uniformly into the spindles. By twisting fibers more consistently, the water frame resulted in yarn that was both smoother and stronger. Yarn made on Arkwright's machine could be used for both the warp and the weft, resulting in the first all-cotton fabric. Initially, Arkwright used horses to turn the rollers and spindles, but he soon adapted the machine to use a waterwheel pushed by a flowing stream or river. Eventually a steam engine supplied the power.

Arkwright was granted a patent for his new machine in 1771. He proved to be a canny businessman, and he eventually earned a fortune producing cotton yarn.

The last step in automating production of yarn was introduced by Samuel Crompton (1753–1827) in 1779. It was called the "spinning mule" since it was a combination of the spinning jenny and the water frame.

The spinning mule used rollers, like Arkwright's, to draw apart slender slivers of cotton, called rovings. In Crompton's machine, four sets of rollers were used in this process. The rovings were then mounted on a moving carriage, borrowed from the spinning jenny, so that the spindles could twist the yarn without pulling too hard on the rovings, thereby avoiding the earlier problem of yarn being pulled apart as it was spun. In Crompton's model, like the spinning jenny, multiple spindles (about 50) were attached to the moving carriage; later, the number of spindles was raised to 150. Later improvements resulted in very large spinning machines, with up to 1,400 spindles among its thirty thousand parts. Such machines were powered by a steam engine.

After 1830, only a few minor changes were made to the spinning mule, and it was the standard machine used to make yarn for more than a century. Not until the mid-1900s was a replacement, called the winder and ring spinner, developed. The last spinning mule was taken out of operation in 1974.

In the production of cotton yarn, there was one more major invention that had an impact: the cotton gin, invented by Eli Whitney (1765–1825), an American. The cotton gin was designed to comb out seeds from the puffs of cotton, called bolls, that were plucked from the plant. The seeds had to be removed before cotton bolls could be carded and used to spin yarn. Removing them required picking them out by hand, one by one, a slow and laborious process that added to the cost of cotton.

In 1792, after graduating from Yale University, Whitney was visiting the Georgia plantation of Mrs. Nathanael Greene, the wife of a Revolutionary War general, where he heard many complaints from neighboring farmers about the time-consuming, labor-intensive job of removing the seeds. Although cotton was a profitable crop, and the land and the climate were ideally suited to growing it, it did not pay to plant very much of it since there was neither enough time nor enough people to remove the seeds from the bolls.

Hearing this, Whitney went about finding a solution. He had grown up on a farm in Connecticut, and he was used to handling machines and working with wood. Whitney

Eli Whitney invented the cotton gin to speed up the process of removing seeds from cotton. *Reproduced by the Library of Congress.*

soon created a workable cotton gin (short for cotton engine). It looked like a rectangular box with a crank handle on the side and rollers lined with teeth inside. As the crank turned the rollers, the cotton fibers were pulled through, but the seeds, too thick to pass between the teeth, were removed. The machine was easy to operate and could remove seeds much faster than a person could by picking out the seeds by hand.

Whitney's invention was an almost instant success. But Whitney did not profit from his invention as he imagined. At first, he offered to process cotton bolls in exchange for part of the price that farmers got for their crop; Whitney asked for forty percent, which was considered too much by most farmers (even though the cotton gin could produce seed-free cotton at far more than twice the speed of humans, resulting in much lower labor costs). Instead, cotton planters made their own copies of the cotton gin without paying Whitney. Although Whitney had a patent on the cotton gin and tried hard to prevent such copying, the cost of enforcing the patent was too great, and Whitney returned to Connecticut without the fortune he had hoped to earn from the cotton gin.

Speeding up the removal of seeds, the cotton gin eliminated a major disadvantage of cotton as an alternative to wool. Thanks to the cotton gin and the spinning mule, cotton cloth became highly popular. Southern farmers began growing more cotton than ever on huge farms called plantations, worked by slaves from Africa, to meet the growing demand.

Weaving

Advances in manufacturing yarn were accompanied by developments in weaving. Indeed, advances in spinning and weaving tended to leap-frog one another: weaving drove the need for more efficient spinning, and as spinning became faster and more productive, improvements in looms were needed to keep pace with the production of yarn.

The first and most dramatic advance in looms was the "flying shuttle," a loom invented in 1733 by Englishman John Kay (1704–1764). Instead of being pushed through the shed, Kay's invention put the shuttle on a wheel that ran along a ledge, called the slay. The weaver pulled a cord to pull the flying shuttle from one side to the other. This process moved the shuttle back and forth quicker than the traditional method and also enabled weavers to make "broadcloth," fabric wider than one person's reach.

A loom equipped with a flying shuttle could weave cloth about twice as fast, with less effort, than the traditional method. It made a single weaver much more productive than with hand looms, a fact that was not lost on traditional weavers. John Kay and his flying shuttle were the target of violence that forced Kay to move to France in 1747, where he died in poverty.

In about 1789 another English inventor, Edmond Cartwright (1743–1823), developed a loom that used a waterwheel for power. Cartwright's power loom substituted water power for the human energy it took to beat the warp, the action of pushing the horizontal yarn tightly against the previous one and shifting the warp yarns to their opposite position. The steady, strong movement of the power loom worked faster than an individual human being and did not require rest. In 1790 a factory was built that used a steam engine instead of a waterwheel to provide the power to Cartwright's power loom. (A steam engine is a device that uses the expansive quality of steam to pump a piston [a solid tube] inside a cylinder [a pipe-like structure] as a means of moving objects; see Chapter 2.)

The result was another jump in productivity, but it came at a price: the power loom needed a waterwheel or steam engine to operate. The machines were too large and too complex to be operated by a single person (the steam engine alone needed someone to tend to it) and too expensive for an individual weaver to buy and install at home. The original factory housing a power loom burned down before it could enter production, but the stage was set for changing the way cloth was made: within ten years, a single factory had been built that contained two hundred power looms.

New ways of working: The factory system

The owners of the new machines installed them in large buildings called manufactories (later shortened to factories). Some of the machines needed to be located near a stream or river to provide the energy to push a waterwheel; others were too large to fit in the cramped house of an individual spinner or weaver. Machines driven by waterwheels or by steam engines did not need to stop and rest, as human-powered machines did.

The rise of the factory system, in which workers were paid on how much time they spent in the factory instead of on the value of the finished products they created, led to a profound change in society, and in the relationship between the individual and his or her work. Work came to represent time spent in a factory, instead of producing fine yarn or fabric, for example. If a single worker could produce much more yarn or cloth in a day using a new machine, the benefit went to the machine's owner; the individual running the machine was paid the same wage regardless of output. And since the new machines often required less skill than hand-operated equipment, owners were able to employ people recently displaced from tiny farms by the enclosure movement that consolidated many smaller farms into larger ones (see Chapter 1).

The owners, having paid for the new, complex machines and the factory, plus the raw material (wool or cotton) and the time of the workers, then collected the difference between the value of the finished product and the cost of the raw materials and labor.

From the viewpoint of Britain's economy as a whole, the new factories led to a dramatic increase in productivity and national wealth. The British economy came to be based on importing raw materials from its overseas colonies and exporting the goods it manufactured from them.

One of England's first large factories, housing a large water frame to spin yarn, was built by Richard Arkwright in Nottingham in 1771. Within twelve years, Arkwright employed five thousand workers. By 1800, new factories were springing up all around northern England, where the city of Manchester became the center of England's new industrial economy. According to an 1823 history of the industry by Richard Guest (*Compendious History of the Cotton Manufacture*, Manchester), by 1818 there were fourteen factories housing about 2,000 looms in the cities of Manchester, Stockport, Middleton, Hyde, Stayley Bridge, and surrounding areas. In just three years, the number of factories had risen to thirty-two, with 5,732 looms. By 1823 there were 10,000 power looms in England.

Guest's book also describes the increase in productivity resulting from the new system—and the potential reduction in the number of people needed to produce a given amount of cloth:

A very good Hand Weaver, a man twenty-five or thirty years of age, will weave two pieces of nine-eighths shirting [fabric suitable for making a shirt] per week, each twenty four yards long.... A Steam Loom Weaver, fifteen years of age, will in the same time weave seven similar pieces. A Steam Loom factory containing two hundred Looms, with the assistance of one hundred persons under twenty years of age, and of twenty-five men will weave seven hundred pieces per week.... To manufacture one hundred similar pieces per week by the hand, it would be necessary to employ at least one hundred and twenty-five Looms, because many of the Weavers are females, and have cooking, washing, cleaning and various other duties to perform; others of them are children and, consequently, unable to weave as much as the men. It requires a man of mature age and a very good Weaver to weave two of the pieces in a week, and there is also an allowance to be made for sickness and other incidents. Thus, eight hundred and seventy-five hand Looms would be required to produce the seven hundred pieces per week; and reckoning the weavers, with their children, and the aged and infirm belonging to them at two and a half to each loom, it may very safely be said, that the work done in a Steam Factory containing two hundred Looms, would, if done by hand Weavers, find employment and support for a population of more than two thousand persons.

In summary, a factory employing 125 people (25 men and 100 children) could do the work of 2,000 people under the old system. It is little wonder that weavers saw the new machines as a threat to their jobs. The stage had been set for social change, and there arose numerous protests against the new machines by workers who had been displaced by them.

The changing relationship between workers and their work

In some ways, machines in a factory might seem to be simply a larger version of a weaver's family operation working from a home. But the greater size and the new technology resulted in a much different relationship between the worker and his or her work.

The factory system involved two major changes. The first and more obvious was that people now worked in a different place than their homes. They went to a large building where the new machines were located. Being employed meant agreeing to spend a fixed amount of time on the job, most often twelve hours a day, six days a week (seventy-two hours a week), or more. A worker who could not, or would not, work received no wages. Whole families might lose their housing (occasionally provided by a factory for people who recently moved into town from the countryside) if the father lost his job. The new system meant that workers lost any sense of independence; they lost the ability to regulate their hours of work, or the quality of work. Just as in the traditional cottage industry, women and children were employed in textile factories, but the parents no longer had the ability to control the time their children spent working.

A second change brought about by the factory system was intense specialization. Instead of a family taking raw wool or cotton and turning it into cloth—and thus being involved in the entire production process—in the factory system, the process was broken down into small parts. A worker might be responsible for replacing the supply of yarn on the looms. Another might be responsible for folding the new material as it came off the loom. No worker participated in the entire process.

Workers became like parts of the machinery they attended. Whatever variety in day-to-day tasks that might have marked the previous system was now eliminated. Each day became a long, uninterrupted repetition of the same small task. The need for skills, much less creativity, was minimized. Some workers went from being highly skilled craftspeople to becoming interchangeable parts of a master machine called the factory. And if a worker failed to behave like part of the machine, the flow of work could be interrupted, at great cost to the factory owner and to the worker.

Just as machine parts were replaced if they wore out or failed, so too were the human parts. Machines, whether driven by a steam-powered engine or flowing water, did not get tired or need to rest, eat lunch, or take a break. In the new factories, the pace of work was set by the machine, with little regard for workers' abilities. To maximize profits, factory owners insisted that the machines be kept working at a steady pace, hour after hour.

Setting the stage for social change

Early factory owners were so focused on making money that they did not give too much consideration to the health and well-being of their workers. Employees were expected to work at least twelve hours a day and to keep pace with the machinery. Factory owners took advantage of the fact that operating the new machines required less skill than was needed to be a master weaver, for example. This meant that the supply of potential workers to operate the machines was larger: factory owners could draw on the thousands of people newly driven off the land by the enclosure movement (see Chapter 1), who were desperate for money to live on.

Workers were not viewed as assets but as an expense to be kept low. Factories paid low wages. Sometimes they employed children, who were expected to work for less money than adults. An additional advantage of employing children was that their small fingers enabled them to work more nimbly on some machines than adults could.

Child labor became a regular feature of the new textile factories that sprang up. This development did not seem particularly revolutionary, as children had done chores on the farms where their families used to live. There was no obvious reason they could not work in a factory. Before the late nineteenth century, children typically did not receive a formal education. Factory workers did not need to read and

The employment of children in places like textile mills did not seem out of the ordinary at first since children had always worked hard on farms. Despite their age, they worked long hours, and they earned less pay than adults. *Reproduced by permission of the Library of Congress.*

write, and children could be put to work earning money for their family and for the factory owner. Many factories in the early Industrial Revolution employed children as young as six or eight years old.

The very fact that machines were housed in factories contributed to major social problems over time. Some factory owners paid wages that barely covered the cost of food and shelter. Factory owners who provided nearby housing for workers often charged rent that was high relative to the wage. In an era when towns were new (sometimes centered around a newly built factory near a stream or river), there were no modern grocery stores. Instead, factory owners opened shops to sell food, and although items in such shops were often overpriced, workers had no alternatives.

The end result of the Industrial Revolution was to convert many highly skilled craftspeople into parts of a master machine called the factory. The factory was a single machine-like system that combined parts made of metal with parts made of flesh and bone. The two worked together in a constant, coordinated, uniform way, day after day, year after year. When a part wore out, whether it was machine or human, it was replaced. Strict rules governed exactly when workers could eat, take a break, or go home.

In these ways, the Industrial Revolution was more than just the introduction of engines and machines to processes like spinning and weaving that had taken place for countless centuries. In ways that were subtle and not so subtle, attitudes began to change. As people working in factories took on aspects of machines, those who employed them began to view their workers as disposable parts, or an economic nuisance. If a superior invention could replace workers and increase output, it was adopted. The fate of the displaced workers was not viewed as the responsibility of the factory owner, any more than the fate of hand-weavers had been the responsibility of the very first factory owners.

Workers no longer lived in villages where they were well-known members of a community, and where their families had lived for generations. Crowded into cities or factory towns sooty from the smoke of coal fires powering steam engines, having little time for anything beyond work, they took on aspects of anonymous parts. In some cases, the workers' views of themselves changed as well. Life was reduced to drudgery, hard work without cessation. Pride in workmanship was replaced by exhaustion at the end of a long day of repetitive tasks.

The end result was that by the end of the first stage of the Industrial Revolution, machines were using the workers, rather than the other way around. In 1854 the American writer Henry David Thoreau (1817–1862) declared in *Walden, Or Life in the Woods:* "Men have become the tools of their tools."

The stage was set for new forms of social and political relationships, and for violent conflict.

For More Information

Books
Bland, Celia. *The Mechanical Age: The Industrial Revolution in England.* New York: Facts on File, 1995.

Bruno, Leonard C. *The Tradition of Technology: Landmarks of Western Technology in the Collections of the Library of Congress.* Washington, D.C.: Library of Congress, 1995.

Cardwell, Donald. *The Norton History of Technology.* New York: Norton, 1994.

Guest, Richard. *A Compendious History of the Cotton Manufacture.* First published 1823. Reprint: London: Cass, 1968. Excerpts found on the Web in the *Modern History Sourcebook,* Paul Halsall, ed. http://www.fordham.edu/halsall/mod/1823cotton.html (accessed on February 12, 2003).

Jennings, Humphrey. *Pandaemonium: The Coming of the Machine as Seen by Contemporary Observers,1660–1886.* Edited by Mary-Lou Jennings and Charles Madge. New York: Free Press, 1985.

Steele, Philip. *Clothes and Crafts in Victorian Times.* Parsippany, NJ: Dillon Press, 1998.

Periodicals

Berg, Maxine. "Small Producer Capitalism in Eighteenth-Century England." *Business History,* January 1993, p. 17.

Fisk, Karen. "Arkwright: Cotton King or Spin Doctor?" *History Today,* March 1998, p. 25.

Griffiths, Trevor, Philip A. Hunt, and Patrick K. O'Brien. "Inventive Activity in the British Textile Industry, 1700–1800." *Journal of Economic History,* December 1992, p. 881.

Reid, Douglas A. "Weddings, Weekdays, Work and Leisure in Urban England, 1791–1911: The Decline of Saint Monday Revisited." *Past and Present,* November 1996, p. 135.

Sullivan, Richard J. "England's 'Age of Invention': The Acceleration of Patents and Patentable Invention during the Industrial Revolution." *Explorations in Economic History,* October 1989, p. 424.

Web Sites

Mokyr, Joel. "The Rise and Fall of the Factory System: Technology, Firms, and Households since the Industrial Revolution." *Northwestern University Department of Economics.* http://www.faculty.econ.northwestern.edu/faculty/mokyr/pittsburgh.PDF (accessed on February 10, 2003).

Social and Political Impact of the First Phase of the Industrial Revolution

4

From 1800 to 1850, the population of England and Wales doubled, from nine million to eighteen million. During the same period, the proportion of people living in cities rose from 10 percent to 50 percent. Put together, the population of the cities of England and Wales rose from about nine hundred thousand to nine million, a 1,000-percent increase, in fifty years.

The increase in population shocked people at the time. As early as 1798, the English economist Thomas Robert Malthus (1766–1834) wrote an essay, "The Principles of Population," predicting widespread famine on the grounds that while population seemed to be proceeding at a geometrical rate (2, 4, 8, 16), food production was only growing at an arithmetical rate (2, 4, 6, 8). Malthus, and many others, feared that the population would rapidly outstrip England's ability to produce enough food to feed the millions of new people. Malthus blamed the lower classes for having too many children and proposed that laws be passed limiting the number of children people were allowed to have.

Words to Know

Anarchism: A social philosophy that advocates voluntary associations among people as a form of self-government, as opposed to central governments dominated by a monarch or other central figure.

Capitalism: A system of organizing a society's economy in which ownership of machines and factories is private, rather than public.

Communism: A form of government in which all the people own property, including both land and capital, in common.

Socialism: A political and economic system in which the people control both the government and also major elements of the economy, such as owning (or tightly regulating) factories.

Although the catastrophe predicted by Malthus never occurred (partly because there was a huge increase in productivity in agriculture, partly because the rate of increase in population slowed), his opinions were widely accepted at the time, particularly his conclusion that poor people were to blame for the profound social changes that accompanied the Industrial Revolution. The jump in population cannot be attributed to industrialization, but industrialization certainly added to the impact of England's shift from a rural, agrarian society to an urban, industrial society as the nineteenth century unfolded.

These social changes had several causes and consequences:

- The consolidation of farmlands as a result of the enclosure movement, in which wealthy aristocrats petitioned the government to own lands that communities used to share, pushed poorer people off the farms and into towns and cities (see Chapter 1).

- The dramatic rise in the number of factories provided jobs for some of these former farmers. These workers were relatively unskilled (compared to master craftspeople), but they could be trained to operate the new machinery being introduced.

- The flow of rural people into cities overwhelmed the physical facilities. Poorly built, inexpensive houses were developed and people crowded into them. Public health facilities, such as adequate sewage systems, could not keep pace with the growth in population.

- England's system of providing for the basic needs of the poor, based on an ancient system of rural parishes (subdivisions of counties corresponding to a local church), could not cope with the sudden rise in both the overall population and the concentration of poor people in cities.

- The nature of work in factories—long hours (sixteen-hour workdays were not uncommon), monotonous labor, widespread employment of children—worsened issues of health. Low wages resulted in crowded housing, inadequate sanitation, and inadequate diets.

- Serious environmental changes took place. Coal was the universal fuel to power factories and heat homes. Soot, a byproduct of burnt coal, covered English cities, turning many buildings black over time and contributing to air pollution, both inside poorly ventilated factories and outside. Lack of sewage treatment plants resulted in raw human waste running into streams and rivers. As late as 1855, a leading English scientist, Michael Faraday (1791–1867), wrote a letter to the editor of the *Times* of London describing a boat ride on the River Thames, which runs through London:

Thomas Robert Malthus. *Reproduced by permission of Getty Images.*

> The appearance and the smell of the water forced themselves at once on my attention. The whole of the river was an opaque pale brown fluid.... The smell was very bad, and common to the whole of the water; it was the same as that which now comes up from the gully-holes in the streets; the whole river was for the time a real sewer.

Two decades before Faraday's letter, in 1833, British surgeon Philip Gaskell had published his observations of the physical conditions of factory workers in *The Manufacturing Population of England:*

> Their complexion is sallow and pallid—with a peculiar flatness of feature, caused by the want of a proper quantity of adipose substance [fat] to cushion out the cheeks. Their stature low—the average height of four hundred men, measured at different times, and different places, being five feet six inches. Their

limbs slender, and playing badly and ungracefully. A very general bowing of the legs. Great numbers of girls and women walking lamely or awkwardly, with raised chests and spinal flexures. Nearly all have flat feet, accompanied with a down-tread, differing very widely from the elasticity of action in the foot and ankle, attendant upon perfect formation.... A spiritless and dejected air, a sprawling and wide action of the legs, and an appearance, taken as a whole, giving the world but "little assurance of a man," or if so, "most sadly cheated of his fair proportions."

At around the same time, in 1836, a factory owner and member of Parliament, John Fielden, wrote *The Curse of the Factory System,* in which he described his own factory and the impact of new laws passed by the British government regarding the maximum work week:

We have never worked more than seventy-one hours a week [just under twelve hours a day, six days a week] before Sir John Hobhouse's Act was passed [in 1831; the bill limited the working hours of children to sixty-four hours a week, or slightly over nine hours a day for six days a week]. We then came down to sixty-nine; and since Lord Althorp's Act [the Factory Act] was passed, in 1833, we have reduced the time of adults to sixty-seven and a half hours a week, and that of children under thirteen years of age to forty-eight hours in the week, though to do this latter has, I must admit, subjected us to much inconvenience, but the elder hands to more, inasmuch as the relief given to the child is in some measure imposed on the adult. But the overworking does not apply to children only; the adults are also overworked. The increased speed given to machinery within the last thirty years, has, in very many instances, doubled the labour of both.

Changes in English society as a result of industrialization gave rise to changes in government as well.

The Reform Bill of 1832

The British Parliament in the early 1800s was a far different institution than it has become. For generations, the Parliament in London included aristocrats and high church officials, sitting in the House of Lords, and wealthy, prominent citizens who sat in the House of Commons. Only people who owned a significant amount of property could vote in parliamentary elections for the House of Commons (no one in the House of Lords was elected; everyone there either inherited a seat as an aristocrat, or became a member by virtue of his position in the Church of England, the official religion). The majority of people, including all women and working men without property, had no voice in government.

The members of Parliament reflected the social structure of England's medieval period (about 500–1400), when social, economic, and political power were based on ownership of land, or on religion. And since members of the House of Commons often represented towns, rather than a specific number of people, changes in England over the centuries had created some odd situations.

For example, centuries of land erosion had caused much of the coastal town of Dunwich to fall into the sea; its population in 1831 had fallen to thirty-two voters. Nevertheless, the town still sent a representative to Parliament, as it had for generations. On the other hand, Manchester, England, had become an important center of manufacturing, with sixty thousand residents. But Manchester had no representation in Parliament, since it was not a large town when the composition of Parliament had last been changed hundreds of years earlier.

Small towns like Dunwich that still sent representatives despite their reduced size were called "rotten boroughs," a term that reflected another fact of British democracy: the absence of a secret ballot. Since it was public knowledge how a person voted, voters could be (and were) bribed to vote for a particular person as a member of Parliament. In some cases, a single wealthy individual controlled Parliamentary representation by monitoring voters to make sure they voted as he had paid them to vote. In other instances, wealthy individuals, such as business owners, traveled to a rotten borough and in effect bought a seat in Parliament by bribing voters in a small town.

The Parliament building in London. In the 1800s, Parliament consisted of prominent aristocrats, church officials, and wealthy citizens. *Reproduced by permission of Susan D. Rock.*

By 1830, the Industrial Revolution had created a new source of social and economic power: ownership of factories. So it was not surprising that wealthy business owners wanted to share in political power as well. The major landmark of political change brought about by the Industrial Revolution was the Reform Bill of 1832.

In November 1830, the leader of the Whig party, an aristocrat named Charles, Earl Grey (1764–1845), organized a campaign to make Parliament more representative of the population. Such a campaign arose from fears that the growing population of cities could lead to a violent revolution by desperate workers who had no voice in government, much like the French Revolution of 1789. During that conflict, mobs of workers, facing starvation, overthrew the king, executed aristocrats, and declared a republic (a system of government in which there is no monarch and officials are elected by the people). The reform movement was opposed by the Conservative Party (also called the Tories), whose parliamentary majority rested partly on Conservative representatives from rotten boroughs.

In 1831, despite Conservative opposition, the House of Commons passed a reform act that would give more people a vote and would send representatives to Parliament from cities like Manchester. But the House of Lords defeated the bill. In response, rioting broke out in several English cities. The Bishop of Exeter complained to the Prime Minister, the Duke of Wellington, that he did not feel safe coming to Bristol—an industrial city, like Manchester, without parliamentary representation—to consecrate a church, due to the threat of violence. Anger over being left out of representation was widely felt, and the bishop told Wellington he had heard of plans for a revolt against land owners among the poorest citizens. This report hardly came as news to the Duke of Wellington. His own house was attacked by a mob that broke thirty windows before it was disbursed by a servant firing a rifle from the roof.

Four months later, the Reform Bill passed, on April 13, 1832, giving industrial cities like Manchester and Liverpool representation in Parliament. But even so, British democracy was sharply limited. Only about 14 percent of British males were qualified to vote (to qualify, a man had to own a minimum amount of property, which excluded most men who worked in factories). Women were not allowed to vote. Some members of Parliament represented fewer than three hundred people, while other members from urban districts such as Liverpool represented over eleven thousand.

However limited in scope, the Reform Act of 1832 was a direct reflection of the widespread changes spurred by the Industrial Revolution. The growth of cities caused by industrialization put in sharp focus how outdated the English parliamentary system had become. And many citizens realized after the act was passed just how much more reform was needed.

The Sadler Report

Although the Reform Bill of 1832 failed to provide factory workers with a vote or any political power, the conditions under which they worked and lived did become a political issue the following year. A member of the House of Commons, Michael Sadler (1780–1835) held hearings in 1832 to highlight the working conditions of children in particular. Even though he lost an election and was no longer a member of Parliament, he published the results of his hearings in 1833 anyway. The published report included the testimony of child factory workers, who told of long hours, low pay, and dangerous working conditions, especially in textile mills.

The Sadler Report caused a storm of public indignation. Some critics faulted him for asking leading questions phrased in a way to elicit the sort of answers he wanted to hear. Sadler's defenders, on the other hand, focused on the fact that children worked for twelve or more hours a day with little rest and barely enough time to eat. And while some factories might have adopted more humane policies, many others were guilty of abusing children, just as Sadler documented. For decades afterward, the testimony of these young workers would be cited as an illustration of how greedy factory owners exploited children.

Sadler's report helped pave the way to legislation that regulated the conditions under which factories could employ

children. Though Sadler lost his seat in Parliament, another politician, Lord Ashley, took up the workers' cause.

The Factory Act of 1833

Lord Ashley (Anthony Ashley Cooper, 1801–1885, known as Lord Ashley until 1851 and later as the Earl of Shaftesbury) was instrumental in persuading Parliament to pass the Factory Act of 1833, which set standards for employment of children in textile factories (and only in textile factories). The act required that children aged thirteen to eighteen could not be employed more than twelve hours a day, during which ninety minutes had to be allowed for meal breaks. Younger children, aged nine through twelve, could only work for nine hours a day, and no child could work between 8:30 P.M. and 5:30 A.M.

This act was bitterly opposed by many factory owners, but other acts followed that imposed even more regulations on the working conditions in factories. The laws were passed to address business practices like those of Richard Arkwright (1732–1792), who made an immense fortune by introducing machinery into textile manufacturing (see Chapter 3). Workers in his factories worked eleven hours a day, from 6 A.M. to 5 P.M. About two-thirds of his employees were children, although Arkwright refused to employ five-year-olds, as some of his competitors did. He waited until children were six to put them to work eleven hours a day. On the other end of the age scale, Arkwright refused to employ anyone over the age of forty.

Factory owners objected that the regulations Parliament passed trampled on their rights as free Englishmen to conduct their businesses as they saw fit, and also violated the rights of other free Englishmen, the workers, from agreeing to work as they chose. The Factory Act of 1833 opened a debate, which has never really ended, over the role of government in regulating economic activity.

Change from within: Robert Owen

Robert Owen (1771–1858), a self-made man and successful factory owner, was one of the earliest industrialists to recognize the need to reform the factory system. Owen had been born into modest circumstances and had come to own a large factory in Newlanark, Scotland, thanks in part to marrying the owner's daughter and borrowing funds to buy a factory from his father-in-law.

Owen was not interested just in making money. He was a member of the Manchester Literary and Philosophical Society, which held meetings to discuss issues of the day, including the plight of workers employed in factories. Owen participated in several experiments that he hoped would improve workers' lives. In 1806, for example, he continued to pay workers' wages even while his factory was closed for several months as a result of a ban on cotton exports to England imposed by the United States. He improved the housing provided to his workers, and he actively worked to combat alcoholism and spousal abuse among his employees. In 1816 Owen established the Institute for the Formation of Character, which provided daytime schooling for children from age two to ten, and offered classes at night for older children and for adults.

Owen's ideas were not popular with most businesspeople. And although some efforts were made in Parliament to pass laws limiting the length of the workday and requiring inspections of factories to make sure regulations were enforced, it took many years for even modest regulations to be passed by Parliament.

In the meantime, Owen tried to take his ideas to the United States, where he hoped for a more welcome reception. In 1824 he acquired the community of New Harmony, Indiana, for $120,000 (equivalent to about $1.8 million in 2003). There he set up small-scale farms and industrial ventures run on the principles of a cooperative, in which the participants/workers owned shares of the businesses and voted on their operations. But within four years the experiment fell into disarray. The community was overcrowded, and people who settled there could not agree among themselves on how to run the ventures.

Owen handed New Harmony over to his sons and returned to England, where he tried to organize labor unions, associations of workers who banded together to bargain with employers for more pay and better working conditions. In 1832 Owen helped organize a coalition of unions (most unions were formed among workers within one industry) called the Grand National Consolidated Trade Union. Within a week it claimed five hundred thousand members, but it soon broke apart as a result of unsuccessful strikes (in which workers would refuse to work in order to force the owners to make some concession, such as better pay or working conditions) and industrial lockouts (in which owners close factories and stop paying wages as a means of discouraging union membership).

Robert Owen also advocated what he called "rational religion," a set of beliefs that contradicted some of the teachings of the official Church of England. His religious beliefs, along with his efforts to organize trade unions, made him highly unpopular among England's ruling classes. He died in 1858 without having achieved his goals, but he left a legacy of efforts on behalf of workers that would eventually inspire others to take up the cause.

Worker challenges to the Industrial Revolution: The Luddites

The efforts of Robert Owen and Michael Sadler largely represented influence from the top down: that is, efforts by wealthy or influential men to improve the lot of ordinary workers. But long before the British Parliament acted, some workers had begun taking things into their own hands. The first spontaneous uprising of workers started in 1811 with the Luddites.

The Luddites were mostly skilled textile workers who felt their jobs were threatened by new knitting machines introduced into their industry. As Richard Guest described in 1823 in *A Compendious History of the Cotton Manufacture,* new water- and steam-powered textile machines made it possible to produce much more fabric using far fewer workers than had been the case before (see Chapter 3). Seen from the viewpoint of a national economy, this development was good news: the productivity of workers increased enormously. But seen from the viewpoint of a skilled spinner or weaver, the new machines and factories meant that their skills and strength were no longer needed: their work could be done by boys or girls for far less pay. The new looms could produce far more fabric in a day or week, with fewer workers, than the hand-operated looms ever could. It was hard to imagine that the demand for fabric would increase so rapidly; it was easy to imagine that skilled workers would lose their jobs in home-based workshops.

Early in 1811 owners of textile mills near Nottingham, England, began receiving letters from someone who called himself General Ned Ludd (sometimes written as Nedd

Ludd), complaining that the new machines were costing people their jobs. No one knew for certain who Ned Ludd was; some thought it was the name of a slow-witted boy in the area who had been teased by other youths.

Typical of the Luddite threats was a letter delivered in November 1811 to a manufacturer named Charles Lacy of Nottingham. The writer accused Lacy of engaging in "divers [diverse] fraudulent, and oppressiv [oppresive], Acts—whereby he has reduced to poverty and Misery Seven Hundred of our beloved Brethren." The Luddites accused Lacy of gaining riches through the misery of his "Fellow Creatures," and threatened to kill Lacy unless he distributed to unemployed workers £15,000 (the pound is the unit of British currency; £15,000 was equivalent to several hundred thousand U.S. dollars in 2003 prices).

In March 1811 the letters had given way to vandalism. The first Luddite attacks were apparently carried out by men who had made stockings. The attacks coincided with a dramatic fall in the demand for the knee stockings men wore with breeches, which were knee-length pants common during the eighteenth century, as long trousers became fashionable instead. Few nights passed without someone breaking into a textile factory and smashing one of the new machines designed to knit stockings. As time went on, the attacks spread to the counties of Yorkshire, Lancashire, Leicestershire, and Derbyshire, and the attackers became known as Luddites.

Factory owners offered rewards for the capture of the vandals. In February 1812 the British Parliament passed the Frame Breaking Act, which made destroying a textile machine punishable by death. As a measure of how seriously the government took the Luddites, twelve thousand troops were sent to protect the factories in areas where Luddites were active. Still the attacks persisted.

On April 11, 1812, Luddites attacked Rawfords Mill, owned by William Cartwright, in Brighouse, England. Cartwright had placed armed guards around his factory, and they fought against the attackers, killing two. A week later, another factory owner, William Horsfall, was murdered in the same area. The authorities arrested more than one hundred workers and charged sixty-four people with crimes connected to the attacks. Eventually, three men were executed for Horsfall's murder, and fourteen others were hanged for the attack on Rawfords Mill.

Nevertheless, the violence continued. On April 20, 1812, workers attacked a factory owned by Emanuel Burton near Manchester. Armed guards killed three of the attackers. The next day, workers returned and burned down Burton's house. Troops were dispatched, and seven more people died. An attack on another mill that week resulted in twelve arrests and four executions.

Gradually the attacks diminished, perhaps in response to the legal crackdown. But periodic attacks were recorded as late as 1817.

Significance of the Luddites

Historians, with the advantage of knowing what came next, are divided over the significance of the Luddites. Did they represent an English version of a possible revolution, like the one that had overturned the monarchy in France in 1789? Were they the forerunners of trade unions, in which workers banded together to bargain for better pay and working conditions in factories? Or were they simply a reaction to social change, without any lasting significance?

The period of the Luddites was marked by other economic and political strains unrelated to industrialization. Britain was still waging war against the French emperor Napoléon Bonaparte (Napoléon I; 1769–1821), who was fighting to dominate Europe. As a result, the value of British wool exports had fallen dramatically, causing many to be put out of work regardless of the new machines. A series of bad harvests had driven up the price of food to a level that caused workers to have difficulty buying enough to eat.

Despite differing views on their historical significance, the Luddites did inspire a new word in the English vocabulary: today, "Luddite" is taken to mean someone who is opposed to new technology. And the Luddites did signal that the new inventions of the industrial era could, and would, inspire unanticipated social reactions.

Socialism: Workers as a political force

The Luddites responded to the Industrial Revolution with direct action: smashing machines. Industrialization in England as well as in Europe also gave rise to the idea that workers should have political power. The memory of the French Revolution of 1789, in which mobs of ordinary people toppled the monarchy and executed many aristocrats, was still fresh in most people's minds. Although factory owners were making progress in gaining political power (through the Reform Act of 1832, for example), ordinary factory workers were not.

The growth of industrialization had a significant impact on the lives of ordinary workers. Many had been forced off small farms by the enclosure movement and into cities, where they lived in dismal housing and worked long hours under dangerous conditions. Women and children worked alongside men, but the combined wages of a whole family could not pay for more than a dingy, dark little house in an overcrowded neighborhood blackened from the soot of coal fires. These urban workers shared much in common with serfs, the poor agricultural workers of the Middle Ages who were virtual slaves, owning no property and unable to move elsewhere.

As this new class of workers grew in number, several writers and thinkers began advocating not only political representation for workers, but also government control over the new factories. The twin ideas of including all men (political rights for women was an idea that came somewhat later) in politics as equals (as was already happening in the United States), and of exerting government control over industry came to be known by an all-encompassing label: socialism. From about 1820 onwards, the term socialism was applied to a variety of ideas and political movements that advocated solutions to social problems; these solutions ranged from the peaceful acquisition of influence through parliamentary elections to violent revolution and the seizure of all private property.

Realizing that ordinary workers far outnumbered property owners, both traditional land-owning aristocrats and the newly wealthy factory owners looked on all forms of socialism as a threat to their power and influence. The notion of violent revolution under the name of socialism sent tremors down the spines of the aristocrats and factory owners alike.

English citizens both wealthy and poor clearly remembered the events of July 1789, when mobs in Paris stormed Bastille prison, seized arms, and took power from the French monarch, Louis XVI. The French Revolution adopted the slogan "liberty, brotherhood, equality," and rounded up aristocrats to be killed. A bread shortage in Paris had sparked the revolution, which soon took on a much larger dimension to include democratic rule by all citizens, not just the wealthy. For the wealthy classes in 1820, the French Revolution was a nightmare they did not want to repeat. For some socialists, it was a dream to be realized throughout Europe. (In France, where it started, the general Napoléon Bonaparte had seized power and tried to extend French rule throughout Europe; a coalition of European monarchies opposed him, and Bonaparte was finally defeated by England in 1815, a date that was recent history for those living in 1830s England.)

The Chartists

One group of reformers that advocated peaceful social change by granting the power to vote to all workers were called Chartists. They were active in England from 1838 to 1848, and they presented a series of petitions (or "charters") to Parliament advocating political change. The Chartists reasoned that the Reform Act of 1832 did not go far enough in extending political power outside a small group of the wealthy and aristocrats. The Chartists also recognized that the Parliament, in 1833, had adopted some regulations that applied to the textile industry. The Chartists wanted more stringent regulations that would also extend to other industries.

The Chartists presented three separate petitions to Parliament, in 1839, 1842, and 1848. The first, titled the "People's Charter," was written in 1838 largely by William Lovett (1800-1877) for the London Workingman's Association. The petition demanded that Parliament adopt a secret ballot, annual elections, an end to the requirement that members of the British Parliament must own property, equal-sized election districts, and the right of every man to vote in Parliamentary elections. Many of these demands may seem ordinary and obvious now, but in 1838 they were viewed as dangerous and radical by many in the English ruling class.

In February 1838, the Chartists held their first public meeting to get signatures on the petition. At their meeting, the Chartists adopted a slogan: "Peaceably if we may, forcibly if we must," which sounded like a threat to many. They had to be careful that not more than fifty people attended a meeting in order not to violate one of the Gagging Acts, laws that banned meetings of more than fifty people. The government instituted the Gagging Acts to prevent workers from banding together to fight the government or their employers. Some Chartists advocated more radical actions, such as a general strike (in which all workers would simultaneously refuse to work) or the election of a "Peoples' Parliament" that would challenge the existing Parliament.

In July 1839, the petition with more than one and a quarter million signatures was presented to Parliament. Two months later, the House of Commons took a vote on whether or not to accept the demands of the petition. The vote was 46 in favor, 235 against. Defeated, the national organization that brought the petition dissolved itself in September.

But the ideas put forward in the petition gained popularity. Local groups of Chartists continued to agitate for change that would deliver political power to working people. Chartists submitted a petition to Parliament again in 1842, claiming to have over thirty-one million signatures, and they submitted a third petition in 1848. On both occasions, the petition was rejected by Parliament. Some legislators ridiculed the effort.

The Chartists encountered many obstacles in pursuing their cause. Organizers of the Chartists were mostly skilled workers, and they were unable to bring in others to their cause. The Chartists were often divided by different priorities (such as political representation or factory regulation), as well as by personality clashes among individual members. Chartism died out as a movement after 1848 without achieving its goals, but much of its program was eventually incorporated into election-law reforms passed in the 1860s. Chartism was an example of the peaceful, gradual adoption of socialist goals, and it was a forerunner of today's British Labour Party.

Revolution: A violent alternative

Just as the Chartists were failing to persuade the British Parliament to adopt their ideas for sharing power and improving the lives of workers, on the European continent a much different approach to bringing about political change was being advocated by a German political philosopher named Karl Marx (1818–1883). Marx's idea was much closer to the French Revolution: workers violently overturning the government, seizing all private property, and ruling without regard to the aristocracy or business elite. Marx thought that workers of all nations had much in common and should unite in a single worldwide government that ignored traditional national boundaries. He also thought that a victory by workers was inevitable, dictated by natural laws that govern the evolution of human society, comparable to the law of gravity and other laws that govern the physical world. Viewing himself as a social scientist, he called his proposed system "scientific socialism," although it is better known as

Young protestors in late twentieth-century China invoke the image of Karl Marx, who advocated workers overturning government and seizing private property to rule without class distinction. *Reproduced by permission of AP/Wide World Photos.*

communism. Communism eventually became a major force in world history.

A native of Germany, Marx grew up in a middle-class household and studied law before turning to writing newspaper articles in 1842. In his articles, Marx criticized the government of the Rhineland, a region of Germany, which had not yet been united into a single country. At the same time, Marx became involved in movements demanding political and economic power for workers. Most European rulers did not permit freedom of expression in the 1840s, and Marx soon had to flee Germany to avoid arrest.

In 1848, Europe was plunged into crisis. For the prior three years, poor harvests and a sharp slowdown in economic activity created rising tensions, as many people could not afford food. In February, the king of France, Louis Phillipe, resigned rather than face an armed revolt by his army in the face of widespread social discontent. His son, the new king, in turn declared a Second Republic (the first had been declared in 1789). In March 1848, working people revolted in Vienna, Berlin, Milan, and Venice. In Hungary, workers demanded independence from the Austrian empire, as did Croats, Czechs, and Romanians, all of whom were under Austrian rule.

To Karl Marx, these spontaneous revolutions against the established order seemed like the worker rebellion that he had predicted would come as a result of oppression of workers during the Industrial Revolution. Staying in London, where English laws protected him from arrest as a political agitator, Marx and a colleague, Friedrich Engels (1820–1895), wrote a document titled *The Communist Manifesto* on behalf of the small German Communist Party. (A manifesto is a statement of political principles.) In it, Marx and Engels urged workers to seize not only political power, but also private property, using violence if necessary.

The Communist Manifesto introduced two ideas that Marx would later expand upon in a much larger work called *Das Kapital* (*Capital*). The first idea was that the laws of history dictated that workers would eventually gain both political power and control of factories, which Marx called "the means of production." The second idea was class warfare, the notion that workers were engaged in a war against property owners, including factory owners. Marx saw the economic interests of workers and owners as being in conflict; he also thought political institutions, such as parliaments, were simply a means to protect one set of economic interests from another. He therefore saw gaining political power and gaining economic power as the same thing.

Moreover, Marx wrote that workers in all nations had the same basic economic interests (enough food to eat, decent housing, safe working conditions), and he urged workers to forget their different nationalities and instead band together in a global effort to seize the "means of production," and to hold them in common. In Marx's vision, no individual would own a factory in the future; everyone would have a share (be a part owner) by virtue of being alive.

This idea of common ownership of property was not unique to Marx, but he was one of its most persuasive advocates. For almost 150 years after he wrote *The Communist Manifesto,* the names Marx and communism struck fear into the hearts of property owners worldwide. It was under the banner of communism that revolutionaries seized power in Russia in 1917 and in China in 1949. In both Russia and China, brutal dictators eventually took control, curtailing individual civil rights and leading to the deaths of millions of their political foes. Their behavior was equated with communism, and a long military and economic struggle ensued with the United States in a conflict that came to be known as the Cold War.

Marx was not the only writer advocating revolution as a response to the Industrial Revolution. Mikhail Bakunin (1814–1876) was a Russian social philosopher who urged replacement of strong central governments with voluntary associations of workers who would cooperate in running factories as well as small local governments. Bakunin's theories were called anarchism, and they inspired generations of workers who opposed the strong worker-dominated governments advocated by Marx. (To be fair, Marx thought that central governments would eventually wither away since their initial purpose was to safeguard private property. But Marx saw the disappearance of strong government as an eventual result of worker control, rather than as the means to achieve it.) Bakunin made a career of calling for revolution, but his theories, unlike those of Marx, were never put into place.

Capitalist, Bourgeoisie, and Proletariat: New Ways of Describing Society

Karl Marx was largely responsible for introducing three new terms to describe elements of society: capitalist, bourgeoisie, and proletariat.

"Capitalist" was the term used to describe a person who owned a factory or a significant share in a company (that is, a person who put up much of the money to finance the factory and therefore would reap his share of the profits). Capital is the term used to describe wealth that is in the form of money, as opposed to wealth in the form of land, which traditionally was the measure of riches in most European countries. Capitalists worried about any move by the government or by the populace to seize control of their property, just as aristocrats had worried that peasants could band together to seize control of their land. Before the Industrial Revolution, some individuals accumulated fortunes as merchants, buying goods in one place and selling them for a higher price elsewhere, but merchants seldom had a way to spend their money, except to buy gold. When the Industrial Revolution created the need to buy expensive machinery and to build factories, suddenly monetary wealth had a new outlet. People who owned capital could invest it in factories and earn even more money through the profits of new industrial enterprises. Thus, capitalism—the new privately owned system of factories and machinery—became a means of earning great fortunes.

Trade unions

One of the most influential and lasting means by which workers tried to improve their lives was the trade union. The essential idea of unions was that while a single worker had no influence over a factory owner—one worker could easily be dismissed and replaced by another—all of the factory's workers acting together could unite and disrupt a factory's smooth operation by refusing to work unless their demands were met.

The concept of associations of workers has an ancient history, going back at least as far as the medieval period (about 400–1500). During that time guilds, associations of skilled workers that set rules and standards for work, regulated a system of apprentices (beginners), journeymen (advanced learners), and masters by which people could learn a skill (such as weaving or masonry) and, in effect, become certified as competent. Often, sons followed their fathers into a trade; women were seldom allowed membership.

Marx used the French word "bourgeoisie" (pronounced boor-zhwah-ZEE) to describe the social class or group that owned capital. The term originated from a German word meaning someone who lives in a town (*burg*). Marx used the term to describe the entire group of wealthy factory owners (including people who owned shares in factories) who shared an interest in protecting their wealth from being taken over or controlled by the workers. The bourgeoisie were a kind of urban equivalent to the rural aristocracy.

"Proletariat" was the term Marx used to describe factory workers. The proletariat represented a new class of people who owned no property and depended on their wages to live. Many members of the proletariat had formerly lived in the country and worked the land. As a result of the Industrial Revolution, these so-called common people had moved into cities, where they lived miserable lives working long hours for low pay in factories. Marx thought that the proletariat would rise up and lead society to a new, idealistic future in which all people were treated as equals.

Although Marx's predictions failed to come into being, these terms entered the vocabulary of many people, not just radical socialists, as a means of describing divisions in society brought about by the Industrial Revolution.

As the Industrial Revolution challenged the dominance of some of these crafts, members of guilds tried to maintain their longtime role in society. At the same time, the new factory owners were eager to replace master craftsmen with the new machines, which could be operated by anyone (meaning, anyone who would work for lower pay).

In response to early efforts by workers to come together to promote their economic interests, England passed laws as early as 1799, called the Combination Acts, that outlawed such worker associations. There followed a long struggle between advocates of labor and advocates of industry. The Combination Acts were repealed in 1824, then reinstated in 1825. In 1817 Parliament passed the Gagging Acts, which barred meetings of more than fifty people, and in 1819 Parliament passed a series of laws aimed against popular discontent. The acts of 1819 banned meetings for purposes of training (as for a popular militia, for example) and increased the penalties for speeches or articles thought to be blasphemous (against religion) or seditious (advocating antigovernment action). Organizing labor unions often fell into these categories.

Trade unions would not exert a decisive influence until well into the second stage of the Industrial Revolution, the period after 1850 (see Chapter 7).

For More Information

Books

Buer, M. C. *Health, Wealth and Population in the Early Days of the Industrial Revolution.* London: Routledge and K. Paul, 1968.

Fielden, John. *The Curse of the Factory System.* First published in 1836. Reprint: Portland, OR: International Specialized Book Services, 1969.

Foster, John. *Class Struggle and the Industrial Revolution: Early Industrial Capitalism in Three English Towns.* New York: St. Martin's Press, 1975.

Gaskell, P. *The Manufacturing Population of England.* First published in 1833. Reprint: New York: Arno Press, 1972.

Guest, Richard. *A Compendious History of the Cotton Manufacture.* First published in 1823. Reprint: London: Cass, 1968. Excerpts found on the Web in the *Modern History Sourcebook,* Paul Halsall, ed. http://www.fordham.edu/halsell/mod/1823cotton.html (accessed on February 12, 2003).

Landauer, Carl. *European Socialism: A History of Ideas and Movements from the Industrial Revolution to Hitler's Seizure of Power.* Berkeley: University of California Press, 1959.

Nardinelli, Clark. *Child Labor and the Industrial Revolution.* Bloomington: Indiana University Press, 1990.

Sale, Kirkpatrick. *Rebels against the Future: The Luddites and Their War on the Industrial Revolution: Lessons for the Computer Age.* Reading, MA: Addison-Wesley, 1995.

Taylor, Philip A. M. *The Industrial Revolution in Britain: Triumph or Disaster?* Lexington, MA: Heath, 1970.

Wrigley, E. A. *Continuity, Chance and Change: The Character of the Industrial Revolution in England.* Cambridge, UK: Cambridge University Press, 1988.

Periodicals

Cassidy, John. "The Return of Karl Marx." *New Yorker,* October 20, 1997, p. 248.

"Karl Marx: The Prophet of Capitalism." *Economist,* December 25, 1999, p. 38.

Phillips, John A., and Charles Wetherell. "The Great Reform Act of 1832 and the Political Modernization of England." *American Historical Review,* April 1995, p. 411.

Tilly, Louise A. "Women, Women's History, and the Industrial Revolution." *Social Research,* Spring 1994, p. 115.

Watson, Bruce. "For a While, the Luddites Had a Smashing Success." *Smithsonian,* April 1993, p. 140.

Web Sites
Binfield, Kevin, ed. "Texts of the Nottinghamshire Luddites." *Murray State University.* http://campus.murraystate.edu/academic/faculty/kevin.binfield/luddites_sample.htm (accessed on February 6, 2003).

Faraday, Michael. "Observations on the Filth of the Thames, contained in a Letter Addressed to the Editor of 'The Times' Newspaper, by Professor Faraday." *Faraday's Letter to the Times.* http://dbhs.wvusd.k12.ca.us/Chem-History/Faraday-Letter.html (accessed on February 12, 2003).

"The Life of the Industrial Worker in Nineteenth-Century England." *The Victorian Web: Literature, History, and Culture in the Age of Victoria.* http://65.107.211.206/victorian/history/workers2.html (accessed on February 12, 2003).

"The Origins of the Industrial Revolution in England." *The History Guide: Lectures on Modern European Intellectual History.* http://www.historyguide.org/intellect/lecture17a.html (accessed on February 12, 2003).

The Second Phase of the Industrial Revolution: 1850–1940

5

The practices of using engines as substitutes for animal and human muscle power and of using machines to produce goods took on a different character after about 1850. Sometimes called the second Industrial Revolution (or the second phase of the Industrial Revolution), this new phase differed from the original in several ways, and marked an important shift in the progress of the revolution.

With the rapid spread of the Industrial Revolution from Great Britain to the United States and Europe came a wave of inventions, some of which were new, many of which simply improved upon existing machines. Advances in science, particularly in chemistry, led to widespread changes, especially in agriculture and medicine. Petroleum became an important source of energy, leading to a new class of mobile machines (notably automobiles and trucks). Electricity was developed into a new means of delivering energy, leading to the introduction of small motors as well as superior lighting for both factories and houses. A new process of stringing together several inventions to create complex systems revolutionized manufacturing, transportation, and communications, and helped to create new business enterprises that were much larger than anything that had come before.

Taken together, these changes accelerated the impact of the Industrial Revolution on society throughout Europe and North America. Whereas everyday life for most people had changed relatively little from 1700 to 1800, it changed profoundly from 1800 to 1900 and beyond.

The United States: The stage is set for rapid growth

During the nineteenth century, the United States grew rapidly, from 5.3 million people in 1800 to 76.2 million in 1900. During the same period, the land area of the United States increased from 891,000 square miles (2,307,690 square kilometers) in 1791 to 3,021,295 square miles (7,825,154 square kilometers) in 1900 (excluding Alaska and Hawaii). The increase in size primarily was a result of the Louisiana Purchase (the acquisition by President Thomas Jefferson in 1803 of French-held lands in North America), the Texas war for independence from Mexico (1832–36), and war between the United States and Mexico (1846–48), which together expanded the area of the United States from a few states on the Atlantic coast to vast tracts of land stretching all the way to the Pacific Ocean.

The dual increases in population and land area provided the United States with a huge internal market for manufactured goods, as well as a large domestic supply of raw materials. The expansion encouraged immigration as well as westward migration. The task of feeding, clothing, and supplying the rapidly growing population with goods enabled the Industrial Revolution in the United States to reach heights unmatched by any other country.

In the first half of the nineteenth century, the growth of industry was concentrated in the Northeast. Agriculture continued to dominate in the South, although the southern states were affected by industrialization as northern textile mills demanded more and more supplies of raw materials. Industrialization also spawned divisions between North and South. Southern cotton planters were convinced that slave labor was required to keep their agricultural economy growing, even as slavery became a political and moral issue in the North. Manufacturers in the North favored tariffs, or taxes, to raise the price of imports, mostly from Britain, while Southern planters resented paying higher prices so that businesses in the North could benefit. Southern planters also did not like hurting some of the biggest customers, who were located in Britain. Settlers in the West were mainly interested in raising grain (especially wheat) and cattle, and they favored federal help in paying for the expansion of railroads that brought their crops to market.

British inventions leave home

British authorities had been quick to recognize the value of the early inventions that began to transform the British economy during the first stage of the Industrial Revolution. To try to maintain their advantage over other countries, the British government passed several laws that prohibited the export of both textile machines and the design plans for these machines. But the laws proved impossible to enforce, and even before 1800 British inventions began showing up in Europe and the United States. An Englishman named Samuel Slater (1768–1835) helped speed the industrialization process along in the United States.

Samuel Slater: The man with a memory for machinery

Samuel Slater was born in Belper, England, in 1768. At age fourteen he went to work for Jedediah Strutt, who owned a cotton mill in Belper with the highly successful businessman and inventor Richard Arkwright (1732–1792). Arkwright had developed the water frame, a machine for making thread from cotton. The water frame was powered by a waterwheel, which turned as water in a flowing river or stream pushed against slats in the wheel, putting the attached machinery in motion (see Chapter 3). Well versed in the operation and design of Arkwright's machinery, Slater eventually became the supervisor of machinery and mill construction at the mill.

To maintain its control over textile machinery, Britain made it illegal for textile workers to leave the country. Mean-

Samuel Slater. *Reproduced by permission of the Library of Congress.*

while, however, investors in the United States were offering rewards for anyone who could deliver plans for a textile mill. In 1789 Slater had decided that the British textile industry had reached its limits, and he thought he had a brighter future in the United States. He slipped into a disguise and left England on a two-month voyage, landing first in New York and later moving to Rhode Island. There a businessman named Moses Brown was one of those offering a reward for help in building a textile mill.

Improving on Arkwright's design, which Slater had memorized, Slater and Brown designed machinery to card (clean and untangle the fibers) and spin cotton into thread. The two men together established a textile mill, and in 1793 Slater built his own mill on the Blackstone River in Pawtucket, Rhode Island, a step widely regarded as the start of the Industrial Revolution in the United States. Slater not only knew how to design the machinery, he was also expert at running a mill. He eventually owned several cotton mills, and he went so far as to establish a new town called Slatersville, Rhode Island, a few miles northeast of the state capital, Providence.

There was no shortage of streams and rivers in New England to provide water power to run the frames, and within a decade of Slater's establishing his first mill, there were eighty mills operating in New England, firmly establishing the American Industrial Revolution. The fact that the mills were established in that region would eventually have enormous political implications for the United States: New England mills were put in competition with Britain for both the cotton grown on plantations in the southern states and for the sales of finished fabric.

In most ways, the Industrial Revolution in America had proceeded along the same basic path as in England. The United States had more of its own raw materials, such as

cotton, and a large territory that it was populating with Europeans by driving out Native Americans. Britain had access to cheap raw materials and room to grow through its large overseas empire.

The spread of the idea of the Industrial Revolution was not limited to the United States, however. Businesspeople in Europe were also eager to take advantage of the wealth brought by the Industrial Revolution by copying machines they observed in Britain. These business owners in turn developed new machines, or improved upon the original concepts embodied in the English originals.

Striking oil! A new era begins

Demand for coal increased throughout the Industrial Revolution. It was the primary source of energy for the growing number of steam engines and, later, for electricity-generating plants. One factor in Britain's early success in

Samuel Slater's Rhode Island mill, which he reconstructed from his memory of a British mill, is generally regarded as the starting point of the Industrial Revolution in the United States. *Reproduced by permission of the Rhode Island Tourist Division.*

Discontinuous versus Continuous Inventions

In the first stage of the Industrial Revolution, the steam engine and new textile machines marked a drastic departure from the way work had been done for centuries. Steam-driven engines gave people a form of strength and power never before experienced. Textile machines enabled a single worker to produce vastly more thread and cloth than ever before.

The inventions that make possible dramatic changes are sometimes called "discontinuous." Instead of resulting in slight change or improvement along a steady path, discontinuous inventions seem to come from nowhere and profoundly change the world. A "continuous" invention is one that either improves upon an older invention, or uses an older invention in a new way. Whereas discontinuous inventions are rare, sets of small improvements to existing inventions for use in other applications are much more common.

The 1800s saw many continuous inventions. As the steam engine and spinning and weaving machines came into widespread use (see Chapters 2 and 3), England, Europe, and the United States entered into a new period in which small refinements were made to older inventions. In general, the second stage of the Industrial Revolution was marked by a large number of continuous inventions, rather than by discontinuous ones.

industrialization was its plentiful supply of coal. The United States also had vast supplies of coal under the Appalachian Mountains of Pennsylvania and western Virginia (present-day West Virginia) and elsewhere. Other countries, such as France and Germany, had abundant supplies as well.

In 1859 Edwin L. Drake (1819–1880), a retired railroad conductor, made a momentous discovery in the town of Titusville, Pennsylvania: an underground deposit of liquid petroleum (oil). It was not the first time oil was noticed in North America. Native Americans had long used oil that seeped to the Earth's surface for medicine, and even for fuel. Early European explorers also found oil seeping from surface rocks or gathered in pools. The early frontiersman Kit Carson (1809–1868) sold oil to lubricate wagon wheels.

Drake's discovery marked the beginning of the American oil industry, and a sharp turning point in the Industrial Revolution. The fact that the United States, unlike other leading industrialized countries such as Britain, France, Belgium, and Germany, has some of the world's largest underground petroleum reservoirs is one reason for America's rapid industrial growth in the second half of the nineteenth century and into the twentieth.

What oil brought: The internal combustion engine

The development of the internal combustion engine coincided approximately with the discovery of the first oil wells in North America. After wells established a steady supply of oil, there came new techniques to refine (process) the crude oil into a variety of useful substances, including kerosene (burned in lamps), gasoline (as fuel for internal combustion engines), and, later, plastic. In the United States, the internal combustion engine became the major successor to the steam engine perfected by James Watt (1736–1819; see Chapter 2). It eventually changed the character of industrialization.

Internal combustion engines differ in a fundamental way from their predecessor, the steam engine. In a steam engine, coal is burned in a separate chamber outside the engine (external combustion) to convert its inherent energy into steam. Steam is inserted under the piston, where the steam's expansion pushes the piston (a solid, tubular piece of metal that slides up and down, or back and forth, inside a hollow cylinder) to the other end. As the steam cools, it contracts and creates a vacuum, which pulls the piston back down. In the internal combustion engine, the process is similar, but a mixture of gasoline and oxygen is squirted under the piston and ignited by an electric spark. The combustion (explosion) of the gasoline and oxygen push against the piston. In both engines, a metal rod attached to the piston transfers this motion, via a series of gears, to other types of motion, such as the circular motion of a vehicle's wheels. This process is repeated over and over, hundreds of times a minute; most internal combustion engines use several sets of cylinders and pistons (four, six, or eight in modern automobile engines, for example) to generate more power.

Internal combustion engines can be made much smaller and lighter than steam engines (as small as a lawn mower or chain saw, for example), partly because they do

Gottlieb Daimler (in back) of Germany developed an internal combustion engine similar to the engines used in modern automobiles. *Reproduced by permission of the Library of Congress.*

not require a coal fire heating water in order to create steam. They are also easier and quicker to start and stop (no need to start coal burning or to cool it down), and better suited for smaller-scale uses, such as automobiles and trucks. And because internal combustion engines are smaller and lighter, they can be used on smaller vehicles that can run virtually anywhere over roads, unlike very heavy steam-drive locomotives that require railroad tracks.

The idea of the internal combustion engine was not new in the 1800s. The Dutch scientist Christiaan Huygens (1629–1695) experimented with such an engine as early as 1680. But the real breakthrough came in 1859, when a French engineer, Jean-Joseph-Étienne Lenoir (1822–1900), built an internal combustion engine that could operate continuously. Lenoir's engine used coal gas (made by processing coal) as fuel. Three years later, another Frenchman, Alphonse-Eugène Beau de Rochas (1815–1893), patented another version of an internal combustion engine. In 1879 a German engineer,

Nikolaus Otto (1832–1891), developed another successful engine known as the "Otto cycle." Some historians credit Otto as being the true inventor of the internal combustion engine.

The greatest jump forward in internal combustion technology occurred in 1889, when a German engineer, Gottlieb Daimler (1834–1900), developed an engine that resembles the motors in twenty-first-century cars. Daimler's engine was small compared to a steam engine, and it operated continuously, for as long as petroleum was available to fuel it. Daimler connected his engine to a two-wheeled vehicle. In 1885 he used his motor to drive a four-wheeled vehicle, which is generally recognized as the prototype of the first modern automobile. (Daimler's name remains current in the form of DaimlerChrysler, the company that manufactures Mercedes-Benz and Chrysler automobiles.)

One advantage of Daimler's design was that it provided a better balance of power to weight; that is, a lighter engine could produce more energy. Excessive weight was always a serious drawback of the steam engine. Steam could produce tremendous energy (to propel a train, for example), but steam engines tended to be large and heavy in order to withstand the pressures of the steam, as well as to carry large quantities of water to convert to steam and coal to heat the water.

Manufacturing automobiles, in turn, became the largest industry of the twentieth century. The automobile, a direct result of the Industrial Revolution, is an invention that brought about some of the most profound social changes associated with living in the industrialized world of North America, Europe, and Japan. For example, cars enabled individuals to live relatively far from their place of employment, facilitating the growth of suburbs and the concentration of poorer workers in city centers.

The electric era

Just as the discovery of oil enabled rapid changes brought about by motorized transportation, another form of energy that was developed in the second half of the nineteenth century resulted in equally dramatic social and economic changes: electricity.

Electricity is a form of energy caused by the presence of electrical charges in matter. Electrical energy can be generated from mechanical energy by a machine called a generator. A generator burns coal, oil, or natural gas, or uses nuclear energy, to boil water to make steam. The steam is then used to drive a turbine, a large shaft mounted with a series of blades that fan out from the center. As steam strikes the vanes, it causes the central shaft to rotate. If the central shaft is then attached to a very large magnet (a piece of metal that attracts iron or steel), it causes the magnet to rotate around a central armature (coils of wire wrapped around a metal core), generating electricity. The electricity flowing through wires delivers energy in a form that can be used to light lamps and to drive motors, both large and small.

Electricity is used today to run appliances in homes and machines in factories, but when it was first developed, it powered a communications revolution. The telegraph, a device invented in the mid-1800s that uses electricity to send instantaneous messages over long distances, minimized the constraints of time and distance, much as locomotives and steamboats had done for travel and shipping. The telegraph, like the telephone that came a generation later, enabled businesses to take orders, buy raw materials, and otherwise treat a whole country—and eventually the entire world—as if it were a local marketplace.

With the telegraph came improved transportation systems (the telegraph was crucial in helping railroad operators coordinate the movement of trains over railroad tracks) and the building of large central factories (where raw materials from far away could be transported by rail and manufactured goods could be delivered to distant customers). Through the telegraph, businesspeople could learn of new opportunities in new markets far away (or of disasters that might threaten their business) and respond quickly. Thus, technology helped stretch the limits of the human imagination, which was perhaps the greatest change of all to come out of the Industrial Revolution.

Samuel F. B. Morse is credited with the successful introduction of the telegraph. *Reproduced by permission of the Library of Congress.*

"What hath God wrought?" The telegraph

In the twenty-first century, instantaneous communications are taken for granted. Telephones are everywhere, and the Internet makes it possible to send messages, sounds, and pictures almost instantly nearly anywhere in the world. It is easy to overlook the novelty, and importance, of rapid communication when it first became available in the mid-1800s.

The person widely credited with the successful introduction of the telegraph was an American, Samuel F. B. Morse (1791–1872). In his early life, Morse was a moderately successful portrait painter who had moved from his

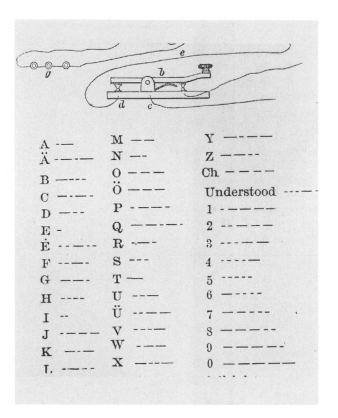

A	.—	M	——	Y	—.——
Ä	.—.—	N	—.	Z	——..
B	—...	O	———	Ch	————
C	—.—.	Ö	———.	Understood	...—.
D	—..	P	.——.	1	.————
E	.	Q	——.—	2	..———
É	..—..	R	.—.	3	...——
F	..—.	S	...	4	....—
G	——.	T	—	5	.....
H	....	U	..—	6	—....
I	..	Ü	..——	7	——...
J	.———	V	...—	8	———..
K	—.—	W	.——	9	————.
L	.—..	X	—..—	0	—————

The Morse Code alphabet guide. *Reproduced by permission of the Library of Congress.*

home in Pennsylvania to pursue an art career in Britain. In 1832, sailing back to the United States from England, Morse heard about discoveries involving electromagnets made the previous year by the English scientist Michael Faraday (1791–1867). Electromagnets are temporary magnets that consist of a core of metal, such as iron, surrounded by a coil of wire. When an electric current is applied to the coil, it turns the metal into a magnet (which attracts, or sometimes repels, other metals), which could then perform a task, such as lifting a weight or causing another piece of iron to move.

Over the next three years, Morse worked on the concept of varying the flow of electricity over wires in order to send a signal. As is so often the case, it is impossible to credit one person alone with an invention, including the telegraph. Experiments dating to 1753 had tried to use electricity and magnetism as a means of communication. Some early devices used multiple wires to transmit messages (one used twenty-six wires, one for every letter of the alphabet). Early pioneers included William Sturgeon (1783–1850) of England, who in 1825 turned a small piece of iron, weighing just 7 ounces (198.4 grams), into an electromagnet by sending electric current through a wire from a battery. The little electromagnet was able to lift a piece of iron that weighed 9 pounds (4 kilograms). In 1830 the American physicist Joseph Henry (1797–1878) went a step further and sent a current through a wire a mile long, "magnetizing" a piece of metal that struck a bell (that is, sent a signal).

Nevertheless, it was Morse who put together a complete system of sending and receiving signals over a distance. His telegraph consisted of an energy source (a battery), an electromagnet, and an electric switch known as a key. As the key came in contact with the metal plate beneath it, an elec-

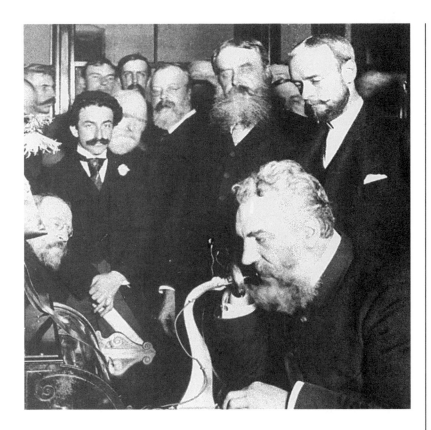

Alexander Graham Bell (sitting) tests his invention, the telephone. *Reproduced by permission of U.S. National Aeronautics and Space Administration.*

tric circuit (path) was completed. Electricity flowed out of the telegraph, into external electrical wires, and to waiting receivers. As the current came into the receiver, it caused the magnet to pull down a device that made a clicking sound (or punched a hole in a strip of paper). Morse also worked out a successful code (known as Morse code), comprising combinations of long and short bursts of electricity created by tapping on the key. Trained operators translated the combinations of longer and shorter bursts into letters, thereby sending and receiving messages. In 1843, Morse persuaded the U.S. Congress to provide funding to establish a demonstration of his system.

The following year, on May 1, 1844, a telegraph message was sent from Annapolis, Maryland, to Washington, D.C., a distance of about forty miles (sixty-four kilometers), announcing that Henry Clay had been nominated to run for president (Clay eventually lost). Still later, a more famous message went the other way, from Washington to Baltimore, when Morse, using Morse code, sent a message taken from the Old Testament, the first part of the Bible, that said: "What hath God wrought?"

Thus began intense competition to spread the telegraph throughout the United States. Morse and his business associates raised private funds to extend the telegraph all the way to New York, via Philadelphia, Pennsylvania. Small telegraph companies began linking smaller cities throughout the East, South, and Midwest.

Railroads played a key role in developing the telegraph. First, railroads let telegraph companies set up poles and string wires beside their tracks. Second, they used the telegraph to control train traffic: at the time, most railroads had a single pair of tracks between two points; they needed fast communications to avoid head-on, or even rear-end, collisions.

Morse's system printed the codes on a ribbon of paper, and operators learned to translate the series of dots and dashes into letters, at the rate of about forty-five words per minute. By 1914 that speed had increased to nearly one hundred words per minute. (In 2003 a high-speed cable modem connected to the Internet could transmit around one-and-a-half million words per minute.)

The telephone

The story of Alexander Graham Bell (1847–1922), the Scottish-born teacher of the deaf at Boston University, and his telephone is widely known. Instead of electric pulses that came out as dots and dashes, the telephone was able to translate the human voice into electrical impulses that were converted back to sound at the other end of a long wire.

The principle of the telephone had been shown first by Michael Faraday in 1831, but it took another forty-five years to demonstrate its practicality. As with so many inventions, it was an idea that many people were working on simultaneously. In fact, Alexander Graham Bell filed his application for a patent just two hours ahead of another inventor, Elisha Gray (1835–1901). The history of the telephone is also another demonstration of the principle that in the Industrial Revolution, inventing something new was

Coal Gas and Natural Gas

Compared to coal, petroleum, and electricity, flammable gas was a secondary source of energy in the 1800s. At first, a gaseous byproduct of manufacturing coke (a form of refined, or processed, coal that burns hotter than coal itself) called coal gas was collected and distributed by pipelines in many cities. Large outdoor lamps burned coal gas to provide the first effective streetlights; each evening, a lamplighter would come along the street and light the lamps. Coal gas lamps were also used to light stores, factories, and homes. It was many years before electric lighting succeeded in displacing gas light-ing, which was at one time much cheaper and brighter than the first electric lights. Coal gas is seldom manufactured today.

Natural gas (as opposed to manu-factured coal gas), found in huge under-ground reservoirs, is also distributed by pipelines. In areas where it is economical to do so, this naturally occurring gas is used for heating and for cooking, and to generate electricity in power plants. Natur-al gas is almost never used for lighting, but it continues to play an important role in providing energy to industry as well as to individual homes.

never enough. Success went to the person who could expand an invention into a successful business which, in the case of telephones, meant spreading their reach into virtually every home and business in the United States.

In the twenty-first century, the telephone is every-where—even, thanks to wireless (satellite) technology, in people's pockets. It seems odd to suggest that the telegraph, now largely a technology of the past, was actually a more sig-nificant invention than the telephone in the history of the Industrial Revolution. The reason is an issue of timing. The telegraph proved to be critical in helping railroads expand; in turn, rapid and reliable transportation made it feasible to bring in more raw materials and ship out more manufac-tured goods, from ever larger factories. Railroads also played a key role in providing food from faraway farms and ranches to industrial cities in the East.

Considering its importance in modern life, it may be hard to imagine the telephone ranking in second place to the telegraph in the story of industrialization. But it would be hard to point to a change made possible by the telephone that had not already started with the spread of the telegraph.

Electric motors

Electricity, like petroleum, was a key enabling technology of the second phase of the Industrial Revolution. The introduction of electricity and its two main uses aside from communications—electric motors and electric lighting—introduced some of the most dramatic and pervasive social changes of the Industrial Revolution.

Humankind's fascination with electricity has a long history, dating to Greece in 600 B.C.E. The Greeks noticed that rubbing amber against a fur cloth caused particles of straw to cling to the cloth. The mystery of this phenomenon (which is today called static electricity) was not solved until 1600, when an English scientist, William Gilbert (1544–1603), who was Queen Elizabeth I's physician, investigated the phenomenon and first applied the word "electric" in a report about magnetism. In 1752 Benjamin Franklin (1706–1790), the American statesman and inventor, demonstrated that lightning and electricity were the same thing. In 1792 Italian scientist Alessandro Volta (1745–1827) invented the first form of a battery and demonstrated how electricity could flow through a wire connected to it. (The word "volt," a measure of electrical potential, honors Volta's role in advancing knowledge about electricity.)

In 1831 Faraday discovered how to generate a flow of electricity by moving a magnet inside a coil of copper wire. The electrical current generated by Faraday was small, but the principle of the generator was established. It was just a matter of time before generators grew in size and electricity came to power motors.

Unlike steam- or gas-powered engines, many machines during the second half of the Industrial Revolution were powered by electricity. An electric motor uses magnetism to move its parts. Magnets can be made quite small, and therefore electric engines can be made much smaller in scale than either coal-burning steam engines or oil-powered internal combustion engines. Indeed, unlike steam or petroleum-powered engines, electric engines do not require any combustion at the site where they are used (although large generators, which may be located far away, often use steam or petroleum to create electricity). The changes electric power brought to society were enormous: power could be delivered to every factory, business, and house without the need for bulky fuel and huge engines.

Aside from Faraday, two other inventors whose names are associated with electricity greatly advanced the second stage of the Industrial Revolution: Thomas Alva Edison and George Westinghouse. Edison is created with inventing or perfecting many uses for electricity, including a practical light bulb, while Westinghouse was key in developing ways to generate electricity on a large scale.

Thomas Alva Edison

Thomas Alva Edison (1847–1931) was a prolific inventor who found many new ways to use the power of electricity. He also was a successful businessman who succeeded in organizing huge companies to generate electricity and arranged for laboratories to carry on new experiments and find yet more uses of electricity.

By the end of his life, Edison had more than one thousand patents for a wide variety of devices. Some of these inventions, however, had actually been developed by people working for him, or had been purchased by Edison. Moreover, while many of the inventions with which Edison is credited (the light bulb, for example) are undoubtedly an essential part of modern life, they did not necessarily push forward the Industrial Revolution so much as add to the comfort and convenience of everyday life.

Edison did not have an extensive formal education. He had trouble in school and was largely educated at home by his mother, who was a teacher. As a child he disliked mathematics but was fascinated by chemistry. By age twelve he was out of the house, earning money selling newspapers, tobacco, and candy on a railroad that linked Port Huron, Michigan, and Detroit. Waiting for the train to turn around for a return trip gave Edison plenty of time to read on his own, a habit instilled by his mother. He also owned a chemistry set, with which he conducted experiments in the baggage car. Throughout his life, Edison believed in invention by trial and error.

Edison became interested in the newly invented telegraph, which was spreading rapidly to cities in the United States. After Edison saved the son of a stationmaster from falling beneath a train, the grateful father taught him Morse code, allowing Edison to get jobs as a telegraph operator, working in various cities across the United States and Canada. In this environment, Edison's natural tendency to experiment and innovate led to a machine that recorded the clicks coming in over the telegraph wires. He then adapted this technology and developed another machine designed to record the voice votes of legislators. Edison was granted his first patent—for the vote-recording machine—in 1869.

Later that year, in New York City, Edison developed a variation of a "printing telegraph," a device to record information about the price of gold. Edison, working with partners, sold the design for the gold "ticker" to Western Union (the main telegraph company of the era), and he also got a job with the company. A few months later, he modified his gold ticker to record the prices of stocks as they were bought and sold on New York's stock exchanges. This invention had a large potential market, and the president of Western Union rewarded Edison by paying him $40,000, money Edison then used to started his own company across the Hudson River in New Jersey.

Edison's new company manufactured stock tickers and also paid engineers to develop new electrical devices or to improve existing ones. Among machines developed at Edison's company were an early form of mimeograph (a copying machine), an improved typewriter, and a method of sending four telegraph messages across a wire at the same time (instead of just one). As a businessman, Edison was aggressive in obtaining patents for machines developed by his employees, and even for small improvements on existing machines—a practice that helped him gain more patents than any other individual in the history of the U.S. Patent and Trademark Office.

By 1876, profits from his business enabled Edison to set up what he called an "invention factory" in Menlo Park, New Jersey, which was the country's first corporate research laboratory. Having seen how new inventions could earn significant sums of money, Edison set a goal of developing one new invention every four days (he eventually succeeded in inventing something new every five days). The firm's inventions ranged widely and eventually resulted in an improved version of the telephone, the phonograph, and the incandescent light bulb.

An English inventor, Sir Joseph Swan (1828–1914), had come up with the idea of sending electricity through a thin wire encased in a glass bulb, to be used as a lamp. By creating a vacuum inside the bulb (sucking out the air), Swann prevented the wire (called a filament) from catching fire, but the heat of the electricity nevertheless caused filaments to melt or break. Thomas Edison tackled the problem and found that a piece of charred cotton lasted enough hours to make the electric light bulb practicable.

On New Year's Eve, 1879, in Menlo Park, Edison demonstrated his new bulb by lighting street lights along a half-mile stretch, as well as his company's building, with his new bulb. The electricity was supplied by a generator Edison had built and installed in his company headquarters. He thus demonstrated not only the light bulb, but also the principle of generating electricity at a central point and distributing it via wires strung over a significant distance. Two years later, Edison had built an electric generating station in New York City, where he supplied about 85 users with electricity that flowed from about 400 outlets.

It was this last development—central generation of electricity and distribution over a grid, or network, of wires throughout a city—that was Edison's biggest contribution to the Industrial Revolution.

But at the same time, Edison made what proved to be a strategic miscalculation. His error involved the nature of electric current (the flow of electrons over a wire). Edison had built generating equipment that sent electricity in one direction only, a system called direct current (DC). An eccentric immigrant from Croatia named Nikola Tesla (1856–1943), who had come to work for Edison's company in 1884, proposed a different approach: alternating the direction of the current. Tesla demonstrated that while direct current tended to decrease over distance, alternating current (AC) could be

distributed over a much longer distance without losing its power. Using his own invention, Tesla also showed that the current of alternating electricity could be increased at a generating plant, then decreased near the final customer, making AC a more efficient means of distributing electricity.

Edison resisted Tesla's idea, partly because he had already invested money in devices that generated direct current, and partly because he thought (incorrectly) that AC was dangerous. But Tesla kept arguing for his idea, and Edison fired him in 1885, a year after he joined Edison's company.

George Westinghouse and Nikola Tesla

Tesla was a creative genius (he eventually held seven hundred patents) who had a tendency to exhibit odd behavior. He claimed he had communicated with creatures from other planets, for example, and he was terrified of women who wore pearl earrings.

Nikola Tesla's alternating generator could direct a current over a long distance without losing power.
Reproduced by permission of the Library of Congress.

After he was fired by Edison, Tesla arranged to work for the inventor George Westinghouse (1846–1914). Westinghouse had earned a fortune from his invention of the air brake, which used compressed air instead of friction to stop a moving vehicle and was widely used on trains; the airbrake patented in 1869, was one of 400 patents Westinghouse eventually owned. Westinghouse quickly saw the advantages in Tesla's alternating generator. In 1888, Westinghouse bought rights to Tesla's AC generator and agreed to use his fortune to develop the idea in competition with Thomas Edison.

Success did not come at once, however. But in 1893, Tesla and Westinghouse won a contract to provide AC power to the Columbian Exposition in Chicago, a kind of world's fair. Tesla's alternating current system was a huge success, and eventually it won out over Edison's direct current. (DC is still used, however, in batteries, which are normally located very close to the object they are intended to power, such as a flashlight or portable CD player.)

Widespread delivery of electricity made possible not only illumination in factories and homes, but also motors to drive machinery. Electricity took its place alongside the steam engine and the internal combustion engine as one of the key sources of energy driving the Industrial Revolution forward. Tesla's real vindication came in 1917 when he won the top award of the American Institute of Electrical Engineers: the Edison Medal.

Applied science changes the world

The first stage of the Industrial Revolution had been marked by the tinkering of talented individuals with a gift for mechanics. A century later, however, the course of the revolution changed as principles of science—particularly those in the fields of metallurgy and chemistry—were increasingly applied to technology.

George Westinghouse is widely remembered for his work with electricity and for inventing the air brake. *Reproduced by permission of the Library of Congress.*

Metallurgy and steel

Since about 1500 B.C.E., humankind has used iron as the metal of choice for making tools. Iron is an element, one of the fundamental substances of the Earth. It is found buried in the Earth's crust in the form of an ore, which means it is combined with other elements, such as manganese, silicon, phosphorous, sulfur, and especially carbon. Using iron to make objects is a two-step process: first, the iron ore is heated to around 2,800 degrees Fahrenheit (1,538 degrees Celsius) in order to remove impurities, such as sulfur. At this temperature, iron is in a liquid form. The high temperatures cause many other elements to vaporize, leaving a mixture of iron (about ninety-six percent) and carbon (about four percent). After stage one, it is called pig iron (so named because it is poured into containers that resemble baby pigs gathered around their mother).

Pig iron is normally subjected to further treatment to create other forms of the metal, including cast iron and steel. The principal treatment involves reheating pig iron to remove some of its carbon content or to introduce other elements (such as chromium) to give the final product the wanted characteristics. The amount of carbon mixed with the iron in particular affects the character of the end result. Iron may be relatively harder or softer, easier to shape with hammers or nearly impossible to dent, susceptible to bending or resistant to deformation. One mix of iron and carbon results in a product called cast iron, which is poured into shaped molds. Cast iron is widely used to make components of engines, for example.

Steel is another form of processed iron, in which the proportion of carbon has been reduced to less than 2 percent. Unlike cast iron, steel is relatively easy to bend into shapes (such as the exterior body of a car, for example). Steel can be strong even when pressed into thin sheets. Other elements can be added to steel to give it other desired qualities: stainless steel, with its shiny surface, resists rust when exposed to moisture, thanks to the addition of the element chromium. Metals created by mixing together separate elements (such as iron and chromium) are called alloys, and the study of how metals behave and how they can be altered is called metallurgy.

Metallurgists continually seek to develop new forms of metal, iron in particular, in order to make products that overcome specific shortcomings, such as the tendency to rust, or products that provide more advantages (strength combined with light weight, for instance). Humans have been experimenting with metallurgy for thousands of years; iron became the dominant metal for making tools about three thousand years ago, and steel was developed at least two thousand years ago. In some respects metallurgy could be called the science of "cooking" metals—heating iron, for example, cooling it, heating it again, mixing in other elements—in order to produce a product with the wanted characteristics.

In the middle of the nineteenth century, an Englishman named Henry Bessemer (1813–1898) developed a new method to convert pig iron into steel. Bessemer's method reduced the time and cost of processing pig iron into steel, long considered the most desirable form of iron because it is more durable, can withstand greater stress, and can bear greater weight than other forms of the metal. Bessemer's process made steel an economically feasible alternative for making a wide variety of manufactured products.

The key issue in making steel is reducing the carbon content. Doing so requires heating pig iron to around 1,300 degrees Fahrenheit (720 degrees Celsius), which takes both time and fuel (such as coal) burning in a furnace. In 1856 Bessemer discovered that blasting oxygen into molten iron actually increased its temperature and burned away much of the carbon that was still in the iron, resulting in steel. In his patent application Bessemer called his invention "a decarbonization process, utilizing a blast of air." His method involved pouring molten iron into a pear-shaped bucket, then inserting oxygen into the bucket (called a converter) in order to raise the temperature of the liquid iron and burn away impurities, notably carbon. Before Bessemer developed the technique, steel was made by hand in small quantities, typically for weapons (like swords) and hand tools. The process took about three hours and made relatively small quantities of around fifty pounds (twenty-two kilograms) of high quality, but expensive, steel. Steel made using Bessemer's process was not of the highest quality (that is, devoid of impurities), but it was relatively inexpensive to manufacture, and this development enabled steel to replace iron in many applications, including miles of railroad track and the interior framework of tall buildings.

Bessemer was not the only person trying to find a better way to turn pig iron into steel. An American businessman, William Kelly (1811–1888) of Eddyville, Kentucky, owned iron mines and also a furnace for making pig iron. In the early 1850s, he developed a steel-making process very similar to Bessemer's, but he did not apply for a patent until 1857, after Bessemer had received a patent in Britain. The two men quarreled for years over who had the rights to the method, but eventually Kelly ran out of money and dropped

Henry Bessemer. *Reproduced by permission of the Library of Congress.*

out of the battle, clearing the way for Bessemer to license his technique for converting pig iron into steel.

Bessemer's technique was widely adopted and used for more than a century. It was replaced in the 1960s by a newer technique that cut the time needed to heat pig iron from about nine hours to about forty-five minutes. A Scottish-born entrepreneur named Andrew Carnegie (1835–1919) licensed Bessemer's technique and built the largest steel-manufacturing company in the United States, earning one of the world's greatest fortunes from it (see Chapter 6).

Bessemer's invention marked a major turning point in the Industrial Revolution. It came at a perfect time: railroads were being built rapidly, especially across the United States, and engineers soon saw advantages in using steel for rails instead of iron. Steel also came to replace iron in the construction of the new ships, tall buildings, and machine tools that marked the second half of the revolution.

Chemistry

For centuries, people have been fascinated with the nature of substances, and with how their characteristics change when they are heated or put together with other substances. In the Middle Ages (500–1400), some people experimented with ways to turn a cheap metal, lead, into gold, as a means of gaining an instant fortune. Such experiments were called alchemy, and if they worked at all (which was seldom), it was purely by chance.

Chemistry, on the other hand, is the organized, systematic study of the fundamental characteristics of substances. As a continuation of a wave of scientific discovery that had started during the Renaissance (c. 1400–1700), chemistry has led to a wide variety of discoveries, starting in the nineteenth century and continuing ever since. Many of these discoveries solved business problems, or made a major difference in everyday life. Chemists have had a variety of motives. Some chemists experimented from curiosity; others were looking for new materials that could replace more expensive ones and save money in manufacturing goods; still others sought substances that were more reliable or uniform than substances that occur in nature. The notion of using manufactured substances in place of natural ones became a major theme as the Industrial Revolution progressed, and it resulted in the establishment of chemistry laboratories by manufacturing companies looking to increase profits. Targeted research (that is, looking for solutions to specific business problems) grew into an important supplement to more general or fundamental research conducted by scientists working in universities.

One example of this new industrial scientific process came in the search for dyes used to add color to cotton or wool fabric. People had long made dye from plants (imagine squashing red berries and pouring the liquid onto white cloth), but manufacturers in the nineteenth century were looking for specific ways to save money and also to make goods that were uniform (the same shade of red, for example). They turned to chemists to find answers; in the case of dyes, it meant developing artificial chemical substitutes for naturally occurring organic dyes.

Dynamite is another important chemical discovery of the era. Dynamite was developed in 1866 by the Swedish chemist Alfred Nobel (1833–1896). It provided a relatively safe, inexpensive explosive that could be used to tunnel past rocks in a mine or clear away boulders blocking the route of a railroad. But Nobel also had a personal motivation. His bother Emil was killed in 1864 in an explosion of nitroglycerine, an explosive substance invented earlier by the Italian chemist Ascanio Sobrero (1812–1888). Nobel wanted to modify nitroglycerine to make it safer to use. He added silica, which enabled him to manufacture a paste that could be shaped into cylinders. These, in turn, could be inserted into holes drilled by miners or railroad workers to blast apart rocks. Sales of his invention made Nobel a wealthy man, and he later willed part of his fortune to fund the Nobel Peace Prize and other prizes for achievements in science and literature.

The Bessemer process for making steel was used for over a century. *Reproduced by permission of the Library of Congress.*

An American, Charles Goodyear (1800–1860), in 1839 invented a process to treat natural rubber (derived from the sap of rubber trees) called vulcanization. Goodyear's invention kept articles made of rubber from melting at moderately high temperatures (even a hot summer day could cause natural rubber to lose its shape). Vulcanization made rubber, with its natural resilience, a useful material for goods like tires, which gave a much smoother ride than wooden wheels.

Chemistry also yielded a new group of materials, called plastics. In 1869, the American John Wesley Hyatt (1837–1920) was looking for a substitute for ivory from elephant tusks to use in manufacturing billiard balls. Elephants were being slaughtered by the thousands to keep pace with the demand for these balls. Thinking about this problem, Hyatt noticed that when he spun a bottle of collodion (a glue-like solution containing cellulose from plant cells often used in medicine to close small wounds), it congealed into a tough, flexible film. Collodion was not successful for its intended purpose: it was highly flammable and caused billiard balls to explode when they crashed into one another. Hyatt solved this problem by adding camphor, derived from the laurel tree, to make celluloid. Celluloid could be heated and poured into a mold, then cooled, at which point it would retain its new shape (such as that of a billiard ball). It was hard and sturdy, like iron, but much lighter and easier to manufacture.

In 1907, Leo Baekeland (1863–1944), a Belgian-born chemist working in New York, was trying to develop a superior coating for the surface of bowling alleys, which were becoming popular. He combined carbolic acid and formaldehyde to create a substance he called Bakelite resin. The material could be poured into molds; once it cooled, it retained the shape of the mold and resisted heat and corrosion. Bakelite soon found a wide array of uses as a substitute for wood and metal that was relatively inexpensive to manufacture and shape.

By manipulating natural substances, such as cellulose, with heat and by stirring in other substances, chemists developed a wide range of artificial materials that could substitute for natural ones. Rayon, for example, was intentionally developed as a substance with chemical properties similar to the secretions of silkworms in order to manufacture an artificial and less expensive version of silk.

Chemistry has had a major impact on modern life. By developing new substances to replace more expensive older ones, chemistry has made it possible for manufacturers to produce goods at prices that most people can afford. It has made possible some inventions, such as movies (film for moving pictures was an early application of celluloid), that have changed the lives of millions of people. Chemistry has also had a major impact on one of the most fundamental human needs: food.

Railroad workers used dynamite to tunnel past boulders blocking the route. *Reproduced by permission of the National Archives and Records Administration.*

The second agricultural revolution

While the name Industrial Revolution may conjure up visions of urban factories belching smoke, during the nineteenth century important changes also swept across agriculture. These changes fall into three main categories:

- Chemistry, in the form of new fertilizers, pesticides, and herbicides.

- Farm machines, such as the tractor powered by an internal combustion engine, that substituted for the pulling power of horses and oxen and enabled farmers to work larger fields.

- Food preservation techniques that made it possible for farmers to sell food in distant cities, long after it was freshly harvested.

Together, these three developments enabled farmers to efficiently support a growing urban population—a trend that has not stopped. The introduction of machinery and science to agriculture had virtually the same impact as it had earlier on cottage industries: fewer farmers producing more food at a lower price. And as with the Industrial Revolution in towns and cities, small, independent farmers were gradually replaced by much larger farms, often owned by businesses that could afford the latest in machinery, fertilizer, pesticides, and herbicides.

Chemicals

Agriculture benefited enormously from the application of chemistry to industry. In a process that started in the 1820s and continued for nearly a century, German scientists took the lead in developing fertilizers that greatly improved the productivity of land. Some fertilizers were developed from natural substances (such as guano, or bat droppings); others were developed by combining elements (such as nitrogen and hydrogen) into forms that could fertilize fields. In yet another area, chemists developed pesticides (to kill insects) and herbicides (to kill weeds), both of which helped increase the yields from crops.

Machines in the field

As European Americans moved into what seemed to them the empty territory of what is today the American Midwest—and in the process displacing the great herds of bison and the Native American people who hunted them—the size of farms grew significantly. The increase in acreage was made possible in part by introducing a series of machines to farming.

One of the most significant of these inventions was the reaper, developed by Cyrus McCormick (1809–1884) of Virginia, to cut down ripe crops like wheat. The reaper was, in essence, a giant cylinder equipped with blades. As the cylinder rolled across a field, the blades came down and cut wheat stalks at ground level. Previously, people with hand-held tools called scythes (a kind of curved knife at the end of a long handle) did this work. The mechanical reaper enabled one person to do the work of many. And it was designed to gather up the fallen wheat into bundles, saving even more time. Not only could harvesting be completed by about half as many people using scythes, the reaper also saved crops from being ruined by rain after they were cut to the ground. McCormick patented his design in 1834, and three years later he started making the machines on his family estate, selling them door to door. Later he licensed others to build his reaper in other parts of the country. In 1847 McCormick established a factory in Chicago, Illinois, which became one of the leading manufacturing companies of the nineteenth century. McCormick himself became wealthy and later invested in railroads and mining.

The next major invention of the agricultural revolution was the self-polishing cast steel plow. A plow is a tool that is pulled through a field (by a horse or ox prior to the development of powered tractors) in order to cut little trenches, called furrows, in the soil. Seeds can then be planted in the furrows. As the plow's blade (called a plowshare) moves through the soil, bits of dirt or mud tend to stick to it, making it harder to pull and also resulting in a wider furrow than needed for the seeds. This was especially a problem with cast iron plowshares trying to cut through the thick soils of the Midwest. Farmers needed to stop and scrape the plowshare clean in order to proceed through the field. A better version of the plowshare was designed in 1837 by a blacksmith (someone who makes tools out of iron) named John Deere (1804–1886), who had moved to Illinois from his native Vermont the previous year. Noticing that the cast iron plows made in Vermont were ill-suited to the thicker, heavier soils of the Midwest, Deere substituted highly polished steel for the cast iron plowshare. Soil did not cling so easily to the smooth, shiny surface of Deere's plow, making work easier and faster for farmers, who soon bought Deere's plows by the thousands.

Later, Deere was responsible for another innovation: instead of making plow blades only to fill specific orders, he manufactured them in large quantities and traveled around

Cyrus McCormick designed a mechanical reaper that brought the principles of the Industrial Revolution to farming. *Reproduced by permission of the Library of Congress.*

to display and sell them. The company he founded is still in business in the twenty-first century, best known for producing farm tractors.

Mechanical tractors were introduced in 1868 as a replacement for the horse or ox in pulling plows through the field or hauling wagons full of harvested crops into town. Initially tractors were powered by small steam engines, like small locomotives, and they primarily were used like a truck, for hauling loads over roads. Gradually they were also used in fields to pull machines or wagons, replacing farm animals. The first gasoline engines were installed on tractors by the Charter Gasoline Engine Company of Sterling, Illinois, in 1887. Henry Ford (1863–1947), the pioneer of automobile manufacturing, began producing tractors that used gasoline engines in 1907; he called them automobile plows. Gasoline-powered tractors were popular with farmers because they were easier to operate and enabled a single farmer to plant or harvest more land than was possible with either animals or steam-powered tractors.

The history of agriculture in the nineteenth century is filled with many other inventions that brought the advantages of engine power and mechanical help to the farmer. These advantages can be measured. In 1830, for example, it required 250 to 300 man-hours (one person working one hour) to produce one hundred bushels of wheat grown on about five acres of land. A century later it required only about 15 to 20 man-hours to produce the same amount of wheat on the same amount of land.

From farm to table

The third key part of modern agricultural revolution centered around food processing and preservation techniques (such as canning and refrigeration) that allowed farm goods to be delivered to urban customers far away. These developments owed a great deal both to the application of technology and to the organizational changes associated with the Industrial Revolution. Thus the story of food in the nineteenth century is the story of how the techniques of industrialization gave rise to companies that package and preserve food and deliver it to grocery stores.

In the era before the Industrial Revolution, the majority of Americans lived in the countryside. Their food came from the farm they lived on, or perhaps from a farm next door. People ate fresh fruit in the summer or early autumn. In the winter or spring, they ate preserves, fruit that had been cooked and stored in jars. Eggs came fresh from the farm's hen. But people living in crowded cities do not keep chickens or raise their own fruit. In order to provide them with food, methods were developed in the 1800s to ship food from the countryside to cities, and to keep it from rotting on the way.

Food preservation, like many other developments during the second phase of the Industrial Revolution, was the result of many discoveries and inventions rather than one big leap forward. Food preservation was critical to the growth of the United States; combined with efficient transportation over long distances (via railroad), it enabled the United States to support a large population of urban industrial workers.

Canning food, that is, sealing cooked food inside a glass bottle or metal can, protecting it from contaminants in the atmosphere, was developed in 1795 by a French chef, Nicholas-François Appert (c. 1750–1841). Appert was competing for a twelve-thousand-franc prize offered by the French Emperor Napoléon Bonaparte (Napoléon I; 1769–1821), who was searching for a way to preserve food to feed his army. Appert demonstrated a method of putting food (such as fruit) in glass containers, cooking it by putting the jars in boiling water, and then sealing the containers.

A few years later, Peter Durand of Britain demonstrated a similar technique, substituting iron cans coated with tin for Appert's glass bottles. Durand's solution was not ideal, however. Solder (pronounced SOD-er; a metal used to make the cans) resulted in lead poisoning if too much canned food was eaten over a short time. Durand's cans also raised anoth-

Food Preservation

There are five basic ways to prevent food from decaying:

- **Freezing:** Humans have long known that freezing meat, and other food, slows or prevents the chemical process of decay. Archaeologists have uncovered evidence that as long as 10,000 years ago, cave-dwelling humans put slaughtered animals in the coldest part of their caves to preserve the meat by freezing.

- **Heating:** Cooking food (raising its temperature to a certain level) kills many bacteria (microscopic organisms) that might make it unsafe to eat.

For cooked food to remain edible, it must be sealed in glass jars or metal cans to keep it away from airborne organisms that might contaminate it.

- **Dehydrating:** Dehydrating food, or removing the water it contains, has long been used to preserve foods. One example of a dehydrated food is pasta. Pasta is essentially flour and water that is formed into a shape, such as a spaghetti noodle, and then dried. Removing the moisture prevents chemical reactions that result in decay or rotting. When pasta is put into boiling water, the flour is rehydrated to make it edible.

er problem: the production of the cans themselves. Initially, a craftsman could produce perhaps sixty cans per day; later, machines were developed that produced hundreds of cans per minute.

Nonetheless, the canning principle had been established and its use spread. Canned food was widely used to supply armies during the American Civil War (1861–65).

Refrigeration was another nineteenth-century invention that changed the face of food distribution. The scientific principle of refrigeration—transferring heat from one object to another—was developed by the French scientist Nicholas Sadi Carnot (1796–1832) in 1824. But it took many years before mechanical refrigeration replaced the age-old method of using ice to keep certain foods (especially vegetables and meat) relatively fresh and safe to eat. Well into the twentieth century, ice men delivered chunks of ice to homes, where it was stored in insulated ice boxes to help preserve food.

- **Fermentation:** Fermentation uses chemical reactions brought about by acids to avoid spoilage. These acids are typically created as a result of chemical reactions between specific microorganisms, such as bacteria, molds, or yeasts, and basic food materials (such as cow's milk) to create an edible, nutritious substance that resists decay or spoilage (contamination by poisonous bacteria). Cheese is a common example of converting a food substance and preserving it by use of fermentation.

- **Chemicals:** Chemical reactions have been used for centuries to preserve food by killing poisonous bacteria. The oldest and most common chemical used to preserve food is sodium chloride (salt), which was used throughout the Middle Ages (500 to 1400) to store fish and meat. Some spices contain chemicals that also kill poisonous bacteria (as well as providing a lively taste to food).

During the nineteenth century, scientists came to understand the theories behind many of these ancient food preservation techniques and began to apply them on a large scale.

Contemporary home refrigerators and air conditioners are the result of a long process of scientific inquiry and invention. As early as 1805 American inventor Oliver Evans (1755–1819) designed, but never built, a refrigeration machine. The theory behind Evans's system, and the basic principle of refrigeration today, is that whenever a liquid changes into a gas it absorbs heat, thereby cooling its environment. In 1842 a physician, John Gorrie (1803–1855), built a machine in Florida to cool hospital rooms following Evans's basic design.

Although Gorrie did not receive a patent for his system until 1851, refrigerated railroad cars were used to carry milk products as early as the 1840s. J. B. Sutherland of Detroit, Michigan, received the first patent for a refrigerated railroad car in 1867. The temperature-controlled cars enabled Chicago, Omaha, and other midwestern cities to become centers of the emerging meatpacking industry; cattle were raised, slaughtered, and butchered in the West, and then their meat (instead of live cattle, as was done previously) was shipped to cities in the East.

For many years, refrigeration was limited to large machines used in factories, especially in the beer manufacturing industry. By the 1890s increasing water pollution (caused by dumping raw sewage, or human waste, into streams, lakes, and the ocean, for example) made it difficult to find supplies of natural ice that did not pose a health risk all by itself. Consequently, in the 1890s mechanical refrigeration was used to produce ice that was delivered, often daily, to individual homes to keep ice boxes cold.

Later still, principles of refrigeration were extended to cooling the air for comfort. American Willis Carrier (1876–1950), having observed that printing on paper worked better in the cooler temperatures of winter than in the heat of summer, in 1923 devised a method of applying refrigeration to lower the temperature in factories and public buildings (air conditioning), in large part to enhance human comfort.

Refrigeration was an outstanding example of how principles of science were applied over the period of a century to advance the notion that human inventions could change some of the fundamental characteristics of nature, whether it was the natural limitations of muscle power or the temperature of Earth's atmosphere.

For More Information

Books

Berman, Daniel, and Robert Rittner. *The Industrial Revolution: A Global Event.* Los Angeles, CA: National Center for History in the Schools, 1998.

Butterworth, W. E. *Black Gold: The Story of Oil.* New York: Four Winds Press, 1975.

Danhof, Clarence H. *Change in Agriculture: The Northern United States, 1820–1870.* Cambridge, MA: Harvard University Press, 1969.

Davis, Henry B. O. *Electrical and Electronic Technologies: A Chronology of Events and Inventors to 1900.* Metuchen, NJ: Scarecrow Press, 1981.

Dudley, William, ed. *The Industrial Revolution: Opposing Viewpoints.* San Diego, CA: Greenhaven Press, 1998.

Fisher, Douglas A. *The Epic of Steel.* New York: Harper and Row, 1963.

Gross, Ernie. *Advances and Innovations in American Daily Life, 1600s–1930s.* Jefferson, NC: McFarland, 2002.

Horwitz, Elinor L. *On the Land: American Agriculture from Past to Present.* New York: Atheneum, 1980.

Meyer, Herbert W. *A History of Electricity and Magnetism.* Cambridge, MA: MIT Press, 1971.

Muir, Diana. *Reflections in Bullough's Pond: Economy and Ecosystem in New England.* Hanover, NH: University Press of New England, 2000.

Pursell, Carroll W. *The Machine in America: A Social History of Technology.* Baltimore, MD: Johns Hopkins University Press, 1995.

Sharlin, Harold I. *The Making of the Electrical Age: From the Telegraph to Automation.* London and New York: Abelard-Schuman, 1964.

Standage, Tom. *The Victorian Internet: The Remarkable Story of the Telegraph and the Nineteenth Century's On-line Pioneers.* New York: Walker and Co., 1998.

Periodicals

"Before Fridges: The Ice Trade." *Economist,* December 21, 1991, p. 47.

Cummins, Lyle. "Rudolf Diesel—The Man and His Mission." *Diesel Progress,* July 1985, p. D34.

Gray, Paul. "Thomas Edison (1847–1931): His Inventions Not Only Reshaped Modernity but Also Promised a Future Bounded Only by Creativity." *Time,* December 31, 1999, p. 184.

Gustaitis, Joseph. "Samuel Slater: Father of the Industrial Revolution." *American History Illustrated,* May 1989, p. 32.

John, Richard R. "The Politics of Innovation." *Daedalus,* Fall 1998, p. 187.

Johnson, Jeff. "Nikola Tesla: Genius, Visionary, and Eccentric." *Skeptical Inquirer,* Summer 1994, p. 368.

Leone, Marie, et. al. "Edison and Tesla: The Founding Fathers of Electricity." *Electrical World,* January-February 2000, p. 41.

Lieberman, Beth. "The Elemental Sparks." *Smithsonian,* February 2001, p. 44.

"The Memory of Samuel Slater." *Yankee,* August 1999, p. 108.

Morse, Minna Scherlinder. "Chilly Reception: Dr. John Gorrie Found the Competition All Fired Up When He Tried to Market His Ice-Making Machine." *Smithsonian,* July 2002, p. 30.

Rosenberg, Nathan. "The Role of Electricity in Industrial Development." *Energy Journal,* April 1998, p 7.

Usselman, Steven W. "From Novelty to Utility: George Westinghouse and the Business of Innovation during the Age of Edison." *Business History Review,* Summer 1992, p. 251.

Web Sites

"History of American Agriculture, 1776–1990." *U.S. Department of Agriculture Research Service.* http://www.usda.gov/history2/text4.htm (accessed on January 31, 2003).

"The History of Oil." *U.S Department of Energy.* http://www.fe.doe.gov/education/oil_history.html (accessed on January 31, 2003).

"The History of the Automobile: The Internal Combustion Engine and Early Gas-Powered Cars." *About.com.* http://inventors.about.com/library/weekly/aacarsgasa.htm (accessed on February 17, 2003).

"Oil, Our Untapped Energy Wealth." *U.S. Department of Energy.* http://www.fe.doe.gov/education/ (accessed on January 31, 2003).

Taylor, Frederick. *The Principles of Scientific Management.* First published 1911. *Fordham University.* http://www.fordham.edu/halsall/mod/1911taylor.html (accessed on January 31, 2003.)

How Things Got Bigger: Economy of Scale

6

In the one hundred years between 1800 and 1900, things got much bigger. Businesses boomed: a family-run fabric-making operation that was contained in a single cottage in 1800 had turned into an enormous factory housing giant machines and employing hundreds of workers by 1900. Transportation expanded: a horse-drawn cart delivering farm produce to market in 1800 had been replaced, by 1900, with a long train pulled by a huge locomotive puffing great clouds of smoke and steam. Agriculture spread: the family farm grew from a small plot, or several small plots, in 1800 to a several-hundred-acre estate by 1900. And manufacturing accelerated: a single skilled worker making carriages in 1800 had given way, by 1900, to a long assembly line turning out automobiles.

This enormous increase in the size of business enterprises was a key characteristic of the Industrial Revolution. Businesses grew larger partly in order to take advantage of a concept called economy of scale, which refers to the fact that generally it is cheaper to build and operate one very large factory that can turn out many products per hour as opposed to a series of smaller factories that can turn out only a few

Words to Know

Assembly line: A system of manufacturing goods in which many workers, often arranged in different stations along a line, carry out the same precise task over and over on multiple products, as opposed to a single worker carrying out many tasks on one product.

Corporation: A business organization that is given the right to act as if it were a person in certain legal matters, such as buying or selling things or entering into binding agreements (contracts).

Economy of scale: The reduction in cost of a product resulting from mass production.

Interchangeable parts: Identical components of a product that are produced separately from the product itself and then assembled.

Mass production: Making large numbers of identical products, often using a system like an assembly line in a factory, rather than making products one at a time.

Monopoly: A business large enough to be able to control the price of a product without regard to competition.

Muckraker: A journalist who focuses on uncovering corruption, abuse, or other wrong-doing. The term is most often applied to a group of journalists writing about business practices in the late 1890s and early 1900s.

Robber baron: The owner and manager of a very large business that was judged to be a monopoly.

products per hour. It may take just one person to operate a large machine, whereas many people might be needed to operate several smaller machines. Even if the cost of raw materials for each product is the same, when the cost of labor is taken into account, it is cheaper to manufacture products on a large scale.

The American system

The Industrial Revolution was made possible by a series of inventions that allowed machines to substitute for human and animal muscles. An equally important innovation during the second part of the Industrial Revolution was the way machines and humans were organized to mass pro-

duce goods that were once laboriously made one by one. A method of manufacturing pioneered in the United States, called the American system, revolutionized manufacturing by introducing two new ideas: interchangeable parts and the moving assembly line.

Manufacturing is largely a process of assembling multiple parts—sometimes thousands of different parts, as in a car, for example—to make a finished product. A key development during the Industrial Revolution was the concept of making parts interchangeable. Before the Industrial Revolution, skilled workers made products for specific customers. Each part would be made for the specific job. The axle of one carriage, for example, might be similar to the axle of another, but not necessarily identical. The American system changed this. Many axles, for example, would be manufactured separately, each one identical, and then assembled into the finished product, such as an automobile.

The moving assembly line, in which workers put together interchangeable parts to fashion a product quickly, was called the American system.
Reproduced by permission of the Library of Congress.

Interchangeable parts were essential for the other innovation, the moving assembly line. At one time, a worker had to walk around the factory floor to collect parts and assemble a whole product. With a moving assembly line, a product, such as a car, moved along on a platform (such as a conveyor belt) and came to a series of stations where workers were waiting to carry out one specific job, such as installing the axle. Once the part was installed, the partially assembled car moved to the next station, where the next worker would install a different part. In the meantime, the first worker was installing an axle on the next unit moving along the line. The assembly line required each worker to stay in the same place and to carry out the same task over and over again; identical tasks matched identical parts and turned out identical products.

A moving assembly line could significantly increase the output of a factory. The volume of work accomplished by workers in a factory in a single day depended on the speed of the assembly line. If the line moved quickly, workers could produce more products than if the line moved slowly. And the success of the assembly line depended on each particular part being absolutely identical; there was no time for workers to adjust parts to fit individual products.

As part of a system, the moving assembly line and interchangeable parts could result in a highly efficient manufacturing operation, when everything worked as designed by an engineer or business owner. Efforts by factory owners to speed up the line provoked workers, however, who in turn staged work slowdowns to slow the lines (see Chapter 7). Despite their resistance to the American system, workers of the late nineteenth century knew that the days of skilled individuals shaping wooden and metal parts by hand and assembling goods with some measure of their own creativity was virtually over.

The idea of interchangeable parts originated around 1850, but it took several decades to implement fully, mostly because of the expense of creating machines to make the standard parts. Devices that could, for example, stamp out exact copies of a part from a solid piece of metal had to be designed and built. Until these so-called machine tools were fully developed, manufacturing from interchangeable parts in fact added to the cost of goods.

Among the first users of interchangeable parts were makers of firearms, clocks, sewing machines, typewriters, engines, and bicycles. Henry Ford (1863–1947), a pioneer automobile manufacturer, was most famous for his success in making the assembly line system work on a massive scale. His new process reduced the cost of making cars so that Ford's company could produce products that Ford workers could afford to buy. What had once been a luxury item became a product that nearly everyone could hope to own. The Ford Motor Company was a classic illustration of how the idea of economy of scale benefited an entire society. The idea that ordinary American workers could afford to drive private cars helped make the United States the envy of the world.

Henry Ford and the Model T

Henry Ford did not invent the gas-powered automobile, nor did he invent the assembly line. He is credited, however, with developing the moving assembly line. In Ford's factories, piles of interchangeable parts were set out in a line. Starting with a bare chassis (the frame), a new car started moving along the line. Workers at their stations added parts until a completed automobile came out, about ninety minutes later.

Ford Motor Company's famous moving assembly line did not spring up overnight. It evolved over time, and at several different companies. Ford's main idea was to drive down the cost of making cars; the moving assembly line was a means to that end. To accomplish this, Ford hired engineers and consultants to study car production and devise ways to reduce the cost. The first car built by Ford came off the line in October 1913, and Ford constantly sought improvements. Over time, the time required to make a car steadily fell, as did the price. Sales, on the other hand, rose, as workers snapped up the popular "Tin Lizzie," as the Model T was affectionately nicknamed.

Henry Ford was born in 1863 in a farmhouse near Dearborn, Michigan, west of Detroit. His grandfather, John Ford, had immigrated to the United States from Ireland in 1847. Henry grew up on the family farm, where he developed a fascination for machinery. Although he absorbed the values of hard work and individualism on the farm, he said later in life that he never loved farm life.

In 1879, at age 16, Ford left his family and became an apprentice (assistant) in a Detroit machine shop. He also took a job at night repairing watches. In 1880, he went to work for a shipbuilding company, where he learned about engines. Two years later, he worked for the Westinghouse Engine Company, repairing the engines on farmers' tractors.

For a time after 1888, Ford returned to farming life, working on land given to him as a wedding present by his father. But his heart lay in working with machines. It was at just this time that two German inventors, Gottlieb Daimler and Karl Benz, developed the first practicable automobile with a gasoline engine. In 1891, Ford abandoned farming for good and moved back to Detroit, working for the Edison Illuminating Company, where he soon became chief engineer. In the evenings, he worked on building a car with a gasoline engine, and in 1896, he demonstrated it on the streets of Detroit. He called it a Quadricycle.

Ford immediately started working on another car, using money invested by Detroit's mayor and some leading city businessmen. In 1899, Ford helped to organize the Detroit Automobile Company. The firm built twenty cars, then went out of business in 1900. Despite the company's failure, Ford was established as a player in Detroit's infant automobile industry.

In 1901, Ford attracted new investors and organized the Henry Ford Company; he owned one-sixth of the stock and worked as chief engineer. But after a year, Ford fell out with the investors and quit. The company agreed to stop using his name, and took a new one: the Cadillac Motor Car Company. Ford then turned to building race cars; one of his vehicles set a new speed record of over 60 miles an hour (132 kph).

In 1902, Ford organized a partnership to make cars with the goal of competing with the Oldsmobile, a modestly priced car already in production. From the very beginning, Ford bought parts from independent machine shops in Detroit, including a shop owned by the brothers John and Horace Dodge (they supplied 650 chassis, the frame on which the parts of a car sit). From the first moment, the Ford Motor Company was based on the practice of assembling parts into a finished automobile. Henry Ford's most

important contribution to the industry (and to the Industrial Revolution) was finding better, cheaper, faster ways to assemble parts.

Without doubt Henry Ford revolutionized not only the automobile industry, but also the face of America, by manufacturing cars that many workers could aspire to own. Ford's most famous product was the Model T, introduced in 1908 at a price of $950. Over the next nineteen years, Ford sold 15.5 million Model Ts in the United States alone. Ford's manufacturing techniques drove down the price of a Model T to as low as $280 in 1915. (In 2003 prices, the Model T went from about $18,900 in 1908 to a low of about $4,900 in 1915.) Of course, the Model T produced in 1915 hardly compares to contemporary cars. It was slow, it lacked power (often drivers had to get out and push it up steep hills), the passenger space lacked any of the comforts of a modern car (such as a heater or air-conditioning), and after 1913 it came

The Model T from the Ford Motor Company became the symbol of the advantages of assembly line production, and it marked the beginning of affordable cars for most citizens.
Reproduced by permission of the Corbis Corporation.

only in one color: black. (Ford once famously quipped that the Model T came in any color the customer wanted, as long as it was black.) By manufacturing inexpensive cars, Ford put them within economic reach of his workers.

In 1914 Ford introduced the $5.00 work day. He began paying his workers $5.00 a day for eight hours of work (about $11.25 an hour in 2003 prices), roughly twice what other manufacturers were paying automobile assemblers at the time.

Not only did the $5.00 a day Ford was paying improve the living conditions of his workers, that wage enabled the workers to buy the products they were making. Ford was building a customer base among his own employees.

The car culture

Ford's moving assembly line system was soon copied by other manufacturers. The relatively inexpensive automobiles Ford and, later, other automakers produced revolutionized American life in the twentieth century. The automobile made it possible for everyone, not just the wealthy, to move much more quickly and travel greater distances. Instead of living within walking distance of work, people could move to a more rural locale and drive to work in the city. Thus was born the suburb, a residential area on the outskirts of a city.

The automobile created a tremendous demand for a whole new infrastructure of paved highways, gasoline stations, repair shops, tire dealers, and insurance agents, to say nothing of parking garages, parking meters, and meter maids. Within a few short decades, the existence of hundreds of thousands of cars created a need for larger, improved roads and highways (cars did not do well in mud or snow) to carry drivers from suburb to city. As suburbs spread farther from traditional city centers, drivers demanded wider roads that sliced through the middle of cities to reduce traffic jams.

The automobile industry also spurred the rapid growth of the petroleum industry since cars that were steadily growing in size and weight required more fuel. Gradually, U.S. underground reserves of petroleum began to dwindle, and foreign supplies were sought. U.S. companies began to exploit the extensive oil reserves in the Middle East in the late 1930s, and by 1946 oil would replace coal as the primary fuel in the world.

Frederick Taylor advised businesses to apply engineering principles to their organization and to treat humans as if they were parts of a machine while compensating them reasonably. *Reproduced by permission of the Orion Publishing Group, Ltd.*

Frederick Taylor and Scientific Management

In 1911 an engineer named Frederick Taylor (1856–1915) published a collection of essays titled *The Principles of Scientific Management*. Taylor was an early example of a management consultant, someone who offers advice to business owners and managers on how to make more money. Taylor's advice was particularly well received, and he had an enormous impact on the way industrial companies were organized.

Taylor began his book by saying: "The principal object of management should be to secure the maximum prosperity for the employer, coupled with the maximum prosperity for each employee." In his view, a key way to improve a factory's efficiency (that is, to increase the value of goods produced by more than the cost of producing them) was to reduce the time spent in production. The way to accomplish this, according to Taylor, was to break down each step in manufacturing to its basic tasks and then assign those tasks to workers best able to perform them. For example, if a worker is good at putting nuts on bolts, then that worker should do that and only that. No further thought or variation would be needed or allowed.

Taylor believed that a key role of managers in enterprises was to study the process and eliminate inefficiencies. One inefficiency was the time wasted when individual workers stopped to think about what they were doing. Thinking not only took up valuable time (paid for by the employer), but also introduced the possibility of variations in the process. Taylor advocated that the manager should use engineering skills to determine the single most efficient way of completing a process, and then ensure that each individual engaged in the enterprise did his or her job exactly

The cost of purchasing, maintaining, and fueling a car had to be added to the family budget, both as a means of getting to work and as a way of maintaining prestige as larger autos became status symbols. People started doing more and more in their cars: eating at drive-in restaurants, watching films at drive-in movie theaters, doing their banking at drive-up teller windows, and even picking up their clothing at drive-through dry cleaners.

Concerns began to arise in the 1960s about the impact of air pollution from automobile emissions (poisonous byproducts of burning gasoline and oil) as the number of cars continued to escalate. Many families had begun owning as designed. This method was "scientific management."

Taylor also was concerned that workers might think it was to their advantage to work more slowly and produce less than they were capable of producing, as a means of keeping their jobs (that is, they feared that if they were too efficient the manager might think he needed fewer workers and let some workers go). Taylor was eager to persuade workers that producing more would not harm their economic interests, nor the interests of their fellow workers, but instead would result in greater rewards.

Taylor's book was widely read and became highly influential. A whole corps of management consultants went to work figuring out the "best" way of doing a task, and designing ways of implementing that best way. One result of using Taylor's method was to minimize or eliminate the possibility that an individual worker might think about his (or her) job and experiment with different—and possibly better—ways of working.

Although Taylor repeatedly insisted that workers must be rewarded financially for their role in increasing the profitability of the business by doing things in a scientific way, that part of his scheme was not always adopted by factory owners. Sometimes factory owners just adopted Taylor's recommendations for changes in the production system—for example, that workers be allowed to perform only the one task at which they excel—which were not readily accepted by most workers. Because factory owners accepted only part of Taylor's approach, scientific management contributed to the shift from treating workers as individual skilled craftspeople to treating them as interchangeable parts of the larger machine.

two or three cars, greatly increasing the number of automobiles spewing exhaust and snarling traffic on highway networks. By the 1960s cars were fully integrated into the economic structure—even into the architecture—of the most advanced nations. Whole cities were built around the assumption that workers would drive to their workplaces.

Highway trucking emerged as an alternative to railroads for delivering raw materials and finished goods, just as railroads had emerged as an alternative to canals in the middle of the nineteenth century. The railroads that had generated huge fortunes in the mid-1800s (see Chapter 5) began to suffer as larger and larger rigs took to the roads. The rise of the trucking industry led to a period of rapid consolidation of railroad companies as they competed with the trucks and tried to stay in business.

Networks

Alongside the American system of manufacturing grew another concept central to the second stage of the Industrial Revolution: the network. Among the most important networks of the nineteenth century were the telegraph network, the telephone network, the electricity network (the grid), and the railroad network. The twentieth century gave rise to three other important networks: radio networks, television networks, and the Internet, a network of links between computers made possible by adopting standardized computer codes to transfer digital information to points around the world.

The essential idea behind a network is the distribution of something, whether messages, products, or energy. Usually networks evolve gradually. In the cases above, shortly after the invention upon which the network was based was perfected, businesspeople rushed to try to turn the new technology into a profitable enterprise. They started to deliver telegraph service, for example, from one point to another. In doing so, they built a leg of the network that was to come, whether they were aware of doing so or not. In the early days of networks it was too ambitious even to think of building a network that connected all points; that process took place a bit later on.

The stories of the network industries have several things in common. At first, each was grossly overbuilt in and around major urban areas. Photographs from the late 1800s show a thick mass of wires strung in New York City, where several companies were competing to deliver electricity. In the case of railroads, many short lines connected only two cities, between which there was a demonstrable need for fast, efficient travel. Initially there were several companies that competed to deliver telegrams between major cities.

At the same time, networks shared another feature: the enormous cost of building them in the first place, and the relatively low cost of operating them once they were built.

This feature was especially true of railroads, where land had to be acquired, cleared, and made relatively level so that iron, and later steel, rails could be laid—an enormous expense before the first dollar could be collected for delivering passengers or goods. These projects were often simply too expensive to be undertaken by individuals, or even groups of individuals. Instead, local and state governments were enlisted, and many early railroads were built with money borrowed by state governments. The governments judged that it was important to have a railroad in order to support the many other industries in the state that relied on transportation to distribute both manufactured goods and agricultural products.

Yet another feature of networks is the need to be complete. What good is a telephone if you can call some people but not others? Initially, some businesses required several telephones in order to be in touch with all their customers and suppliers. Completeness means compatibility. In the case of railroads, if the tracks are not the same width in all cases, locomotives and cars cannot make use of all tracks—they cannot continue when the width of tracks changes. The same is true of other networks. All telephones work with any long-distance service; on the Internet, E-mail messages can travel from one local provider to a computer using a different provider. In the United States, all electrical appliances are made to use 110 volts of electricity, which is the standard delivered on the electricity network.

Consequently, the rise of networks during the second half of the Industrial Revolution gave rise to standards, the idea that on a single network, all objects will conform to the needs of the network. All light bulbs work in compatible lamps, for example. Customers can switch between one brand of bulb and another without worrying about whether the bulbs will fit, or whether the electricity will be of the right power. Lamp manufacturers cooperate by making sure all brands of bulbs can be used in their products. All railroad cars in the United States and Canada can run on any set of tracks, regardless of who manufactured the cars and on whose tracks they are running: the gauge (width) is the same on all. (There are a handful of historical exceptions to this rule. In the nineteenth century, some railroads in the Rocky Mountains, built to serve mines, were built to a different standard—narrow gauge—which was judged easier to build under the circumstances. Today, narrow-gauge railroads are relegated to tourist attractions.)

Building, maintaining, and using a network is not just a technical issue. It is also an important business issue. Individual businesspeople, sometimes aided by the government, voluntarily agree to accept a certain set of standards in order to be on the network. It is easy to imagine a better telephone receiver, one that sends stereo-quality sound and music, for example. But it does not exist. The reason is that in order to be useful, every telephone needs to be able to send and receive to every other telephone, and the agreed-upon standard does not support stereo-quality telephones.

In some cases, dual networks exist side by side. One example is videotapes: for a long time there were two standards, VHS and Betamax. VHS tapes could only be played in a VHS videotape player; and Betamax tapes could only be played in a Betamax player. Eventually, the VHS standard gained the upper hand (even though some people thought Betamax offered a better picture), video rental stores began stocking only VHS tapes, and the Betamax video player disappeared. Videotapes were not judged to be as socially important as some of the other networks (they needn't be regulated for public welfare and safety reasons, for example), and so government left it up to the marketplace to battle it out. Eventually there was a kind of videotape network that included stores that rent and sell videotapes that conform to the standard.

As the Industrial Revolution continued to progress, the idea of networks gave rise to the idea that a few businesspeople acting together could control key networks, railroads in particular, and charge whatever they wished for access. A related idea was building an enterprise so large that its economies of scale would give it a monopoly on the market: the enterprise could control the price of the product it sold without interference from competitors. A few businesspeople came close to successfully monopolizing the railroad market in the late 1800s, and they became famous in the process.

All aboard! The railroads story

The growth of railroads in the second half of the nineteenth century illustrates many of the positive and the

negative features of the Industrial Revolution. In the United States, railroads tied together the Atlantic and Pacific coasts, gave life to whole industries, and created a whole new class of business owners: the robber barons, wealthy industrialists like Andrew Carnegie and John D. Rockefeller.

As Americans—and the boundary of the United States—moved westward in the first half of the nineteenth century, railroads followed. The growth of agriculture, coal mining, and iron mining in the Midwest largely dictated where railroads headed. Railroads were built to haul grain from Ohio; coal from Pennsylvania; iron ore from Minnesota; and later, meat from Chicago, Illinois, to the West. Chicago became the focal point of the railroad network, as it was a port city on Lake Michigan. East Coast port cities like New York; Baltimore, Maryland; and Boston, Massachusetts, however, were anxious to maintain their importance as ports. In order to keep Boston's status intact, railroad promoters there went door to door to solicit funds to build new

The tracks of the first transcontinental railroad are joined at Promontory in the Utah territory, 1869.
Reproduced by permission of the National Archives and Records Administration.

The Importance of Transportation

The ability to move goods rapidly over long distances was critical to the progression of the Industrial Revolution. After 1850, railroads expanded dramatically with the development of the steam engine. The railroads at first competed with shipping businesses that used waterways to haul raw materials and manufactured goods, but soon railroads overwhelmed the competition. Later, in the twentieth century, trucks would replace railroads as the primary mover of freight, and automobiles would come to play a central role in everyday life.

In preindustrial society, the movement of people and goods was limited to the speed, strength, and endurance of animals, mostly horses and oxen. Goods were hauled in wagons that could travel only during the day and at speeds of less than 5 miles an hour, and there were pauses to feed and water the animals. Alternatively, sailing ships could carry large cargoes, but they depended on uncertain winds.

The available modes of transportation meant that most industries were local in nature. The size of a single enterprise was limited, in part, by the cost and speed of shipping things over long distances. The train and the steamship, and later the automobile and the truck, revolutionized transportation, and thus were major contributors to the success of industrialization.

railroads linking that city to Albany, New York, at the eastern end of the Erie Canal, a traditional inland shipping route to the Midwest.

As the railroad network expanded, so did the competition—and, surprisingly, the cooperation—among the companies building the railroads. Various entrepreneurs sought to make a fortune by building tracks connecting all the major cities and towns of America and by taking customers away from their competitors by offering inexpensive shipping. At the same time, though, a railroad is a natural network; people want to be able to ship goods between any two points, and doing so often meant using more than one railroad company for a product to reach its final destination. Consequently, railroad company heads would compete with one another at one time, then sit down together to agree on standards at another time.

During the decades between 1860 and 1890, American railroad owners effectively created a national network by agreeing to standards. For example, railroad standards dictated that the distance between tracks (gauge) would be 4 feet, 8½ inches, and that railroad cars would have brakes and compatible coupling devices so they could fit together. Operations were also standardized, including the use of common signals, schedules, and even time. (In about 1880 railroads agreed to set the minute hands on all their clocks and watches to the same time, a "standard time," instead of relying on local jewelers along the line who set their clocks to noon when the sun was directly overhead.) Standards were also set in business affairs: there was a set cost for using another company's freight cars, and all companies agreed to sell "through" tickets so that a passenger could buy a ticket at the start of a journey that used several different railroads.

At first, building railroads was seen both as a business opportunity and as a social necessity for some cities and towns. There was intense competition among lines for hauling freight from the West to the East. Smaller lines, linking cities with towns, were bought up by the "main line" companies, creating a series of parallel rail networks. For example, the New York Central Railroad (from which New York City's Grand Central Station derives its name) was assembled by Commodore Cornelius Vanderbilt (1794–1877) in 1853; Vanderbilt purchased and merged several smaller lines in New York State to link New York City with Buffalo, then an important shipping port on Lake Erie.

Building a railroad was, of course, highly expensive. Land had to be acquired, a roadbed had to be built by clearing the land, tracks had to be laid, and engines and cars had to be purchased. Some small railroads could never make a profit after paying for their initial investment; others were barely profitable, and in the case of economic slowdowns (called "panics" in the 1800s), they operated on the verge of bankruptcy or went out of business altogether.

The finances of railroads, in fact, came to be even more important than their actual operations. In the late 1800s, building a network to enable long-distance shipping became central to the railroad industry. Thus, long after the technology had been improved and the rails laid, railroads came to be dominated by financiers, people whose interests were in buying and selling companies, rather than operating them.

The robber barons

At the end of the nineteenth century, a handful of businesspeople managed to control enormous business empires and to accumulate some of the greatest fortunes yet seen. So great was their influence over such key industries as steel, railroads, and oil that they came to be seen as a challenge to the government of the United States. Known as robber barons at the time, they not only shaped the later Industrial Revolution, they came to symbolize its excesses. Three of the best known robber barons were Andrew Carnegie (1835–1919), John D. Rockefeller (1839–1937), and J. P. Morgan (1837–1913).

Andrew Carnegie and steel

The life story of Andrew Carnegie is the classic American dream come true: poor little Scottish lad comes to the United States with no money, works hard, gets into the steel business, and ends up a billionaire who can't give away his fortune fast enough before he dies.

Strangely, Carnegie's story started when his father became a victim of industrialization. The family weaving business in Scotland was forced out of business by the new textile mills when Carnegie was a young boy. The Carnegies picked up stakes and moved to Pittsburgh, Pennsylvania, where they had relatives.

In Pittsburgh Andrew went to work in a textile factory at age thirteen, earning $1.20 a week. His origins were humble, but Carnegie was smart and ambitious. He went through a series of jobs after leaving the textile mill. He delivered telegraph messages, and then was promoted to sending messages. So great was his telegraphy skill that he was offered a job as general assistant to an executive of the Pennsylvania Railroad. Riding the train, he happened to meet an inventor with an idea for a specially made car with seats that folded into beds at night. Carnegie took the idea to his boss, who snapped it up. For his trouble, Carnegie was paid $5,000 as a bonus, a huge amount at the time.

Carnegie did not spend his bonus. Instead, he invested it in many companies that were founded during the American Civil War (1861–65) and were growing rapidly. By age twenty, he owned stock in dozens of companies. He was offered a job as general superintendent of the Pennsylvania Railroad, but instead he decided to follow the advice he later gave to others: "Put all your eggs in one basket—and watch that basket." In Carnegie's case, the basket was filled with steel mills.

Carnegie knew from his railroad work that cast iron rails were prone to cracking. On a trip to England, Carnegie saw the new Bessemer process for making inexpensive steel, which was lighter, stronger, and longer-lasting than iron (see Chapter 5). Carnegie obtained the rights to use the process and returned to the United States, where he built a steel mill of his own. Soon he was supplying steel rails to railroads. Always a shrewd businessperson, Carnegie also bought coal mines, rather than pay someone else for the chief fuel used in making steel.

Carnegie was generally known as a good employer, but he was not fond of labor unions, groups of workers who banded together to negotiate better pay and working conditions from their employers. Labor unions found there was strength in numbers: an employer could fire one worker who asked for a raise, but generally he would not fire all the workers in a factory if together they all asked for a raise. In 1892 steelworkers at his Homestead facility, near Pittsburgh, went on strike, refusing to work until a new union contract was signed The issue was not limited to pay; the

Andrew Carnegie built the world's largest steel company and was one of the world's most generous philanthropists. *Reproduced by permission of Getty Images.*

The Muckrakers

For a period of about twenty years, between 1890 and 1910, a group of journalists writing for national magazines specialized in revealing the business practices of the giant corporations, called trusts. The trusts had monopolies on the markets they were in, meaning they were large enough, and powerful enough, to be able to control the price of their products without regard to the competition. These investigative journalists also wrote articles about how some businesses engaged in unsafe practices (especially in the food industry), and they described the utterly miserable conditions in which some poor workers were forced to live. As a group, these journalists were called "muckrakers," a term first applied to them by U.S. president Theodore Roosevelt (1858–1919) in 1906. Roosevelt was defending his political allies following a series of *Cosmopolitan* magazine articles in written by David Graham Phillips (1867–1911). Phillips re-

vealed that some Senators received payments from companies in exchange for arguing on behalf of the companies before the Senate.

One of the earliest of the muckrakers was the Danish-born journalist Jacob Riis (pronounced reese; 1849–1914), who took photos and wrote stories about immigrants in New York City. Riis described the lives of the poorest immigrants, who often went without food and who lived jammed in tiny apartments that lacked bathrooms. Published in 1890 as the book *How the Other Half Lives,* Riis's work presented a stark, even shocking, contrast between the country's image of itself and the realities of life for the poor. Among fans of Riis was Theodore Roosevelt, who was then governor of New York. Riis's work led to broad public acceptance of government programs to help the poor and to impose minimum standards for landlords renting out apartments.

Homestead strike became a contest of wills between Carnegie's manager, Henry Clay Frick (1849–1919), and the union over whether the company could eliminate the union altogether by refusing to sign a contract. The strike started while Carnegie was vacationing in Scotland (some union sympathizers thought he arranged his vacation specifically to be away when a new union contract was due to be signed). Violence broke out, and eighteen strikers and guards were killed. Eventually, state militiamen (called the National Guard today) were sent to the site to restore order, and to end the strike.

Ida Tarbell (1857–1944) was a journalist born in western Pennsylvania whose father made barrels in which oil was hauled. She wrote an in-depth study of the Standard Oil Trust, published in nineteen installments between November 1902 and October 1904 in *McClure's Magazine* (the articles were collected into book form in 1904). Her articles exposed how Standard Oil's business practices drove smaller competitors out of business (her own father had been one such competitor) in violation of federal law. Her work paved the way for the Roosevelt administration to enforce the 1890 Sherman Antitrust Act and break up the oil monopoly into several smaller companies.

Perhaps the greatest of the muckrakers was American writer Upton Sinclair (1878–1968). In 1906 he published the novel *The Jungle,* a harrowing tale about immigrant workers in Chicago's stockyards, where cattle were slaughtered and butchered for shipment to markets. While Sinclair's point was the misery of immigrant workers, middle-class readers were horrified to read his account of the filthy conditions of the meatpacking industry that provided their Sunday roast beef. Popular sentiment caused the federal government to pass the Food and Drug Act in 1906, regulating the preparation of food and sending government inspectors into businesses to make sure they obeyed the law.

The influence of the muckrakers, many of whom published their articles in *McClure's Magazine,* began to fade after about 1906. But their articles, photographs, and books had helped to bring about an important change in public perception of big business, and they opened the door to politicians like Theodore Roosevelt and his cousin Franklin Delano Roosevelt to institute new laws that made the government a third player, alongside business owners and workers, in the new economy of the Industrial Revolution.

Carnegie later claimed that had he known what was happening in Homestead, he would never have let the violence go so far. Two years after the strike, Carnegie fired Frick. But in the meantime, Carnegie Steel had become the largest steel company in the world, and Carnegie had become immensely wealthy. Not only did he own the steel plants, he owned the mines in Minnesota where the iron ore was mined as well as the boats and railroad used to haul the ore to his plants. And while the market for steel rails was declining, new uses for steel were springing up, including the beams used to build the skyscrapers that were just coming into style.

Today we would call Carnegie Steel a vertically integrated company. Carnegie gathered under one company the raw materials (iron from Minnesota), the transport (boats to carry the ore across the Great Lakes to Pennsylvania and a railroad to take it to his plants in Pittsburgh), and the manufacturing facilities (steel mills in Pittsburgh) that made an essential commodity with applications nearly everywhere.

In 1901 the New York financier J. P. Morgan hatched a scheme to corral virtually all steel production in one company; acquiring Carnegie's company was vital to the plan. Morgan enlisted one of Carnegie's assistants to approach the steel magnate to find out how much Carnegie wanted for his steel company. Carnegie thought about it overnight, then scribbled a figure on a piece of paper: $480 million (worth about $10.3 billion in 2003 prices). He sent the paper with his assistant to Morgan, and the banker accepted the price.

After selling his company, Carnegie, then sixty-five, turned his attention to giving away his fortune. He contributed money to build 1,679 libraries throughout the United States. About 70 percent of the libraries financed by Carnegie were built in small towns of fewer than 10,000 people. He also donated money to build Carnegie Hall in New York City, still a premier auditorium for music; he contributed to Tuskegee Institute, a school for African Americans in Alabama; and he founded the Carnegie Institute of Technology in Pittsburgh, Pennsylvania (now part of Carnegie-Mellon University).

In 1889 Carnegie wrote an essay titled *The Gospel of Wealth.* Having gained a fabulous fortune after starting with nothing (except for high intelligence, a pleasing personality, and a huge dose of luck), Carnegie praised the Industrial Revolution. He acknowledged that the rich lived in huge houses, but he justified this on the grounds that in these mansions the fine arts could find a home. He expressed the opinion that workers, too, were better off than before the Industrial Revolution, even if they were not as well off as people who controlled huge companies. And Carnegie had a solution for the enormous inequalities of wealth: the rich should give away their fortunes in ways that benefit those less well off. It was a lesson he followed twelve years after writing the essay.

After he had died, on November 11, 1919, it was discovered that his net worth was about $23 million. Carnegie was hardly poor at his death, but he had managed to give away more than 90 percent of his fortune.

John D. Rockefeller and oil

In 1859 Edwin L. Drake (1819–1880), a retired railroad conductor, discovered oil in Titusville, Pennsylvania (see Chapter 5); at about the same time two young men in Cleveland, Ohio, Maurice Clark and his neighbor, a young accountant named John D. Rockefeller, were opening a small wholesale grocery business with $1,000 of Rockefeller's own savings and $1,000 from his father. Fifty years later, Rockefeller was one of the richest men in the world, and perhaps the richest man ever. His fortune was estimated at about $50 billion (in 2003 dollars), his name a synonym for fabulous wealth. It wasn't groceries that made Rockefeller rich; it was oil.

Rockefeller was not exactly an oil man: he was a money man. It was his expertise in business, in buying companies and arranging deals, that succeeded in creating the Standard Oil Trust, a series of related companies that controlled practically all the oil in the United States at a time when the Industrial Revolution was beginning to run on oil.

Just as the Industrial Revolution could not have proceeded without technical innovations, it could not have succeeded without money, great heaps of it, to build machines, factories, railroads, telegraph lines: the entire infrastructure that transformed society in Europe and North America in the course of 150 years. At the beginning of the Industrial Revolution, one clever inventor might have been able to raise enough money to start a company, and then earn enough money from that company to make it bigger. But as the scale of business grew, more complicated financial arrangements were needed. The Standard Oil story is about the influence of finance.

Four years after opening their wholesale grocery business, Rockefeller and Clark decided to get into the fast-growing oil business by building an oil refinery in Cleveland (kerosene lamps were becoming very popular, and refineries

John D. Rockefeller amassed his enormous fortune by building the Standard Oil Company, establishing as close to a monopoly on the oil industry as was ever created. *Reproduced by permission of the Library of Congress.*

made kerosene from the oil that was pumped from the ground). They brought in a third partner, Samuel Andrews, who had experience in oil refining, and later two brothers of Clark joined them. Rockefeller, the former bookkeeper, was eager to see the company grow, and he always looked for another opportunity to increase profits. He built his own oil barrels, for example, and even bought land where oak trees, used for making the barrels, grew. He built kilns where the trees grew, in order to dry the freshly cut lumber and save on the cost of shipping the lumber to his barrel-making shop. But the main way to grow as a business, Rockefeller thought, was to buy other oil-related companies.

In 1865, however, Rockefeller ran into opposition from the Clark brothers, who did not want to borrow money to buy more refineries. Rockefeller paid the partners $72,000 (about $862,000 in 2003 prices) for their shares in the company, and he became the sole owner. Five years later, Rockefeller and several new partners formed a new company with $1 million in capital (monetary assets), and they began buying other refineries in Cleveland. Within five years the new firm, named the Standard Oil Company, had bought all the other refineries in the city. Besides kerosene, Standard Oil also made paint and glue, which were by-products of oil refining. But the future still lay ahead: the gas-powered internal combustion engine was not perfected until 1885.

For the next two decades, Rockefeller assembled a large collection of companies related to the petroleum business. He especially concentrated on buying and building companies that marketed oil. His companies had agreements among each other that divided the United States into regions where the companies did not compete with one another.

Rockefeller also made deals with railroads that gave him secret discounts on shipping oil, discounts that competitors did not receive. Consequently, Rockefeller's costs were lower, and he could afford to drive smaller competitors out of business by underpricing them. Occasionally Rockefeller would keep his ownership of a company secret, in order to obtain business information from competitors who never realized they were dealing with a Rockefeller subsidiary. Some details of Rockefeller's business dealings have never been uncovered, although a series of articles written by Ida Tarbell and published in *McClure's* magazine between 1902 and 1904 had carefully documented ways in which Rockefeller operated. These articles had aroused public sentiment against the man who controlled about 75 percent of the oil business in the United States.

In 1906, the administration of President Theodore Roosevelt went to a federal court in Missouri, successfully making the case that Standard Oil violated the Sherman Antitrust Act by restraining (limiting) competition. Two years later, in 1911, the Supreme Court agreed with the lower court. The Supreme Court ruled that Rockefeller's company was guilty of limiting competition among formerly competitive companies by fixing the cost of transporting oil, the prices paid for oil, and the prices charged for products—actions that together the court described as an "unreasonable" restraint of trade. The court ordered that Standard Oil be broken apart into its constituent firms, which would have to compete with each other. Some of the separated companies, such as Standard of Ohio (Sohio), Standard Oil of California (Chevron), and Standard Oil of New York (Mobil), were quite large by themselves. Eventually, some of these separated companies merged together again, but these mergers were limited, and they did not take place for at least twenty years. The combination of firms created by Rockefeller was never fully reassembled.

J. P. Morgan and just about everything

While John D. Rockefeller used finance to build a fortune based on an actual activity—pumping, refining, shipping, and selling oil products—another business titan of the same period built his influence wholly on paper.

J. P. Morgan exerted significant influence over the Industrial Revolution through finance—lending money, acquiring stock, and building monopolies in railroads and steel.
Reproduced by permission of the Corbis Corporation.

Though John Pierpont Morgan, universally known as J. P. Morgan, was not nearly as wealthy as Rockefeller, Morgan held far more economic power.

Morgan's father, Junius Spencer Morgan, himself came from a wealthy New England family, and became even wealthier by helping to direct British investments in the rapidly growing American economy. Pierpont, as J. P. was called, was trained from the beginning to carry on the family tradition, and so he did. The principal business of the Morgans was to help collect the huge sums of money needed to finance expensive new enterprises, especially railroads. As railroad companies faltered (as a result, perhaps, of spending too much money and gaining too little business), the Morgans were there again, to buy up the failing companies and consolidate them into larger enterprises (today one might say larger networks). So far as is known, J. P. Morgan never drove a railroad spike, never shoveled a lump of coal into a locomotive, never designed any improvement to an industrial system. He did, however, arrange to have written very large checks.

Morgan and his company arranged the financing that put together corporate giants such as American Telephone and Telegraph (AT&T), International Harvester (successor to Cyrus McCormick's company), General Electric (founded by Thomas Alva Edison), Westinghouse Electric, and, most famously, United States Steel, the result of Morgan's combining Andrew Carnegie's steel company with several smaller firms. It was during Morgan's heyday that most big corporations moved their headquarters from the towns where they were founded to New York City, to be close to the stock markets of Wall Street and the sources of money needed to pay for business expansion or to scoop up faltering competitors.

Morgan was famously opposed to competition. He thought that when Andrew Carnegie constantly drove down the price of steel to ruin his competitors, he jeopardized those businesses as well as their workers. Morgan maintained that it was better to control industries in a trust (a monopoly) to avoid chaos in business and the pain it entailed.

For all his power and influence, Morgan did not die with a fabulous fortune. His wealth at the time of his death in 1913 was estimated at $80 million. He was far from being a pauper, but his fortune was less than one-tenth that of Rockefeller who, as the story goes, sniffed when he heard of Morgan's demise: "And to think, he wasn't even a rich man."

For More Information

Books

Chernow, Ron. *Titan: The Life of John D. Rockefeller, Sr.* New York: Random House, 1998.

Hoyt, Edwin Palmer, Jr. *The House of Morgan.* New York: Dodd, Mead, 1966.

Krass, Peter. *Carnegie.* New York: John Wiley and Sons, 2002.

Lacey, Robert. *Ford, the Men and the Machine.* Boston: Little, Brown, 1986.

Quackenbush, Robert. *Along Came the Model T! How Henry Ford Put the World on Wheels.* New York: Parents' Magazine Press, 1978.

Periodicals

Cookson, Gillian. "The Transatlantic Telegraph Cable." *History Today,* March 2000, p. 44.

Harrington, Ann. "The Big Ideas: Ever Since Frederick Taylor Pulled Out His Stopwatch, Big Thinkers Have Been Coming Up with New—Though Not Always Better—Ways to Manage People and Business." *Fortune,* November 22, 1999, p. 152.

Holzmann, Bjorn Pehrson. "The First Data Networks." *Scientific American,* January 1994, p. 124.

"The Making of the Modern Company." *Business Week,* August 28, 2000, p. 98.

Samuelson, Robert J. "The Assembly Line." *Newsweek,* Winter 1997, p. 18.

Schutz, Howard. "Giants in Collision: The Northern Pacific Panic of 1901." *American History Illustrated,* September 1986, p. 28.

Tedlow, Richard S. "What the Titans Can Teach Us." *Harvard Business Review,* December 2001, p. 70.

Winter, Drew. "The Mass Production Revolution: Forget the Machine: 'The Line' Changed the World." *Ward's Auto World,* May 1996, p. 101.

Web Sites

Carnegie, Andrew. "The Gospel of Wealth, 1889." *University of California at Los Angeles: Bruin Online.* http://www.bol.ucla.edu/~ya4f/carnegie.html (accessed on February 18, 2003).

"John D. Rockefeller, 1839–1937." *The Rockefeller University: The Rockefeller Archive Center.* http://www.rockefeller.edu/archive.ctr/jdrsrbio.html (accessed on February 18, 2003).

Taylor, Frederick. "The Principles of Scientific Management." *Internet Modern History Sourcebook.* http://www.fordham.edu/halsall/mod/1911taylor.html (accessed on February 21, 2003).

Social and Political Impact of the Second Phase of the Industrial Revolution

7

By the year 1900, the impact of the Industrial Revolution was felt across the United States. Practically every aspect of everyday life had altered dramatically over the past century. Enormous fortunes had been made by the owners of factories, natural resources (notably oil), and business networks such as railroads. People who once were scattered among scores of small farms in the countryside were now living in cities, working for employers who in many respects viewed their employees as living parts of a complex machine called the factory. Those who still lived in rural areas used new machinery and chemicals to raise crops or livestock that would be transported to faraway markets. In the United States, 40 percent of the population lived in cities, up from just 6 percent in 1800. In the next twenty years, the majority of Americans would be found residing in urban areas.

Such profound transformations hardly went unnoticed. The reality of the Industrial Revolution was reflected in changes in government and politics, as well as in new social organizations that were established independent of the government.

Words to Know

Anarchism: A social philosophy that advocates voluntary associations among people as a form of self-government, as opposed to central governments dominated by a monarch or other central figure.

Capitalism: A system of organizing a society's economy under which ownership in machines and factories is private, rather than public.

Communism: A form of government in which all the people own property, including both land and capital, in common.

Labor union: A voluntary association of workers who join together to apply pressure on their employer for improved pay, shorter hours, or other advantages.

Monopoly: A business large enough to be able to control the price of a product without regard to competition.

Pension: A monthly payment made to employees who retire from a company

after reaching a certain age or after working a certain number of years for that company.

Socialism: A political and economic system in which the people control both the government and also major elements of the economy, such as owning (or tightly regulating) factories.

Social work: Efforts to alleviate a variety of problems often encountered by poorer people, such as unemployment, poverty, and lack of housing.

Strike: The refusal to work by members of a labor union who aim to close down a factory or other facility as a means of putting pressure on the employer to grant higher pay or other improvements in work conditions.

Strikebreakers: Workers who take the places of employees who are on strike. They are hired by company owners in an effort to defeat strikers.

Tariff: A tax on imports.

Society in the industrial era

In 1914 automobile giant Henry Ford (1863– 1947) made headline news when he started paying workers $5.00 a day—roughly double what other manufacturers were paying at the time. The average non-Ford laborer earned less than $800 a year for a six-day workweek. (Ford paid his workers better in part so they could afford to buy the cars they were making, generating more sales—and profits—for Ford.) Calculated in 2003 dollars, in 1914 a Ford worker earned around

$28,000 a year while a typical worker earned around $14,000 a year.

The life of a typical worker at the turn of the twentieth century was difficult. Pay was low, hours were long, and working conditions were brutal and often wildly unsafe. The dangers of factories were dramatized at 4:30 P.M. on March 25, 1911, when a fire broke out inside the Triangle Shirtwaist Company located on the top three floors of the Asch Building in New York City. There, five hundred employees, mostly Jewish immigrant women aged thirteen to twenty-three, sewed women's shirts. Fueled by all the fabric, the fire spread rapidly to all three floors of the factory. Within fifteen minutes, 146 women had died. Many jumped to their deaths; others tried to slide down elevator cables, but lost their grip; many were burned to death. Firemen tried to rescue the women, but their ladders reached only to the sixth floor, one floor below the factory, and women jumping from the windows tore through fire nets as they plummeted, holding hands in groups of three or four.

Workers at the Ford plant in Highland Park, Michigan, assemble parts in 1914, the year Henry Ford began paying his workers $5.00 per day, more than twice their previous pay.
Reproduced by permission of the Library of Congress.

The combination of low pay for long hours (ten hours a day, six days a week was typical) and unsafe working conditions was characteristic of the second phase of the Industrial Revolution. In addition, workers who lost a job suddenly found themselves without any income. Paid vacations and health insurance were unknown. When a person grew old and wanted to retire, it was necessary to have personal savings to live on; companies did not pay pensions to retired employees. Nor was work steady. If employers lacked orders for products, workers were told not to come in. No work, no pay. A worker who fell ill was not paid for that day and might lose his or her job to someone who could work. Many workers went for weeks every year without work, or pay, because his or her employer had shut down during a slow period. Even for higher-paid middle-class occupations, such as

accountants, for whom daily life was more comfortable, economic disaster was often as close as one missed paycheck.

Housing conditions in the cities were often as dismal as those of the factories. Multiple families crammed into two- and three-room apartments, often without natural light or ventilation. Indoor plumbing was rare except in the homes of the middle class (such as those of doctors). People seldom bathed or washed their hair (once a month would have been common for working-class women in 1900). Sometimes, as in the case of cigar makers in New York City, tiny apartments were also the workplace, where the father and mother devoted one room to rolling tobacco leaves into cigars, used the other room for living and sleeping, and had a small kitchen off to the side.

Most working families needed the pay of both father and mother—and sometimes the children as well—to avoid starvation or being thrown into the street when the rent went unpaid. Work often began at a young age: thirteen, ten, or even six. The census of 1900 showed that almost 20 percent of children aged ten to fifteen who lived in urban areas worked full time.

In many respects, people living on farms were not much better off. Their incomes also were low, and they lacked modern things that provided comfort and enjoyment. On the other hand, farm houses were not crowded together, and farmers were able to grow their own food. But many farmers were subject to losing their farms to the banks that had loaned them money to live on until their crops came in. If the crops failed because of drought or plant disease, farmers became refugees headed for the city to find work.

The workers respond

Almost from the beginning of the Industrial Revolution, the people most directly affected by industrialization had responded. One initial approach was taken by the Luddites in England, who tried to wreck the new textile machines they blamed for the loss of their traditional jobs (see Chapter 4).

But the most widespread, and eventually the most effective, approach to fight the leaders of industrialization was to form a labor union. Unions are organizations of workers who have banded together to bargain with an employer for higher wages, shorter hours, and other improvements in their working conditions. The reasoning behind a union is that an individual worker can easily be dismissed, but a large group of workers stands a chance of success by threatening not to work until their demands are met.

Business owners strongly resisted unions. They did not appreciate efforts to curb their power over the terms and conditions of work, or to raise the cost of hiring workers. Employers bitterly opposed unions at every opportunity. Workers who tried to form a union were often fired immediately and banned from the premises, sending a strong message to other workers that union activities would cost them their jobs. To most business owners, labor was a commodity to be bought and sold, just like raw materials, and workers who tried to gain bargaining leverage by joining a union were treated as a threat to the power and economic well-being of industrialists.

Workers also tried to improve their lives through politics. In Europe, members of the socialist movement had long campaigned governments to assume ownership and control of large companies, and they fought for worker control over government through democratic elections—or through violent revolution (see Chapter 4). Socialists, who sought political and economic equality for all people, were also active in the United States, but they were not as successful in elections as their counterparts in Europe.

In the campaign to defeat socialism in the United States, some opponents linked it to the "Old World" of Europe, where most socialist theorists had originated, thereby suggesting that socialism was unpatriotic. These opponents scoffed at a "foreign" idea of collective action by workers that contradicted the American ideal of rugged individualism. The cultural ideal of the United States as a fresh new beginning, a place where brave individuals came in order to strike out into the wilderness and create a living as a pioneer farmer, was deeply embedded in American culture in the late nineteenth century. These ideas were often promoted in newspapers and magazines of the era. In addition to the public opposition to unions and socialism, it was not so uncommon in the second half of the nineteenth century for business owners to try to influence government officials by offering bribes in the form of cash, lucrative stock in new ventures, or employment after an officeholder left the government.

Throughout the last half of the nineteenth century, the issue of industrial workers was intertwined with the issue of immigration. Tens of thousands of Europeans landed in the

United States eager to find jobs and a better life. They often were willing to work for low wages, any wages, in order to buy food for their families. Employers used the fresh supply of inexpensive labor to combat the influence of trade unions and to keep wages low. It seemed there were always more workers willing to take jobs than there were jobs to go around. And because many industrial jobs required few skills or language training, immigration supplied a steady stream of qualified workers willing to forgo labor union membership for a job. (On the other hand, some of those who were most effective in building the influence of labor unions, including Samuel Gompers, were immigrants.)

American labor unions

The history of American labor unions is almost as long, and as complex, as the history of the Industrial Revolution itself. It is a story that took place through negotiations, violence, and political elections. It is the story of an ongoing struggle between workers and business owners for a share of the wealth created as a result of industrialization. There would be no history of labor unions without industrialization, just as there would be no story of industrialization without workers.

From the very beginning—and continuing into the present day—those who invented the new machinery or invested money to build new factories saw their workers as a cost of doing business. And just as the business owners tried to buy the least expensive raw materials, so did they try to save money on the cost of hiring workers. At the same time, the workers who operated the new machinery wanted to earn as much money as possible from their jobs. Thus there has always been a conflict between owners and workers. (Throughout history owners have sometimes disputed this idea; workers seldom have.) Sometimes the conflict has been resolved peacefully, oftentimes it has not. Even Henry Ford, who voluntarily doubled his workers' pay in 1914, was the target of bitter clashes a few years later between his company and unions representing his workers.

Like the growth of companies and industries during the Industrial Revolution, the growth of unions was uneven and disorganized. Efforts to organize workers to bargain for higher wages, shorter hours, and better conditions usually focused on a single company, or industry, or region. Early attempts to combine several unions into national organizations met with mixed results. The expansion of unions, and their influence, often took place through well-publicized events such as strikes, riots, or disasters, which in turn attracted workers from other companies or industries to join union ranks. (In a strike, union members acting as a group refuse to work in order to force a company to meet the union's demands, such as higher pay or shorter hours.)

Early government responses to unionization

While workers were organizing trade unions, employers often turned to the government for help in defeating them. As early as 1806, the activities of a group of Philadelphia shoemakers were found guilty of violating common law by joining together to demand higher wages. (Common law is the body of old English customs that were legally enforceable, even without a specific law.) Workers were viewed as individuals who should agree to work for certain wages, or not work at all. English law, like governments in general, frowned on unofficial groups getting together to achieve their objectives. Such groups were labeled criminal conspiracies and punished. This opposition to organized labor characterized U.S. law as well.

Official attitudes began to shift slightly by 1842, when the Massachusetts state supreme court ruled that another group of shoemakers had not violated the law by refusing to work for any company that paid less than the shoemakers' agreed-upon minimum wage. A shoemaking company that went out of business as a result sued the workers and lost.

After the Civil War, the federal government sometimes took a more aggressive stand against unions as strikes became more frequent, a sign of the growing influence of unions. Many strikes in the period from 1865 to 1900 turned violent as strikers tried to physically stop nonunion people from entering a struck company, or as companies hired private guards to escort strikebreakers (workers hired to replace the striking employees) through picket lines. Both the federal government and state governments often responded by sending the police or army troops to restore order, which usually meant breaking up union picket lines and defeating the strike.

It was not until 1935 that federal laws were passed giving labor unions the right to strike and to maintain picket lines (but not to interfere physically with strikebreakers). These laws were passed as part of the program called the New Deal of President Franklin D. Roosevelt (1882–1945), who came to power during a period of high unemployment called the Great Depression.

The Knights of Labor and the Haymarket Square Riot (1886)

A number of notable incidents went into building the union movement in the United States. In 1869, Uriah Stephens and some fellow garment workers in Philadelphia had founded the Noble Order of the Knights of Labor. The union was open to anyone (with the exception of bankers, lawyers, professional gamblers, liquor dealers—or stockholders). In this respect it differed from existing unions of workers with specific skills, such as cigar making, carpenters, or plumbers. Within twenty years, the Knights of Labor had seven hundred thousand members. Its main goal was reducing the workday to eight hours from the usual ten.

On May 1, 1886, members of the union went on strike against the McCormick Harvester factory in Chicago, Illinois, in an effort to reduce the workday to eight hours. Two days later, fighting broke out at the factory and police who were on the scene monitoring the strike opened fire, killing four people. The next day, May 4, the Knights of Labor organized a demonstration at Haymarket Square in Chicago to protest the shootings. The rally started at 4:30 in the afternoon, and at around 10:00 that night police moved in to demand that the rally end. Suddenly a bomb exploded among the police, killing seven. In the consequent riot, about sixty more policemen were injured, most of them by bullets fired by other policemen.

The Chicago district attorney, strongly backed by a press campaign led by the publisher of the *Chicago Tribune* newspaper, seized on the incident as an opportunity to get rid of labor organizers, some of whom advocated anarchism

The Pullman Strike of 1894

One milestone in the history of American labor unions was the 1894 strike against the Pullman Palace Car Company of Pullman, Illinois. The company, owned by George Pullman (1831–1897), manufactured and operated luxurious railroad passenger cars. Pullman had built a town near Chicago, named after himself, which had a population of about 12,000. He rented modest homes to his workers and larger homes to factory managers, and he built a grand hotel where he lived when he was in town and where visitors stayed. He even built a church and rented the space to different denominations, which took turns for Sunday services. It was, in Pullman's view, a model town.

Pullman thought his town made good business sense. "Such advantages and surroundings made better workmen by removing from them the feeling of discontent and desire for change which so generally characterize the American workman; thus protecting the employer from loss of time and money consequent upon intemperance, labor strikes, and dissatisfaction," he said.

In 1893 an economic downturn (the term "recession" was used a century later to describe this phenomenon) had reduced the demand for Pullman's cars. Consequently, the company laid off (let go) some workers and reduced the pay of others by 25 percent. Rents for housing in his company town, however, did not come down; money was still taken from now-reduced paychecks. This squeeze made many workers desperate, and in 1894 Pullman's workers organized a local branch of the American Railway Union.

On May 9, 1894, a committee of the union met with Pullman and demanded that wages be restored. Pullman refused, but he agreed to look into other complaints about the behavior of foremen in his shops. The day after the meeting, three members of the union delegation who had met with Pullman were fired. In response, the union members at Pullman Palace Car Company went on strike.

The Pullman workers asked other railroad workers to refuse to work on trains that were pulling Pullman's cars, and in June, the American Railway Union, led by Eugene Debs (1855–1926), agreed. The result was a widespread shutdown of U.S. railroads, including those that delivered mail.

and socialism. (Anarchism and socialism were political philosophies that advocated democratic control over economic institutions, as well as political institutions. Anarchists believed in the elimination of government institutions

With the Pullman company refusing to bargain with the strikers on either the issue of reduced wages or the rent the company charged to its workers to live in company-owned houses near the Pullman factory, occasional fights erupted between frustrated workers and the armed guards hired by the railroads. Some trains were set on fire.

On July 2, two federal judges, Peter S. Grosscup and William A. Woods, issued an order barring leaders of the American Railway Union from encouraging members to interfere with railroad traffic. (Technically, the strike was against the Pullman Company; refusing to let trains operated by other companies run as a means of putting pressure on the Pullman Company was called a secondary strike, and was declared illegal.) The government cited a law against business monopolies in obtaining the order, arguing that the railway union was acting as a monopoly by using its power to strike against railroad operators that were not part of the Pullman company.

The next day, July 3, despite opposition from the governor of Illinois and the mayor of Chicago, President Grover Cleveland (1837–1908) sent twelve thousand troops (about half the U.S. Army) to Chica-

go to restore order. The mail started moving again, but the strike that had affected the entire nation's railroad traffic was defeated.

The union leader Debs was arrested for refusing to obey the judges' order to end the strike, and he was sentenced to six months in jail. There, he spent his time reading and as a result became a socialist. After his release from jail, Debs went on to become the most popular socialist leader in the country, eventually running for president in five elections between 1900 and 1920. He never won more than a small percentage of the popular vote.

After the strike, Pullman insisted that workers promise not to join any union as a condition of going back to work, and he refused to rehire local union leaders. Most of the strikers went back to work at their old wages. With its leader Debs in jail, the Amerian Railway Union soon disbanded, having failed to achieve the Pullman workers' demands.

The Pullman strike was a major setback in efforts to organize workers. George Pullman died two years later. He ordered that his grave be lined in concrete, fearing that resentful union members might try to vandalize it.

in favor of voluntary associations; socialists believed that government, controlled democratically, should own and operate major businesses. Business owners viewed both as threats to their property and prosperity.) Police arrested eight

Mary Harris Jones, known as Mother Jones, organized workers in many industries across the United States during her long fight for the rights of laborers.
Reproduced by permission of the Library of Congress.

well-known socialists and anarchists and charged them with murdering the policemen.

Despite a lack of proof connecting the accused men with the bomb, all eight were found guilty. Seven were sentenced to hang (the eighth was sentenced to fifteen years in prison). Four of them were hanged on November 11, 1887, one committed suicide in jail, and the remaining two were pardoned (freed) by the governor of Illinois, John Altgeld (1847–1902), six years later. The governor showed that the trial had been a travesty of justice, and that the judge had allowed citizens with strong prejudices against unions to serve on the jury, while the prosecution never offered any proof that the accused had anything to do with the bomb.

The Haymarket Square incident marked the end of the Knights of Labor. It also was a setback for the campaign for the eight-hour workday.

Mother Jones and the coal miners

The history of unions in coal mines was often marked by violence, both in eastern mines (largely in Pennsylvania) and in the West, especially in Colorado. The list of strikes that resulted in violence from both the miners and the mine owners is a long one. In 1877 ten union activists were hanged in Pennsylvania; in 1892 eighteen miners and private guards died during the Homestead Strike near Homestead, Pennsylvania. Also that year, striking miners dynamited the Frisco Mill in Coeur d'Alene, Idaho. The year 1893 saw the first of several violent strikes in Cripple Creek, Colorado. In 1897 nineteen striking coal miners were killed and thirty-six were wounded by a posse (an armed band) hired by the mine owner near Lattimer, Pennsylvania. In 1898 fourteen were killed and twenty-five wounded in violence at a

coal mine strike near Virden, Illinois. In 1899 and again in 1901 U.S. troops occupied the region around Coeur d'Alene. In 1902 fourteen miners were killed and twenty-two were wounded at Pana, Illinois. The following year troops quelled rioting by striking miners at Cripple Creek. In 1904 six miners were killed during a battle between striking miners and militiamen (the National Guard) at Dunnville, Colorado. In 1914 company guards and Colorado militiamen fired into a union tent at Ludlow, Colorado, killing nineteen, including twelve children.

Into this atmosphere marched Mary Harris Jones (1830–1930), one of the most colorful characters in the history of labor unions. Once called "the grandmother of all agitators," Jones the former schoolteacher and seamstress traveled the United States organizing coal miners, textile workers, and railroad workers into unions and campaigning on behalf of child workers. Her prim, petite figure and snow-white hair, which she kept under a bonnet, prompted the nickname

Young coal mine workers gather. Coal miners that attempted to unionize were often met with violence, culminating in the 1914 incident at Ludlow, Colorado. *Reproduced by permission of the Library of Congress.*

Mother Jones. Her modest appearance masked an unstoppable passion to achieve what she saw as social justice.

Mother Jones was a native of Ireland and the widow of George Jones, himself a union organizer in Memphis, Tennessee, who had died alongside their children in a yellow fever epidemic in 1867. Jones moved from Memphis to Chicago and devoted the rest of her long life to organizing workers to achieve higher pay and shorter hours. Although she battled for the rights of all workers, her special concern was coal miners, and in 1890 she became a paid organizer for the United Mineworkers Union.

One of Jones's most famous campaigns took place in 1903, when at age seventy-three she led a long march of textile workers, half of them children, from Kensington, Pennsylvania, near Philadelphia, to President Theodore Roosevelt's house in Oyster Bay, New York, on Long Island. The march served to attract national attention to the plight of women and children working in factories.

Samuel Gompers and the American Federation of Labor

Samuel Gompers (1850–1924) came to New York from a London slum, the son of a cigar maker. Forced to drop out of school at age ten in order to earn money for his family, he is known today as the founder of the Federation of Labor and the union leader who focused attention on purely union issues, like pay, benefits, and shorter hours, without concentrating on basic political changes, as the socialists favored.

In New York Gompers and his family lived in another slum where families were jammed into two- or three-room apartments. As a cigar maker, Gompers often took the role of a "reader"; other cigar makers would set aside some of their own production for him in exchange for having Gompers read books out loud to them, in order to relieve the boredom of their work. In this way, Gompers educated himself on the job.

In 1864 Gompers joined the cigar makers' union, and ten years later he became the president of its local chapter (branch). Gompers set about making the union a more important force in workers' lives. He insisted that union

members pay more to belong, so that the union had funds to operate, recruit new members, and pay union officials who worked full time on union affairs. He also set aside funds that were used to help cigar makers who were injured, fell ill, or lost work. The union, for Gompers, did more than demand higher pay for workers; it also became a kind of social welfare organization, a role that was largely taken over by the government sixty years later.

By 1881 Gompers was active in establishing a union of unions, the Federation of Organized Trades and Labor Unions of the United States and Canada. This organization was an alliance of unions that represented skilled workers, such as cigar makers, carpenters, and plumbers, regardless of their employer. In this way, Gompers's organization resembled medieval guilds (associations of skilled craftsmen that set rules and standards for their work). In 1886 this organization became the American Federation of Labor (AFL). Gompers served as its president, a post he held for the rest of his

Samuel Gompers (center) shown with other leaders of the American Federation of Labor in 1918.
Reproduced by permission of the Library of Congress.

life, with the exception of one year. That year was 1895, during a national economic slowdown that made progress by unions exceptionally difficult. The labor federation defeated Gompers's bid for reelection to a one-year term as union president and instead chose John McBride, who favored a more political, socialist-oriented approach. The following year, Gompers stood for reelection and defeated McBride.

Although Gompers started out believing that unions should limit their activities to strictly economic goals, he later shifted his position and encouraged the AFL to stand behind politicians who promised to support laws favorable to workers. The union first played an active role in politics in the election of 1908, when the AFL supported William Jennings Bryan (1860–1925), a democrat who favored such union goals as an eight-hour maximum work day. Despite union support, Bryan lost to the Republican candidate, William Howard Taft (1857–1930).

John L. Lewis and the Congress of Industrial Organizations

The counterpart of Samuel Gompers's notion of organizing skilled workers around their particular skills (cigar makers, bricklayers, carpenters, and so forth) was the Congress of Industrial Organizations (CIO), which aimed to organize all workers based on the industry they worked for (such as miners, railroad workers, steelworkers) regardless of their individual skills. In some respects, the CIO was a reflection of the second phase of the Industrial Revolution, since it focused on workers in so-called mass-production industries like coal, steel, automobiles, rubber, glass, and textiles.

The founding father of the CIO was John L. Lewis (1880–1969), president of the United Mine Workers Union. Mine workers—primarily coal miners—had a long history of union organization that included many incidents of violence. Miners were a special case among workers, since many lived in towns owned by mine operators and faced constant dangers inside the mines. When they went out on strike, miners were often ready to use their fists to stop strikebreakers, workers hired by mine owners to replace striking employees. Because coal was vital both to industrial operations

(notably railroads and steel mills) and for domestic purposes
(for heating homes), government intervention in coal workers' strikes was not unusual.

The United Mine Workers Union had been formed in
1890 through the merger of two other mine workers' unions.
The United Mine Workers Union already had a long history
of success—it achieved an eight-hour workday through a
strike in 1898—when Lewis became its president in 1920.

Lewis would hold that position for the next forty years. Among his greatest successes was convincing mine owners to pay for a union-operated health and welfare fund called the United Mine Workers' Health and Retirement Fund, which paid for miners' medical bills and provided a $100 monthly pension for miners who stopped working after age sixty-two. The fund paid for hospitals in coal mining regions and established health clinics, staffed by doctors hired by the union and paid for by employer contributions.

In 1935 the United Mine Workers Union led in the formation of the CIO, a federation of other unions organized by industry: the International Typographical Union; Amalgamated Clothing Workers; International Ladies' Garment Workers; United Textile Workers; Oil Field, Gas Well, and Refinery Workers; United Hatters, Cap, and Millinery Workers; and International Mine, Mill, and Smelter Workers. The new CIO in turn became affiliated with the American Federation of Labor, but it was not a happy alliance. The CIO was expelled from the AFL in 1937, and five years later, in 1942, the United Mine Workers Union withdrew from the CIO. In 1942 the federal government seized coal mines to end a strike that was viewed as crippling the U.S. economy at a time when the nation was fighting World War II.

The CIO and its member unions represented labor's most serious challenge to the power of industrialists since the first fabric factory was set up in Rhode Island. First, the CIO represented huge numbers of workers and initiated an aggressive drive to sign up more. Second, member unions could shut down key industries (steel, automobile, and coal, for example), and in turn have a huge impact on the rest of the U.S. economy. Third, the CIO was active politically. From the mid-1930s it focused its efforts on influencing the Democratic Party to adopt positions that favored its members (as opposed to the owners of factories, whom the Republicans favored). After World War II, when the Republican Party achieved a majority in Congress, Ohio senator Robert Taft (a Republican and son of the former president) tried to counter union influence by passing the Taft-Hartley Act of 1947, which amended the 1935 National Labor Relations Act and imposed new limits on union rights. (The National Labor Relations Act of 1935 gave workers the right to organize and

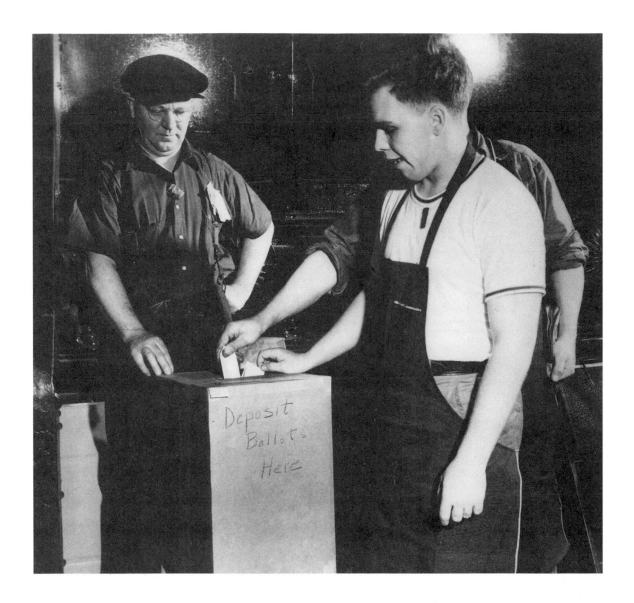

belong to unions; the Taft-Hartley Act put limits on how unions could go about achieving their goals.)

Part of the new influence of unions resulted from a relative new weapon in their armory that formerly was exclusive to business owners: money. When John L. Lewis had formed the United Mine Workers' Health and Retirement Fund in 1946, it was created by an agreement with the federal government, which had temporarily seized control of some coal mines that had been shut down by a United Mine

A worker at an auto plant casts his ballot during an election for plant representation on the National Labor Relations Board. *Reproduced by permission of the Library of Congress.*

Workers strike. Fearing a national emergency without continuing supplies of coal, President Harry Truman (1884–1972) took over operation of the mines on May 22, 1946, and threatened to draft striking miners into the army. The strike was soon settled, and establishment of the Health and Retirement Fund was part of the settlement. (After the settlement, the government returned control of the mines to their owners.) Taking advantage of the emergency, Lewis successfully bargained for payments by employers to contribute money to a union fund that would in turn pay union members a pension (pay that continues after retirement) after age 62. Having the union control the fund meant that workers would still receive a pension, even if the company for which they worked had gone out of business.

The union pension funds came to be enormous pools of money that fund managers invested, sometimes in the very companies that were paying into the fund. In this way, the unions came to own large parts of important businesses. In effect, the workers who were once pitted against the wealthy had become part-owners of their own companies. The funds also gave workers a stake in the economic well-being of these businesses, a factor that separated some unions from the political theories of socialism that called for the government to take over and run companies.

Approaches besides unions

Labor unions were not the only response by workers wishing to alleviate the misery of their living conditions. Two other approaches involved forming voluntary associations (sometimes along ethnic lines) called fraternal orders and engaging in efforts known as social work that helped those in need.

Voluntary associations have a history dating back to sixteenth-century England. They were organized by working people as social organizations, and also to provide economic benefits to members' families in case of sickness or premature death.

Among the organizations with English origins that took root in the United States were the Independent Order of Odd Fellows (brought to the United States in 1819), the Ancient Order of Foresters (American branch founded in Philadelphia in 1838), and the Freemasons, a large secret society with uncertain origins. Purely American counterparts were established in the 1830s, including the Improved Order of Red Men (formed in 1833), Ancient Order of Hibernians in America (1836), the Knights of Pythias (1864), the Benevolent and Protective Order of Elks (1868), Knights of Columbus (1882), and the Fraternal Order of Eagles (1898). Many of these organizations are still active.

The original purpose of voluntary groups was not strictly related to labor issues or the Industrial Revolution (although the Knights of Labor, 1869, took its name and organization from other fraternal groups and for a time viewed itself as a secret society open to laborers). The fraternal orders did, however, offer life insurance and medical insurance to members, filling a gap created by the surging population and lack of government alternatives.

Jane Addams, along with her friend Ellen Starr, established Hull House in Chicago. *Reproduced by permission of the Library of Congress.*

Hull House was among the first examples of what we today call social work, efforts to help the social conditions of people without necessarily addressing the root causes, such as pay or unemployment. The founder of Hull House was Jane Addams (1860–1935), who came from a well-to-do family in Cedarville, Iowa. On a trip to London, England, she visited Toynbee House, a settlement house in a London slum that provided some essential services and counseling to poor workers. She returned to the United States determined to set up a similar house in the slums of Chicago.

In 1889 Addams and a friend, Ellen Starr, rented part of an old mansion in Chicago and called it Hull House. Their purpose, they declared, as quoted in *Twenty Years at Hull-House,* was "to provide a center for higher civic and social life, to institute and maintain educational and philanthropic [charity] enterprises, and to investigate and improve the conditions in the industrial districts of Chicago." At Hull House a worker could get a hot lunch, leave a child in day care, learn English, and receive medical care and legal advice. Later Addams added kindergarten classes, evening classes for adults, an employment bureau, even an art gallery, a gymnasium, a book bindery, and a music school.

Hull House pioneered many social services provided today by government agencies as well as by churches and volunteers. Jane Addams herself made the connection between the specific services provided by Hull House and the larger issue of human welfare in the new factory system created by the Industrial Revolution. Addams campaigned vigorously for laws governing child labor, mandatory schooling for children, factory safety inspections, and labor unions. She also became a leading campaigner for the right of women to vote, which was finally achieved in 1920.

The impact of industrialization on government

When the transplanted Englishman Samuel Slater (1768–1835) established a textile mill in Rhode Island in 1797, he did more than open a fabric-making business: he set the stage for a long argument over the proper role of government in economic affairs. Even though Scottish economist Adam Smith (1723–1790) had argued in 1776 in *The Wealth of Nations* that governments should refrain from meddling in economic matters, the reality is that people have come to expect the government to do something to improve the economy. (For more on Slater see Chapter 5; for more on Smith see Chapter 1.)

The responses of the federal government to the Industrial Revolution can be divided into four broad categories:

- Encouraging the growth of industry by taxing imported manufactured goods (1820–1860).

- Aiding industrial growth and discouraging organized labor (1865–1900).

- Asserting controls over private business through regulation (1900–1911).

- Actively alleviating suffering resulting from economic depression (1932 to present).

These government activities are not mutually exclusive. Government has tried to stimulate economic growth almost since the beginning of the United States, with some presidential administrations being more active than others. For much of the nation's history, agriculture was more important, and engaged more people, than industrialization. Sometimes, agriculture and industry have been in conflict, and industry did not always carry the day. Attitudes toward organized labor have been hostile or friendly, largely depending on the political party in power. Government programs such as pensions (social security) and unemployment insurance were started during the presidency of Democrat President Franklin Delano Roosevelt (in office from 1933 to 1945); they have continued, and even expanded, in the decades since, during both Democratic and Republican administrations. The job of government has come to be seen as helping people as well as helping businesses expand.

In *The Wealth of Nations,* Adam Smith argued that governments should not interfere in economic matters. *Reproduced by permission of the Library of Congress.*

The period of U.S. history since 1952 (a year marked by the election of Republican Dwight D. Eisenhower as president) might be best described as post-industrial, a period when the rapid changes brought about by the Industrial Revolution slowed. During this period, industrial production was gradually moving to Asia, to be replaced in the United States by new industries such as computer technologies and entertainment, as well as by service industries such as health care and finance (see Chapter 8).

The United States and the great tariff debate

The role of government changed significantly over the course of the Industrial Revolution, or, more exactly, notions of what the government should do about the economy changed. In the 1750s, as the Industrial Revolution was just underway in England, the makeup of the English Parliament (governing body) reflected the main economic influence of the time: major landowners, the aristocracy, inherited seats in the House of Lords and shared power with the king. Even the House of Commons, despite its name, did not represent the common man but reflected the power of wealth: people in England were not allowed to vote in parliamentary elections unless they could show they had a certain amount of wealth, an amount that enabled knights and middle-class merchants to vote, but not farm workers or factory workers (see Chapter 4).

The chief concerns of the British government in the 1700s were protecting the country from foreign attack and protecting private property from possible attempts by the poor to seize wealth via a revolution, or even via a democratic vote. Alleviating suffering among the poor was a lesser issue, carried out in England under the so-called Poor Laws that distributed government money to the very poor and sick through local churches (remembering that the Church of England was, and is, the official church of England and is supported by the government).

In the United States, as more and more industrial enterprises opened (especially in New England) to manufacture goods (especially cloth), the government confronted the issue of whether, and how, to help these struggling companies succeed against larger, more established competitors in Britain. The problem was that English factories could produce cloth and ship it to the United States less expensively than native factories could make it. What was the government to do, if anything?

The most popular answer (popular among the New England factory owners, anyway) was to wipe out England's advantage by taxing goods imported into the United States. Such taxes, which had the effect of raising the price of imported materials (such as cotton fabric), are called tariffs, and they continue to be applied in the twenty-first century. (In 2002, for example, the U.S. government imposed a 30 percent tariff on some types of imported steel to help U.S. manufacturers compete against foreign companies).

The issue of tariffs contributed to the conflict between North and South that eventually helped lead to civil war in 1861. In the 1820s, newly built textile factories could not compete with imported English cloth, which was cheaper despite the cost of transportation. In northern states, where the textile factories were located, this was a problem—Americans were tempted to go for the lower price of imported English cloth.

But getting cheaper cloth was not a problem for people in the South. Southern cotton plantations supplied the raw material, cotton, for factories in Britain as well as in New England, and Southerners saw no reason to pay more for fabric (as a result of tariffs) in order to benefit businesses in New England.

In 1816 the U.S. Congress passed a tariff act that imposed a 25 percent tax on imports. Part of the aim was to pay the government's bills, but another goal was to help industries in the United States compete with foreign competitors. In 1825 Representative Henry Clay (1777–1852) of Kentucky, who strongly believed that the government should help encourage economic growth, helped pass a law that set tariffs on imported iron, wool, cotton, and hemp (hemp is a tough fiber used to make rope and certain types of fabric) even higher (at 35 percent). In 1828, the tariff on manufactured goods was raised again, to 50 percent.

Tariffs on imported manufactured goods were unpopular with many people in the South, who resented paying higher prices for manufactured goods without gaining any of the economic benefits that flowed to manufacturers in the North. John C. Calhoun (1782–1850), vice president under Andrew Jackson (1767–1845), wrote an essay in 1828 titled "South Carolina Exposition and Protest," in which he argued that the tariff of 1828 violated the U.S. Constitution, and that therefore a state had the right to nullify it (declare it invalid), or else secede from the United States (pull out of or break away from the country). Calhoun's constitutional argument was that the tariff unfairly benefited some states at the expense of others, which he viewed as unconstitutional. Because the Northern states were already growing in population faster than the Southern states, which entitled them to send more members to the House of Representatives, Calhoun foresaw a day when some states could, in effect, gang up on the others. Calhoun's protest raised the idea of secession (a state withdrawing from the United States) for the first time. The debate over tariffs continued right up to the early 1860s and was one of the issues that led to the American Civil War (1861–65).

Government economic intervention

After the Civil War, the Republican Party largely dominated the federal government. (In the seventy-two years from 1861 to 1933, a Republican was president for fifty-six years, a Democrat for sixteen years. Only two Democrats, Grover Cleveland and Woodrow Wilson, were elected in that period, each of whom served two terms.) For the most part, the Republican Party, which was formed in 1854, adopted policies favorable to the emerging industrial corporations of the era. On the one hand, the Republicans believed in letting business alone to pursue their interests as they saw fit, without government interference. On the other hand, the Republicans resisted efforts supported by workers to pass laws that would limit the length of the work day or provide protection for women and children employed in factories.

Tariffs and other taxes

As in the 1820s, after the Civil War, tariffs were increasingly placed on specific goods to benefit specific industries and sometimes to appease voters in a particular state or congressional district. From 1865 to 1900 federal tariffs averaged 47 percent of the price of imports. By raising the price for manufactured goods particularly, tariffs aided new manufacturing companies. As these companies became more profitable, they found it easier to attract new investments. Tariff collections also had the advantage of raising money to pay off loans taken out to finance the Civil War, to provide pensions for Union war veterans, to pay for the war against Native Americans as the country expanded westward, and to bankroll public improvements such as highways (themselves an indirect way of supporting industry).

In the twentieth century, the federal government turned to other taxes (or reductions in taxes) to influence the behavior of consumers and businesses alike. Taxes were cut to make more money available to be spent (by both businesses and consumers), or to encourage businesses to invest in new factories as a means of stimulating economic growth. Whether politicians favored tax breaks for individuals or for businesses, there was little argument that the government should play an active role in helping to manage the overall economy.

Trust Busters

Prior to 1890 it was perfectly legal for corporations to band together and behave in ways that promoted their own interests, such as agreeing not to lower prices on goods they all manufactured. Other businesses tried to achieve monopolies by buying up the competition or driving smaller competitors out of business. The unprecedented size and influence of the companies that had monopolies on markets raised concerns that such companies (called trusts in that era) could seriously harm consumers by raising prices higher and higher since they had no competition (see Chapter 6).

To contain the power of these industrial leaders, the U.S. Congress passed the Sherman Antitrust Act in 1890 and the Clayton Act and the Federal Trade Commission Act in 1914. The Sherman Antitrust Act made it illegal for companies to conspire with one another to set (fix) prices on goods sold across state lines. Other activities that became illegal were group boycotts, in which two companies refused to do business with a third company as a means of driving that third company out of business, and horizontal market division, in which companies agreed to stay out of each other's geographical areas.

Despite passage of the Sherman Antitrust Act, little was done to enforce it until the administration of President Theodore Roosevelt (1901–09). Roosevelt became known as a "trust buster" for the legal challenges he mounted against monopolies. In the 1904 case *Northern Securities Co.* v. *United States*, the government had claimed that Northern Securities Company had violated the Sherman Antitrust Act by bringing under common ownership two railroad companies, the Northern Pacific Railroad and the Great Northern Railroad, that ran roughly parallel tracks east and west across the northern tier of states. The government wanted the company

President Theodore Roosevelt vigorously challenged the hold that monopolies had in the business world during his administration. *Reproduced by permission of the Library of Congress.*

broken up in order to restore competition between the two constituent companies, and thereby to avoid higher prices for both passengers and companies shipping freight by rail. The Supreme Court agreed with the government's argument and ordered that Northern Securities be dissolved and that the two railroads once again be operated as separate companies.

The Roosevelt administration's most famous case was *Standard Oil Co. v. United States*. In 1906 the government filed a suit in federal court, charging that the Standard Oil Trust, a group of thirty-four oil companies owned or controlled by the financier John D. Rockefeller (1839–1937), violated the Sherman Antitrust Act by limiting competition.

Starting in 1868, with the Standard Oil Company incorporated in Ohio, Rockefeller had steadily bought a series of oil refineries and other companies associated with the petroleum business. At first, the main product was kerosene, used in lamps. With the development of the automobile, another product derived from oil, gasoline, became highly profitable.

Rockefeller often used the word Standard in company names. In his company, Rockefeller assigned certain geographical areas to each company; other companies owned by Rockefeller were not allowed to compete in those areas.

In 1882, Rockefeller had formed the Standard Oil Company of New Jersey in order to take advantage of a New Jersey law that let corporations own other companies. Over the next two decades, Rockefeller came to control enough of the U.S. oil industry that he could largely dictate prices, even if it meant using profits from one area of the country to drive competitors out of business in another.

In 1911, the Supreme Court issued its ruling in the case, agreeing with the government and ordering that Standard Oil be broken up into independent companies. The ruling also included guidelines about how companies could use the name Standard in their new operations. The result of the breakup of Standard Oil was the formation of oil companies that were in operation ninety years later, with such names as Sohio (Standard of Ohio) and Standard Oil Co. New York (Mobil). Eventually, starting in the 1930s, some of these separate companies merged, but the enormous combination created by John D. Rockefeller was never reassembled.

The government's role in assisting workers

Should the government take a leading role in helping people suffering from unemployment, poverty, or homelessness? In the newly organized United States of 1776, the role of government was seen as being minimal: protect the new nation from foreign attack and look after issues that might arise as a result of commerce that crossed state or international boundaries. No provision was made in the Constitution for aiding large numbers of people in cities who were without jobs, money, food, or homes. The Founding Fathers had never seen such problems, which arose as unwelcome results of the Industrial Revolution.

The social problems arising from industrialization began to be seen in the nineteenth century. Often, the affected workers were immigrants who had flooded into big cities; thus it was often easier to blame poverty and unemployment on immigration rather than on shortcomings of industrialization. If the urban poor posed any problem, it was more often seen as one of crime or potential rioting, which was an issue for the police. Charity was assigned to churches or to voluntary social workers, like Jane Addams.

In October 1929 an event took place that eventually challenged whether the system of private ownership of business could survive. On October 29, prices on the New York Stock exchange plunged. The causes of the stock market crash, as it was known, were complex. Stock prices had risen sharply in the preceding six months, and many investors had borrowed money from banks to buy stocks, expecting to sell them at higher prices, repay the loans, and make a tidy profit.

But in early October, prices stopped rising. Many investors decided that stocks were over-priced. As investors

realized that prices had reached a peak, they started selling shares to take advantage of prices that were still high. The basic law of supply and demand set in: there were more stocks for sale than investors to buy them, and as a result prices started falling. On October 29, the drop in prices was severe.

Investors, including many ordinary people, owed banks for the money they had borrowed to buy the stocks. But the money had disappeared. Even after selling their stocks, investors did not have enough to repay the loans. In just two weeks, from October 29 to November 13 (when prices finally stopped falling), more than thirty billion dollars in value simply disappeared.

The fact that so many loans had gone bad posed a problem for banks. The source of the loans was depositors' money, which was now gone. As depositors went to withdraw money from banks, some institutions did not have the cash and closed their doors.

Within a few years, economic activity had dropped sharply. Eager to protect their savings, most people were reluctant to buy things, and companies laid off workers by the thousands. The sight of so many unemployed caused a further contraction of sales, which led to more layoffs. Companies, foreseeing much reduced demand, laid off workers.

By 1932, at least 25 percent of workers did not have a job, and many others could only find part-time work. People endured the humiliation of standing in long lines to get a handout of bread just to keep their families from starving. The traditional advice to the unemployed—"Get a job!—" was a mockery: there were no jobs to get.

To make things even worse, a severe drought that lasted for most of the 1930s hit states in the West and Southwest. Many farmers saw their crops dry up and die for lack of rain. Enormous clouds of dust that looked like tornadoes swept through Oklahoma, forcing families off their farms

Men seeking financial assistance wait outside a federal relief office during the Great Depression.
Reproduced by permission of the Library of Congress.

The Phenomenon of the Crash

Although the Industrial Revolution overall resulted in economic growth, it also had an unwelcome side effect: the economic slowdown. Economic growth means that factories are producing more and more. People who invest in such enterprises see the value of their investments rise steadily. But any hint of an end to this growth often causes investors to try to sell their shares in companies (for fear the company might eventually go out of business). When this selling becomes widespread, the result is an economic slowdown.

There are many words used to describe this cycle: panic, crash, depression, and recession. All these words represent the same basic thing: a widespread and relatively sudden decrease in economic activity. Driven partly by fear of what might happen in the future, consumers order fewer goods, manufacturers produce less and hire fewer workers. Workers who do not have jobs purchase less (and may cause their neighbors to buy less, for fear of what might happen to them), which causes other manufacturers to order fewer goods. The cycle of fear feeds on itself, sometimes for several years.

In the United States, notable periods of economic slowdown have occurred in 1819, 1837, 1857, 1873, 1893, 1914, 1929, 1957, 1982, 1991, and 2001, with other less severe downturns in between.

Experts disagree on what causes an economic slowdown, and on how to stop the cycle and resume growth. They even disagree on precisely when recessions begin and end.

As the second phase of the Industrial Revolution resulted in enormous and into a desperate migration to California, where they were stopped from entering at the state border. The American economic system had broken down almost completely.

In the 1932 presidential election, the Democratic candidate, Franklin Delano Roosevelt (1882–1945), won 88.9 percent of the vote. It was one of the most lopsided elections in U.S. history. Roosevelt had promised the American people a New Deal. The next eight years saw a whirlwind of federal agencies and programs designed to alleviate the suffering of ordinary workers. One of the most familiar was a pension program for retired people called Social Security. The Tennessee Valley Authority built electricity-generating plants powered by growth in individual businesses, economic downturns also became larger, partly because they affected more people who worked in factories.

The downturn that started in 1929 was the worst that had taken place in U.S. history. It created a national emergency, with tens of thousands of people without work or food. Some observers feared that workers would start a revolution, similar to the 1917 communist revolution that had taken place in Russia just twelve years earlier.

President Herbert Hoover (1874–1964), in office only a few months when the stock market crashed, focused on small-scale local efforts to encourage private initiatives to address the needs of workers who could not find work, as well as encouraging so-called character building, suggesting that unemployment was the fault of the workers rather than a national calamity far beyond the control of those out of work.

In 1932, Congress considered a bill to immediately provide a bonus payment to World War I veterans. In May 1932, about 10,000 veterans gathered in Washington to demonstrate their support for the bill. The House of Representatives passed the measure, but the Senate did not. Shortly afterwards, General Douglas MacArthur drove the "bonus marchers" out of the capital, where they were camped on the site of a former recruiting station. MacArthur used tanks and soldiers with bayonets, justifying his controversial tactics on the grounds that he thought the United States was on the verge of a communist revolution.

water falling over dams, and as a result brought electricity to many farms for the first time. The Civilian Conservation Corps provided jobs in federal parks to unemployed urban workers.

Of particular interest to labor unions was the National Labor Relations Act, passed in 1935. The act gave workers the right to organize unions and to go on strike (refuse to work) in order to persuade employers to grant their demands for higher wages or better working conditions. It also established the National Labor Relations Board, giving the federal government a role in helping companies and unions avoid strikes by providing professional mediators. The National Labor Relations Act redressed what had been an imbalance in the U.S. economy.

During World War II many Americans worked in plants and factories in northern cities to help build up American defense forces, as this poster from the era depicts. *Reproduced by permission of the Library of Congress.*

While business owners were covered by laws protecting private property, workers had not previously been given parallel protection in pursuing their interests in the form of unions.

Some New Deal programs worked, some did not. Some people accused Roosevelt of promoting socialism through government control of the economy, others credited him with saving the economy from socialism by alleviating suffering without attacking private ownership of business.

One thing was certain: the role of the government had changed drastically in response to dire emergency.

After Roosevelt's death in 1945, Republicans continued to resist some New Deal programs, or to modify them. In 1947, for example, the Republican-controlled Congress passed the Taft-Hartley Act over President Truman's veto. The act limited the ability of unions to require workers to join the union and pay dues, and the law banned secondary strikes (strikes against companies that were customers or suppliers of the firm that was the initial target of a strike). The Taft-Hartley Act also gave the U.S. Attorney General the power to obtain a court order postponing a strike for eighty days if it threatened the national health or safety. The Act also barred unions from contributing money to political campaigns.

Roosevelt's programs would do little to end the Great Depression. The United States only recovered after World War II broke out in Europe in 1939, when Germany declared war on Poland and eventually drew most of Europe into the fray. With the hostilities came a need for weapons, and lots of them. In 1940 Roosevelt volunteered to produce military supplies and lend them to Britain in its struggle against Germany. In 1941 the United States entered the war, after the Japanese navy attacked the American naval base at Pearl Harbor, Hawaii. The United States geared up in an unprecedented burst of industrial activity, producing ships, planes, tanks, rifles, ammunition, and every other conceivable tool of war. Unemployment was a thing of the past; the gears of industry were humming along.

The second world war in some ways marks the end of the period called the Industrial Revolution. Of course, the industrial economy did not disappear, and the complex process of industrialization continued to spread throughout the world (see Chapter 8). But the revolutionary aspect of the constant stream of new inventions that fundamentally changed people's lives was over in Western Europe, where it was born, and in the United States, where it thrived.

For More Information

Books

Addams, Jane. *Twenty Years at Hull-House*. First published in 1910. Urbana: University of Illinois Press, 1990.

Bloomfield, Maxwell H. *Peaceful Revolution: Constitutional Change and American Culture from Progressivism to the New Deal.* Cambridge, MA: Harvard University Press, 2000.

Dalton, Kathleen. *Theodore Roosevelt: A Strenuous Life.* New York: Knopf, 2002.

Dubofsky, Melvyn, and Warren Van Tine. *John L. Lewis: A Biography.* New York: Quadrangle/New York Times Book Co., 1977.

Gorn, Elliott J. *Mother Jones: The Most Dangerous Woman in America.* New York: Hill and Wang, 2001.

Kindleberger, Charles Poor. *Manias, Panics, and Crashes: A History of Financial Crises.* 4th ed. New York: Wiley, 2000.

Laughlin, Rosemary. *The Pullman Strike of 1894: American Labor Comes of Age.* Greensboro, NC: Morgan Reynolds, 2000.

Laurie, Bruce. *Artisans into Workers: Labor in Nineteenth-Century America.* New York: Hill and Wang, 1989.

Levy, Elizabeth, and Tad Richards. *Struggle and Lose, Struggle and Win: The United Mine Workers.* New York: Four Winds Press, 1977.

Lichtenstein, Nelson. *State of the Union: A Century of American Labor.* Princeton, NJ: Princeton University Press, 2002.

Livesay, Harold C. *Samuel Gompers and Organized Labor in America.* Boston: Little, Brown, 1978.

Stein, Leon. *The Triangle Fire.* Reprint: Ithaca, NY: Cornell University Press, 2001.

Terrill, Tom E. *The Tariff, Politics, and American Foreign Policy, 1874–1901.* Westport, CT: Greenwood Press, 1973.

Periodicals

Gorn, Elliott J. "Mother Jones: The Woman." *Mother Jones,* May 2001, p. 58.

Jefferson, Cowie. "From the Folks Who Brought You the Weekend: A Short, Illustrated History of Labor in the United States." *The American Prospect,* January 1, 2002, p. 41.

"John L. Lewis: A Coal Miner Who Made Unions as Tough as Himself." *Life,* Fall 1990, p. 62.

Web Sites

"African American Labor History Links." *American Federation of State, County and Municipal Employees.* http://www.afscme.org/about/aframlink.htm (accessed on February 20, 2003).

Bread and Roses: Poetry and History of the American Labor Movement. http://www.boondocksnet.com/labor/history/ (accessed on February 20, 2003).

Druley, Laurel. "Losing a Sense of Belonging." *Minnesota Public Radio.* http://news.mpr.org/features/200112/10_mainstreet_ourtown-m/rebekahs.shtml (accessed on February 20, 2003).

"Labor History: The Pullman Strike." *Solidarity.com: Wisconsin's Link to Labor.* http://www.solidarity.com/HisSpr.htm (accessed on February 20, 2003).

The Economy Goes Global: What Next?

8

Traditional revolutions not only have a start date, they have an end date as well. The American Revolution could be said to have ended with the defeat of the British army at Yorktown, Virginia, which left the thirteen former British colonies in North America free to form a new country, the United States. The French Revolution is said to have ended on November 11, 1799, when the French general Napoléon Bonaparte (Napoléon I; 1769–1821) seized control of the government, ending a decade-long experiment in democracy, a political system in which a majority of the people vote to determine the government and its policies. The Industrial Revolution is different. It represents major changes in the way people earn a living, where they live, and even in the way they view the world. The shift from a largely rural society to an urban, industrial one is still continuing, not only in the countries of Europe and North America where it started, but also throughout Asia, Africa, and South America.

The term Industrial Revolution has come to mean different things. It means the substitution of mechanical power, both engines and machines, for animal power (ani-

Words to Know

Automation: A process designed so that one event follows another without active intervention; usually such processes involve machines that carry out tasks by design, rather than with human intervention.

Communism: A form of government in which all the people own property, including both land and capital, in common.

Cottage industry: A system in which skilled craftspeople manufactured goods, such as cloth, from their homes rather than in factories. This scenario was typical of the period before the Industrial Revolution.

Labor union: A voluntary association of workers who join together to apply pressure on their employer for improved pay, shorter hours, or other advantages.

Microchips: A tiny complex of connected electronic components produced on a small slice of material. Microchips are the basic building block of computers.

Service economy: An economic system in which most people are engaged in helping or serving other people, rather than raising food or manufacturing products.

mals and humans). It means the shift from a rural agricultural society to an urban industrial society in which the most important economic activity is making things instead of raising animals or growing crops for food. The Industrial Revolution also represents the start of a new era of history in which people consciously seized control of their lives, using scientific methods to improve their conditions in every aspect.

The substitution of machines for animals and humans

Substituting machines for animal power is one of the easiest aspects of the Industrial Revolution to understand. Starting in the 1700s, textile-making machines and steam engines began to perform work traditionally done by humans and animals. Machines did not replace humans—they were still needed to operate the machines and perform other

One result of the Industrial Revolution was the rise of urban areas. At the beginning of the Industrial Revolution, most people lived in rural areas that supported agriculture, but today the vast majority of people live in urban settings. *Reproduced by permission of Getty Images.*

tasks—but the modern mill or factory was quite different from the traditional family-run business centered in a cottage, or home.

The shift from cottage industry to twenty-first-century industry raises issues about how people feel about their work and the quality of their lives. The introduction of machinery certainly relieved the worker of hard labor, even drudgery, but many say machines also resulted in workers feeling alienated (set apart) from their work and being reduced to acting as parts of a bigger machine. But in the eighteenth century a worker seldom ventured far from his native village, whereas a modern worker conducts his life in a larger area and can travel the globe if he wishes.

The development of engines that rely on oil or coal for energy raises concerns about how long the energy supplies will last and what effect these fuels are having on the environment. The United States has already experienced a noticeable decline in its oil reserves and must import oil from abroad to keep its industrial economy running. Many scientists insist that the Earth is getting warmer as a result of the exhaust from millions upon millions of engines—not just cars, but also coal-burning electric generators and many other industrial machines—and that this so-called global warming could have disastrous environmental consequences.

The environment

Concerns about the impact of the Industrial Revolution on the environment, especially on the atmosphere, are far from new. In Britain, King Edward I (1239–1307) banned the burning of coal in 1272 in response partly to complaints about soot, a by-product of coal that filled the air and darkened the exterior of buildings. The term smog (a combination of smoke and fog) was first used in 1905 in London, England, to describe the unhealthy atmosphere.

In the middle of the twentieth century, the less visible pollutants from automobile exhaust (by-products of burning gasoline) led to laws that forced car manufacturers to modify their designs in order to reduce emissions. The number of cars worldwide, however, has continued to grow.

For decades, the desire to expand industrialization has been at odds with the desire to protect the environment. The battles between the two sides have taken many forms, ranging from laws governing the disposal of dirt and other wastes from coal mining operations (which can block streams and pose a threat of landslides if not properly handled) in West Virginia to laws requiring improved fuel efficiency for cars across the United States.

In the last quarter of the twentieth century, scientists raised concerns that the overall temperature of the Earth might be rising, largely as a result of atmospheric pollution. Global warming raised the prospect that the massive glaciers in the Arctic and Antarctic might melt into the oceans, raising the level of the seas and threatening the many cities situated on coasts. Scientists have called for urgent measures to reduce pollution and to start finding ways to repair the damage already done. Some politicians, on the other hand, insist that global warming has not been proved and resist calls for measures to control pollution because creating machinery that is less harmful to the environmental will cost businesses a lot of money.

The debate over the future of industrialization and the environment continues to be a hot political issue in the first decade of the twenty-first century, even as less-developed countries rapidly expand their industries and, with them, the total amount of pollutants in the atmosphere.

Ironically, the Industrial Revolution was rooted in an earlier environmental issue: the dramatic reduction in the extensive forests of oak trees that once supplied not only lumber to build houses and ships, but also wood to burn for heat in the winter. With the disappearance of the oaks, coal was viewed as a solution to heating needs. The principal motivation for the development of the steam engine developed by Thomas Newcomen (1663–1729) was to pump water from the bottom of coal mines (see Chapter 2). Technology solved one problem, the shortage of firewood, and created another: air pollution due to extensive burning of coal.

For a time after World War II (1939–45), many people thought that nuclear power would substitute for coal and oil (an enormous amount of energy is created by splitting the nucleus of an atom). As people began to question what to do with dangerous waste from nuclear plants and realized that a potential accident could result in the deaths of millions of people, their optimism for nuclear energy somewhat diminished.

The shift from agricultural to urban society

Another aspect of the Industrial Revolution was the shift in human endeavor from growing food to manufacturing objects. Throughout the eighteenth and nineteenth centuries, the majority of people in Europe and the United States were engaged in some aspect of raising food, either for themselves or to sell to others. In the twentieth century, that percentage fell dramatically as a result of new opportunities for work in cities, largely created by industrialization. The number of farmers also decreased as a result of advances in productivity due to the introduction of farm machines, improved farming techniques, and scientific developments such as the creation of artificial fertilizers.

In the first census of the United States, taken in 1790, about 95 percent of the population lived in rural areas (with 5 percent living in cities); by 2000 that figure had declined to just over 20 percent living in rural areas (with 80 percent in larger towns and cities). That someone lives in an urban area does not mean he is engaged in industry, just as someone who lives in a rural area is not necessarily a farmer; a person might live in a city or rural area and serve the people who work in industry or who farm. Since the end of World War II, the greatest change in the U.S. economy has been the growth of this service sector: jobs that are not involved in manufacturing or agriculture, but rather in delivering some type of service. Examples of service industries include health care, financial services such as banking and insurance companies, education, and entertainment (music, movies, video).

Since 1950, service occupations have been the fastest-growing job category in the United States. So strong is the service sector that the percentage of Americans engaged in industrial jobs actually declined in the second half of the twentieth century. Many of these jobs moved to other countries, especially in South Asia (including Malaysia, Indonesia, the Philippines, and India), where few people prior to mid-century worked in industry (the Industrial Revolution didn't come to some of these countries until the twentieth century; see below). Of course, not all industrial jobs have moved overseas: American factories still produce vast quantities of goods ranging from fabric to cars.

A strong argument could be made that this shift away from manufacturing represents the end—or the beginning of the end—of the industrial era in the United States. In western Europe (England, France, Germany, Spain, Italy, Belgium, Holland, Norway, Sweden, and Denmark, for example) a similar trend has taken place. Industrial work is still growing in the countries of eastern Europe (Poland, Hungary, Bulgaria, Romania, and Ukraine, for example) and Asia.

Economists, politicians, and labor union leaders argue over the implications of the shift from manufacturing to service. Can a country like the United States continue to prosper if people are engaged in helping one another, or entertaining one another, while people in other countries are turning raw materials into products? Can new industries based on intellect (thinking), such as pharmaceuticals (medical drugs) and computer software, replace manufacturing as an economic engine? If the answer is yes, then education and training will continue to be important to the future of both individuals and the entire society.

A changing worldview: The idea of progress

In the 1950s the General Electric Company (GE) had a slogan presented on television commercials: "At GE, progress is our most important product." Until the Industrial Revolution, people had little idea of progress. They lived their lives according to the natural cycle of seasons: planting crops in the spring, tending them in summer, harvesting them in fall, getting ready to plant in winter, year after year, century after century.

But with the Industrial Revolution, this cyclical notion of time changed to seeing time as a line, moving from one event to the next, one new invention to the next, each invention bigger, faster, better, improving on the one before. And so life began to be seen as moving forward and generally upward. If progress is the essence of industrialization, then the Industrial Revolution has not yet stopped.

It has been many years since the last important mechanical innovation of the type associated with the Industrial Revolution. Older machines see continuous improvements. But what about the discontinuous innovations, those technologies that seem to rise out of nowhere and change the world. Do they exist today? Perhaps, in the form of computers.

What about computers?

Do computers fit into the Industrial Revolution? Or do they represent a new revolution all on their own? From the time when modern computers were first developed in the 1930s, they have shrunk in size (they used to fill an entire room) and increased in power (early on they were only simple calculators), and they are now everywhere.

In industry, computer technology can be considered as just one step in the long string of improvements to machinery. In the first decade of the twenty-first century, more than half the homes in the United States had a personal computer, and nearly all electronic devices are run by a microchip. A microchip, the fundamental component of a computer, is faster and more reliable than a human being when it comes to coordinating the complex processes required to operate an automated machine. Today the very word automated means that a human being has been replaced by a microchip. Questions still arise, however, about whether a computer can replace a human brain. Face recognition programs, for instance, can be programmed to scan a crowd of people, looking for particular individuals. Programs such as these still need to be created by human beings, but they do demonstrate how a computer can process information quicker and more accurately than can the human brain.

Are computers, then, driving a third stage in the Industrial Revolution? Certainly, factory owners are attracted to the notion of reducing the cost of labor by using computers, the same motivation that led to adoption of most improvements to machines and indeed to the invention of machinery in the first place. And considering that machines have been supplementing, or replacing, human physical power since the eighteenth century, is the replacement of human mental power nothing more (or less) than the next, and perhaps last, stage of the Industrial Revolution?

The revolution marches on: Asia

At the beginning of the twenty-first century, while Europeans and Americans are wondering about the future, or even the present, status of industrialization, some parts of Asia are experiencing for the first time the rapid socioeconomic changes that transformed Europe and North America a century earlier. The story of an industrial revolution in Asia is quite different from that of Europe and North America, however. In Asia, industrialization was largely imported from the West.

Japan

In the mid-nineteenth century, life in Japan had changed little from the preceding two centuries. Japan had experienced none of the intellectual and economic revitalization that occurred in Europe starting in about 1400. Since the mid-1600s, Japan had been ruled by a powerful military leader called a shogun.

In 1851 American navy commodore Matthew C. Perry (1794–1858) was chosen to lead a naval expedition to Japan with the purpose of "opening" Japan to trade. Previously, Western contact with the country was limited to one Dutch trading ship allowed to land each year. The Americans had three goals: to establish Japan as a station where they could take on more supplies of coal for steamships, to assure better treatment for shipwrecked American sailors, and to open trade.

Matthew C. Perry of the U.S. Navy inadvertently brought the Industrial Revolution to Japan by insisting that the Japanese agree to let Navy ships refuel there; Japan imported technology and reformed its society to join the list of industrialized nations. *Reproduced by permission of the Library of Congress.*

Perry arrived in Japan two years later (1853) with a force of five ships. He was determined to persuade Japan's leaders to abandon 250 years of isolation from the world. His success in doing so was remarkable. In the last half of the nineteenth century, Japan's rulers made a conscious decision to transform the country over a short period of time from a traditional rural society into a modern industrial state. They imported Western technology and manufacturing techniques on a large scale, so that fifty years after Perry's expedition Japan had become a leading industrial power. Japan's success was demonstrated in 1904 when it went to war with Russia to achieve influence over Korea and Manchuria (part of China). Japan defeated Russia within a year and established control over the previously Russian-occupied Liaotung peninsula, which juts out into the Yellow Sea between mainland China and the Korean peninsula. By 1941 Japan was so powerful it felt that it could challenge the United States for influence in Asia and attacked Pearl Harbor on December 7, 1941.

After the United States dropped two atomic bombs on Japan in August 1945 to bring World War II to an end, Japan underwent a second rapid transition, to a Western-style democracy. The transition was overseen by the United States military, which governed Japan from 1945 to 1951 and imposed a new constitution that reduced the role of the emperor and instituted democratic rule, much like countries of Western Europe or the United States.

In one hundred years, Japan had imported both an economic system and a political system, making it one of the foremost industrial powers in the world. By 2000, the three largest Japanese car makers (Toyota, Honda, Nissan) challenged their U.S. counterparts (General Motors, Ford, and DaimlerChrysler) for market domination in the United States.

China

China's reaction to meeting the industrialized West was quite different from Japan's. The Chinese had encountered Europeans as early as 1271, when the Italian explorer Marco Polo (1254–1324) opened a land route to establish trade. For hundreds of years, China carefully limited contact with the West. As European powers found sea routes to Asia, China responded by establishing special trading ports, such as Hong Kong, but still limiting Western influence.

Limiting Western influence worked, to the extent that it delayed China's introduction to industrialization, for awhile. By 1900, however, Russia was expanding eastward, helped in part by the establishment of the trans-Siberian railroad (extending from the capital of Russia in the west to the Pacific coast of Russia in the east) while Japan was pressing to extend its influence over Korea and Manchuria.

In the twentieth century, China's isolation from industrialization ended. Today, Chinese factories produce a wide range of goods sold throughout the world, and China's economy is growing rapidly. Unlike in the west, however, where changes in government followed industrialization, in China the government instituted industrialization. The Chinese Communist Party, which came to power in 1948 and has held it ever since, oversaw the start of the shift from a rural agricultural society to an urban, industrial one. In the west, by contrast, communism, an economic philosophy under which the people own all property in common, arose as a reaction to the Industrial Revolution, not as a driving force of it.

Indonesia, Malaysia, the Philippines

The story of industrialization in Indonesia, Malaysia, and the Philippines is quite different from that of either Japan or China. The revolutions in Southeast Asia were almost entirely imported—arriving usually in the form of textile factories—into countries whose main resource so far has proved to be large numbers of people willing to work for small sums of money. Workers, many of them girls or women, sew inexpensive clothing sold in shopping malls across Europe and America. Like in England and the United States, people in Southeast Asia who might once have worked on farms now spend their days in factories earning low wages, while some social activists in the United States and Europe picket retail chains for selling articles made under conditions that exploit workers.

Does industrialization inevitably follow the same path everywhere? Despite the low salaries (by U.S. standards), will the Southeast Asian economies grow over time, just as the United States has evolved from a country with low wages into one with a large middle class? Will the emerging population of urban workers in Southeast Asia successfully push for more political power, just as American workers did in the period from 1830 to 1932? Is it a fundamental feature of industrialization to start with a factory and end up a century later with a society that looks something like the United States or western Europe? Will the time frame be similar, or will social and political changes follow more quickly? These questions remain unanswered.

The Middle East, Africa, and Central and South America

While the nature and speed of an industrial revolution in Asia remains a question, what about the areas of the world where industrialization is not really a factor, areas such as the Middle East, Africa, and Central and South America?

The Middle East

The story of the Industrial Revolution and the Middle East can be told in one word: oil. The largest country (in land area) of the Middle East, Saudi Arabia, also has the world's largest known reserves of underground petroleum. Saudi Arabia on its own has enough reserves to ensure the world's oil supply well into the future. Other countries in the region that also have significant supplies of oil include Iraq, Iran, and Kuwait. But throughout the twentieth century and into the twenty-first, the role of these nations in industrialization has been limited to supplying that one key raw material: oil.

There are several possible explanations for the limited extent of industrialization in the Middle East. One has to do with population. Saudi Arabia, although it covers a large land area, is sparsely populated, with an estimated twelve million people at the turn of the twenty-first century. The population of Iraq is estimated at about sixteen million (less than metropolitan New York, whose population is about twenty-one million); and Iran is thought to have around forty-eight million.

Another explanation is cultural. Most of the Arab-speaking states of the region were part of the Turkish Ottoman Empire (1300–1922), which, in effect, covered most of the Islamic world up to the end of World War I (1914–18). To a great extent, the Ottoman Empire was isolated from the rest of the world and did not go through any of the changes associated with the Renaissance (a period of heightened scholarly and scientific pursuits in Europe, from about 1400 to 1700) and the Industrial Revolution. The role of Islam in the development of Ottoman society (and thus, Middle Eastern society generally) is a subject of debate. What is clear is that adherence to Islam includes closely following social rules recorded in detail in the seventh century by Muhammad (c. 570–632), the founder of the Muslim religion. Some authorities wonder whether these rules are compatible with an industrial society. For example, Islam bars charging interest on loans, that is, the lender charging a borrower a small fee for using the lender's money. Is it feasible to build an in-

Oil flows from this derrick in Iran in 1910. The story of the Industrial Revolution in the Middle East can be told in one word: oil. *Reproduced by permission of the Library of Congress.*

dustrial economy, which requires investing large sums of money, without permitting interest-bearing loans?

Africa

The northern strip of Africa bordering on the Mediterranean Sea is also a region shaped largely by the Ottoman Empire. Countries in the central and southern part of Africa have almost entirely missed the impact of the Industrial Revolution. Many parts of Africa were European colonies from the 1700s until around 1960. European industrial countries viewed these colonies (and others in Asia, such as Vietnam) as sources of raw materials, not as places to establish factories. Whether African states will in the future support an industrial economy remains to be seen. Since the 1950s, Europeans and Americans looking to find inexpensive sources of labor for their factories have gone to southern Asia. The possibility of African countries raising enough money to launch their own industrial revolution seems remote, at least in the early years of the twenty-first century.

Central and South America

For the most part, the countries of Central and South America, like those of Africa, have not participated in the Industrial Revolution. Exceptions would be Chile, Argentina, Peru, Venezuela, and to a lesser extent, Brazil. The reasons for this are similar to the case of Africa. Much of South America was under the rule of Spain until the early nineteenth century. Unlike English colonies in North America, which attracted large numbers of European immigrants eager to industrialize, Spanish colonies generally remained only a source of raw materials, especially gold. Although most Spanish colonies in the western hemisphere achieved independence during the eighteenth century, they were not in a position to attract capital (money to invest in factories) and large populations of workers to support industrialization on a huge scale. In addition, by the turn of the twenty-first century, South America remained south of the main trade routes connecting Europe and North America. Many South American countries have natural features, such as the Andes Mountains or the rainforests of Brazil, that make them inhospitable to large populations or easy transportation.

Agricultural exports, such as coffee, are important to some South American nations, and thus many people work the farms. In the last quarter of the twentieth century, however, some American manufacturers established textile plants in South America (notably in Peru) to take advantage of the region's relative poverty and low wage rates. Working against industrialization in the region is the illegal drug trade. While illicit drugs (notably cocaine) generate huge fortunes for criminals, little of this money makes its way into the economies of countries like Colombia or Peru, where the drugs are cultivated in large measure to serve a market in the United States.

The Industrial Revolution and human psychology

Generations after the American system of manufacturing—with its interchangeable parts and moving assembly line—was introduced, there is evidence that human beings are adapting to the system. In thousands of U.S. classrooms, teachers follow detailed guidelines on what to teach their students, knowing that at the end of the year all students will take the same test to see whether they have learned the same things. Equality in access to education notwithstanding, one argument in favor of such standardized tests is to assure employers that all students coming from the public schools have the same knowledge. Is there an unspoken desire for the schools to produce interchangeable parts?

The fundamental idea of the factory—identical products produced by those working on an assembly line—had by the twenty-first century permeated everyday life. Even food is produced in facilities that are more like factories than farms. Some chickens, for example, are raised in cages and are fed a diet shown to maximize their output (pounds of meat) per input (feed). They are then processed, cooked, and canned or frozen for use at home or in chain restaurants, where all menus are the same and all meals are assembled by workers trained in an identical manner and served to customers who know exactly what they are getting.

The lifestyle brought about by the Industrial Revolution isn't remarkable: it is standard.

For More Information

Books

Bairoch, Paul. *Economics and World History: Myths and Paradoxes.* Chicago: University of Chicago Press, 1993.

Beckmann, George M. *The Modernization of China and Japan*. New York: Harper and Row, 1962.

Chapman, William. *Inventing Japan: The Making of a Postwar Civilization*. New York: Prentice Hall, 1991.

Cohen, Theodore. *Remaking Japan: The American Occupation as New Deal*. New York: Free Press, 1987.

Department of Economic and Social Affairs, Population Division. *World Urbanization Prospects: The 1999 Revision*. New York: United Nations, 2001.

Eckstein, Alexander. *China's Economic Revolution*. New York: Cambridge University Press, 1977.

Fieldhouse, D. K. *The West and the Third World: Trade, Colonialism, Dependence, and Development*. Oxford, UK: Blackwell, 1999.

Johansen, Bruce E. *The Global Warming Desk Reference*. Westport, CT: Greenwood Press, 2002.

Madeley, John. *Big Business, Poor Peoples: The Impact of Transnational Corporations on the World's Poor*. New York: Zed Books, 1999.

McCuen, Marnie. *The World Environment and the Global Economy*. Hudson, WI: Gary E. McCuen Publications, 1999.

Minami, Ryoshin. *The Economic Development of Japan: A Quantitative Study*. New York: St. Martin's Press, 1986.

Morgan, Sally. *Global Warming*. Chicago: Heinemann Library, 2003.

Vernberg, F. John, and Winona Vernberg. *The Coastal Zone: Past, Present, and Future*. Columbia: University of South Carolina Press, 2001.

Periodicals

Britten, Daniel. "Progress and the Invisible Hand: The Philosophy and Economics of Human Advance." *New Statesman,* July 31, 1998, p. 48.

"The Brown Revolution: Urbanisation." *Economist,* May 11, 2002.

Egan, Timothy. "Alaska, No Longer So Frigid, Starts to Crack, Burn and Sag." *New York Times,* June 16, 2002, p. 1.

Forrant, Robert. "The Rise of 'the Rest': Challenges to the West from Late-Industrialization Economies." *Business History Review,* Winter 2001, p. 922.

Gille, Sarah T. "Warming of the Southern Ocean Since the 1950s." *Science,* February 15, 2002, p. 1275.

Kaplan, Morton A., and Robert Selle. "The Emergence of a Global Society." *World and I,* September 1998, p. 18.

Mitchell, John G. "Urban Sprawl." *National Geographic,* July 2001, p. 48.

Revkin, Andrew C. "With White House Approval, E.P.A. Pollution Report Omits Global Warming Section." *New York Times,* September 15, 2002, p. 22.

Web Sites

Buntrock, Dana. "Without Modernity: Japan's Challenging Modernization." *Architronic: The Electronic Journal of Architecture.* http://architronic.saed.kent.edu/PDF/v5n3/v5n3_02.pdf (accessed February 21, 2003).

Clark, Gregory. "The Spread of the Industrial Revolution, 1860–2000." *University of California at Davis: Department of Economics.* http://www.econ.ucdavis.edu/faculty/gclark/ecn110b/readings/chapter5-2002.pdf (accessed February 21, 2003).

"The Long Road to Kyoto: A Brief History of Global Warming and Public Policy." *University of Virginia: Computer Science.* http://www.cs.virginia.edu/~jones/tmp352/projects98/group12/gw4.htm (accessed February 21, 2003).

Urbinato, David. "London's Historic 'Pea-Soupers.'" *U.S. Environmental Protection Agency.* http://www.epa.gov/history/topics/perspect/london.htm (accessed February 21, 2003).

Index

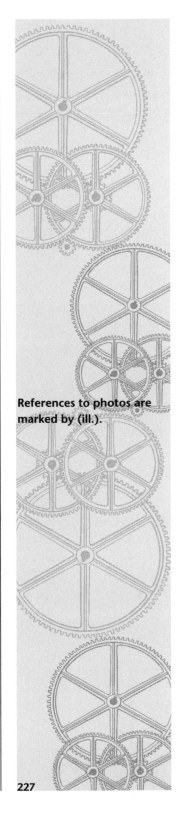

References to photos are marked by (ill.).

Andrews, Samuel 166
Animals 209–210. *See also* Horses
Appert, Nicholas-François 137
Apprentices 10
Aristocracy. *See also* Feudalism;
    Medieval period
    definition of 10
    democracy and 6–7
    Enlightenment and 21–22
    industrialization and 4
    Parliament and 86–87
    progress and 6–7
    religion and 13, 19–20
Arkwright, Richard 72 (ill.)
    cotton mill of 109
    spinning machine and 72, 110
    textile factory of 77, 91
Art 13–14
Ashley, Anthony Ashley Cooper,
    Lord 90–91
Asia 193, 214–215, 216–219. See
    also *specific countries*
Assembly lines 145 (ill.), 173
    (ill.)
    American system and 145, 146
    definition of 144
    Henry Ford and 147, 148–151
    standardization and 223
Automation 210, 216
Automobiles 114 (ill.), 145 (ill.),
    149 (ill.), 150 (ill.)
    air pollution and 152–153, 212
    assembly lines and 147,
        148–151
    competition and 218
    internal combustion engine
        and 115–116
    oil and 3, 151
    society and 116, 151–154, 158
    tires and 132

B

Baekeland, Leo 132
Bakelite 132
Bakunin, Mikhail 101
Beau de Rochas, Alphonse-Eu-
    gène 114
Bell, Alexander Graham 119
    (ill.), 120
Benz, Karl 148

Bessemer, Henry 129–130, 130
    (ill.)
Bessemer process 129–130, 131
    (ill.), 161
Bibles 16–17, 120
Binfield, Kevin 94
Blenkinsop, John 54–55
Boilers 36, 37, 39–40, 42
Bonaparte, Napoléon 95, 97,
    137, 209
Boulton, Matthew 48
Boulton and Watt 59, 60
Bourgeoisie 103
Brakes 126
Brown, Moses 110
Bryan, William Jennings 186
Burton, Emanuel 95
Business 4–5, 6–7, 176, 188, 196.
    See also Finance

C

Cadillac Motor Car Company
    148
Calhoun, John C. 195–196
Canals 51–52, 58
Canning 137–138
Capital 100
Capital 102. *See also* Finance
Capitalism 29–30, 76, 84,
    102–103, 172
Capitalists 102–103. See also *spe-
    cific capitalists*
Carnegie, Andrew 4, 130,
    160–165, 161 (ill.), 168
Carnegie Hall 164
Carnegie-Mellon University 164
Carnegie Steel Company
    161–164
Carnot, Nicholas Sadi 138
Carrier, Willis 140
Cartwright, Edmond 75
Cartwright, William 95
Catch-Me-Who-Can 54
Caus, Salomon de 38
Celluloid 132
Central America 222–223
Charles II 40, 44
Charter Gasoline Engine Compa-
    ny 136
Chartists 97–98
Chemistry 130–133, 134, 139

Henry, Joseph 118
Henry Ford Company 148
Henry the Navigator, Prince 14
Hero 38
Homestead Strike 161–163
Homfray, Samuel 54
Hoover, Herbert 203
Horses 5 (ill.)
  agriculture and 135, 136
  coal mines and 41
  machines and 209–210
  railroads and 51, 53
  spinning machines and 72
  transportation and 158
Horsfall, William 94–95
Hours
  children and 4, 85, 86, 89, 91
  factory system and 4, 78, 85, 86,
    89, 91, 92, 150, 173, 179, 182
  labor unions and 179–182, 187
  strikes and 179, 182, 187
Housing 78, 80, 174–175,
    180–181, 200 (ill.)
How the Other Half Lives 162
Hull House 191–192
Hulls, Jonathan 56
Hume, David 21, 22, 29
Huygens, Christian 44, 114
Hyatt, John Wesley 132

I

Immigration 176–177, 199
India 68
Individualism 176
Indonesia 219
Industrialization (definition of) 64
Industrial Revolution
  beginning of 9–12
  first stage of 1, 112
  overview of 1–2, 209–212
  second stage of 1, 107–108,
    112, 205
  third stage of 2, 193, 215–216
Institute for the Formation of
  Character 92
Interchangeable parts. *See also*
  Standardization
  assembly lines and 145–146,
    146–147
  definition of 144
  humans as 4, 80–81, 223

Interest 19, 220–221. *See also* Finance
Internal combustion engines 1,
  3, 113–116, 148
International Harvester 168
International trade 217, 218. *See
  also* Colonialism; Mercantilism
Internet 2, 117, 154, 155. *See also*
  Computers
Inventions 112, 215–216. See
  also *specific inventions*
Investment. *See* Finance
Iran 220, 221 (ill.)
Iraq 220
Iron. *See also* Steel
  coal and 49, 52
  railroads and 52–53, 157, 161
  steam engines and 45
  steel and 127–130
Islam 220–221

J

Jackson, Andrew 195
Japan 205, 217–218
Jefferson, Thomas 20, 48, 108
Jet engine 57
Joffroy d'Abbans, Marquis de 56
John (king of England) 20
Jolliet, Louis 52
Jones, George 184
Jones, Mary Harris (Mother
  Jones) 182 (ill.), 183–184
The Jungle 163

K

Kay, John 72, 75
Kelly, William 129–130
Knights of Labor 179–182, 191
Kuwait 220

L

Labor 80 (ill.), 133 (ill.), 183
  (ill.), 187 (ill.), 189 (ill.). *See
  also* Labor unions

anarchism and 179–182
benefits for 173–174, 188, 189–190, 191
competition and 93–96
cottage industries and 66–67
factory system and 4, 78–81, 84–85, 85–86
government regulates 103–104, 179, 188–189, 196, 202–205
government suppresses 103–104, 162, 178–179, 179–183, 187, 188, 189–190
guild system and 10, 27–29, 103
immigration and 176–177
as interchangeable parts 4, 80–81, 223
lockouts of 92
Luddites and 93–96
management of 152–153
rights of 6–7
socialism and 96–97, 176, 179–182, 184, 186, 190
textiles and 93–96
voluntary associations of 190–191

Labor unions. *See also* Labor; Strikes
American Federation of Labor 184, 185 (ill.), 185–186, 188
American Railway Union 180–181
business opposition to 161–162, 176
coal and 182–184, 186–188, 189–190
Congress of Industrial Organizations 186, 188–189
definition of 172, 210
early examples of 92–93, 102–104
government and 103–104, 178–179, 181, 186, 188–189, 203–204, 205
Grand National Consolidated Trade Union 92
growth of 177–178
Haymarket Square Riot and 179–182
Homestead Strike and 161–163
hours and 179–182, 187
Knights of Labor 179–182, 191

Luddites and 95
as monopolies 181
Pullman strike and 180–181
purpose of 175–176, 186
railroads and 180–181
United Mine Workers Union 184, 186–188, 189–190
violence and 162–163, 179–183
voluntary associations 190–191
wages and 95, 161–163, 178, 180–181
Lacy, Charles 94
Laissez-faire 10, 29–30, 192
Land 23–24
Latin America 222–223
Laws. *See* Government regulation
Lenoir, Jean-Joseph-Étienne 114
Leonardo da Vinci 13
Lewis, John L. 186–188, 189–190
Lighting
electricity and 123, 125, 127
gas and 121
General Electric and 168
standardization and 155
Literacy 16–17. *See also* Education
Livingston, Robert 58, 60
Locke, John 20, 21
Lockouts 92
London Workingman's Association 97
Looms 64, 68–69, 75–76
Louisiana Purchase 108
Louis Phillipe (king of France) 100
Louis XVI 97
Lovett, William 97
Ludd, Ned 93–94
Luddites 93–96, 175
Lunar Society 48
Luther, Martin 18–19

M

MacArthur, Douglas 203
Machiavelli, Niccolò 13–14, 14 (ill.)
Machines. See also *specific machines*
energy and 33–34, 47f

engines compared with 47
humans and 209–212
interchangeable parts and 146
textiles and 1, 63–66
Magna Carta 6, 20
Malaysia 219
Malthus, Thomas 83–84, 85 (ill.)
Management 147, 152–153
Manchester Literary and Philo-
    sophical Society 91–92
Mannucci, Aldo 17
Manufacturing 145 (ill.). *See also*
    Factory system
    American system of 144–147,
        223
    Henry Ford and 147, 148–151
    plows and 135–136
    society and 213–215
    technology and 3
*The Manufacturing Population of
    England* 85–86
Marquette, Père 52
Marx, Karl 99 (ill.), 99–103
Marxism 99–103. *See also* Social-
    ism
Mass production 144. *See also*
    Factory system; Manufactur-
    ing
McBride, John 186
McClure's magazine 163, 167
McCormick, Cyrus 134–135, 136
    (ill.), 168, 179
McCormick Harvester 179
Mechanical power 3. *See also* Ma-
    chines
Medieval period. *See also* Aristoc-
    racy; Feudalism
    alchemy in 130
    definition of 10
    government in 87
    religion during 13, 14
    Renaissance and 12
    wealth and 22
Mercantilism 10, 20–21, 26–27,
    29–30, 76. *See also* Colonial-
    ism
Merchants 27–29, 67
Metallurgy 127–130. *See also*
    Bessemer process; Steel
Mexican-American War 108
Michelangelo 13
Microchips 210, 216. *See also*
    Computers

Middle Ages. *See* Medieval period
Middle East 151, 220–221
Middleton Railway 52
Military 205
Miller, Patrick 56
Mills 109–111. *See also* Factory
    system; Textiles
Model T 147, 149 (ill.), 149–150,
    150 (ill.)
Monopolies. *See also* Competition
    competition and 4, 156, 162,
        163, 167, 168–169, 197–199
    definition of 144, 172
    government regulation and 4,
        163, 167, 197–199
    J. P. Morgan and 168–169
    labor unions as 181
    muckrakers and 162, 163
    oil and 163, 166–167, 198–199
    railroads and 156, 167,
        197–198
    steel and 168–169
More, Sir Thomas 24
Morgan, J. P. 4, 164, 167–169,
    168 (ill.)
Morgan, Junius Spencer 168
Morland, Samuel 44
Morse, Samuel F. B. 117 (ill.),
    117–120
Morse Code 118 (ill.), 119–120,
    124
Motors. *See* Engines
Movies 133
Muckrakers 144, 162–163
Muhammad 220

N

Napoléon I 95, 97, 137, 209
National Labor Relations Act
    188–189, 203–204
National Labor Relations Board
    203
Native Americans 112, 134, 196
Natural gas 121
Natural law
    control over 140
    definition of 10
    scientific revolution and 14–16
    socialism and 99, 100
    society and 20
Nautilus 58

factory system and 76–78, 146
industrialization and 4
steam engines and 41–42,
44–45
textiles and 67, 71, 75, 76–78,
93, 112
Progress 6–7, 215–216
Proletariat 103
Property 20, 99, 100–101
Protestantism 17–20
Pullman, George 180, 181
Pullman strike 180–181
Pumps 7, 39, 41–43

Q

Quadricycle 148

R

Railroads 53 (ill.), 133 (ill.), 157
(ill.). *See also* Steam locomotives
agriculture and 137, 157
Andrew Carnegie and 160–161
brakes and 126
coal and 51–53, 157
competition and 167, 197–198
development of 50–53
factory system and 52
finance and 154–155,
159–160, 168
food and 121
government and 155, 197–198
Great Northern Railroad
197–198
growth of 156–160
iron and 52–53, 157, 161
labor unions and 180–181
monopolies and 156, 167,
197–198
networks and 154–155,
155–156, 156–160
New York Central Railroad 159
Northern Pacific Railroad
197–198
Northern Securities Company
197–198
Pennsylvania Railroad 160–161
Pullman strike and 180–181

refrigeration and 139–140
standardization and 155–156,
158–159
steam locomotives and 52,
53–56
steel and 130, 163
Stockton and Darlington Rail-
way 55
strikes and 180–181
telegraph and 117, 120, 121
transportation and 50–53, 158
trucking and 153–154, 158
Ramsay, David 38–39
Rawfords Mill 94, 95
Rayon 132
Reapers 134–135
Recessions 193, 199–205, 201
(ill.)
Reform Bill of 1832 88–89
Refrigeration 138–140
Regulation. *See* Government regulation
Religion
Enlightenment and 21, 22
God in 13, 14, 19–20
Islam 220–221
Medieval period and 13, 14
printing press and 16–17
Protestantism 17–20
Reformation and 17–20
Robert Owen and 93
Roman Catholic Church 13,
16–17, 17–20, 21
scientific revolution and 14–15
Renaissance
definition of 10
democracy and 20
England and 40
Enlightenment and 21–22
literacy and 16–17
Middle East and 220
navigation and 14, 20–21
overview of 12–14
progress and 7
Reformation and 17–20
scientific revolution and 13,
14–16, 40, 130–131
steam and 38–41
Republican Party 188, 196, 205
Revolution. *See also* Industrial
Revolution
American Revolution 9, 30, 48,
209

French Revolution 9, 48, 88, 95, 96, 97, 209
  Marxism and 99–103
  Russian Revolution 9, 101, 203
  scientific 13, 14–16, 40, 130–131
  socialism and 96–97
Reynolds, Richard 53
Riis, Jacob 162
Robber barons 4, 144, 157, 160. See also *specific robber barons*
Robison, John 45
Rockefeller, John D. 4, 165–167, 166 (ill.), 169, 198–199
Rods 36, 37, 41, 113
Roman Catholic Church 13, 16–17, 17–20, 21
Roman Empire 12–13
Roosevelt, Franklin Delano 163, 179, 193, 202–205
Roosevelt, Theodore 198 (ill.)
  monopolies and 167, 197–199
  Mother Jones and 184
  muckrakers and 162, 163
Rousseau, Jean-Jacques 21
Rubber 132
Rumsey, James 57
Russia 9, 101, 203, 217–218
Russo-Japanese War 217–218

S

Sadler, Michael 89–90, 93
Sadler Report 89–90
Salt 139
Saudi Arabia 220
Savannah 60–61
Savery, Thomas 42–43
Science
  chemistry and 130–133
  empiricism of 10, 15, 22, 48
  energy and 34
  industrialization and 210
  Lunar Society and 48
  management and 152–153
  metallurgy and 127–130
  Reformation and 18, 19
  Renaissance and 13, 14–16, 40, 130–131
Scythes 135
Service economy 210, 214–215
Seven Years War 23, 30

Sherman Antitrust Act 163, 167, 197–199. *See also* Monopolies
Shipping. *See* Navigation
Sinclair, Upton 163
Slater, Samuel 109–110, 110 (ill.), 192
Slavery 64, 65 (ill.), 74, 108–109
Small, William 48
Smith, Adam 10, 29, 30, 192, 193 (ill.)
Sobrero, Ascanio 131
Socialism. *See also* Communism
  Chartists and 97–98
  definition of 84, 172
  Franklin D. Roosevelt and 204–205
  labor and 96–97, 176, 179–182, 184, 186, 190
  Marxism and 99–103
  wealth and 96–97
Social reform 91–93
Social security 193, 203
Social work 172, 191–192
Society
  automobiles and 116, 151–154, 158
  factory system and 2, 3–6, 64–66, 78–81, 83–86, 171–175
  Great Depression and 199–205
  immigration and 199
  Luddites and 95
  manufacturing and 213–215
  Marxism and 102–103
  natural law and 20
  progress and 6–7
  standardization and 223
  steam locomotives and 55–56
  textiles and 64–66, 78–81
  wealth and 4, 164–165
Somerset, Edward 39–40, 41–42
South America 222–223
"South Carolina Exposition and Protest" 195
Spain 222
Specialization 78–79, 146
Spinning 70 (ill.), 71 (ill.)
  cottage industries and 66–67
  definition of 28, 64
  machines 67, 69–73, 74–75, 109–110
  process of 68

Telegraph 115 (ill.), 117 (ill.), 118 (ill.)
  development of 117–120
  electricity and 116–117, 118–119
  factory system and 117, 121
  finance and 120
  growth of 120
  impact of 121–122
  networks and 154, 155
  patents and 124
  railroads and 117, 120, 121
  Thomas Alva Edison and 124
  transportation and 117, 120, 121

Telephones 117, 119 (ill.), 120–122, 155, 156

Tennessee Valley Authority 202–203

Tesla, Nikola 125–127, 126 (ill.), 127

Textiles 80 (ill.), 90 (ill.), 111 (ill.). *See also* Spinning; Weaving
  agriculture and 63, 66, 108–109, 222
  Asia and 219
  children and 63, 65, 77, 79–80, 89–91, 219
  clothmaking process 67–69
  competition and 93–96
  cottage industries and 28–29, 63, 66–67, 78
  cotton and 66, 67
  dangers of 173
  definition of 64
  dyes for 131
  enclosure movement and 66–67, 76, 79
  factory system and 63–66, 76–78, 90–91, 192, 219, 222
  government regulation and 109–110
  labor and 93–96
  Luddites and 93–96
  mechanization of 1, 63–66, 67–76, 109–111
  Mother Jones and 184
  productivity and 67, 71, 75, 76–78, 93, 112
  society and 64–66, 78–81
  specialization and 78–79
  steam engines and 72, 75–76, 109, 112
  tariffs and 194–196
  wages and 79, 80
  water and 72, 75, 76, 109, 110
  wool and 66, 67

"Texts of the Nottinghamshire Luddites" 94

Thoreau, Henry David 81

Time 6–7, 215

Tires 132

Torpedoes 59–60

Toynbee, Arnold 11

Toynbee House 191

Tractors 136

Trade 217, 218. *See also* Colonialism; Mercantilism

Trade unions. *See* Labor unions

Trains. *See* Railroads

Transportation. *See also* Automobiles; Navigation; Railroads
  agriculture and 137, 157
  automobiles and 151, 158
  energy and 34
  oil and 3, 151
  overview of 3, 158
  railroads and 50–53, 158
  steamboats and 56–61, 158
  steam engines and 3, 50, 158
  steam locomotives and 52, 53–56, 158
  steel and 130
  telegraph and 117, 120, 121
  trucking and 153–154, 158

Treatise on the Improvement of Canal Navigation, A 58

Trevithick, Richard 53–54

Triangle Shirtwaist Company 173, 174 (ill.)

Trucking 153–154, 158

Truman, Harry 190, 205

Trusts. *See* Monopolies

Tull, Jethro 25

Tuskegee Institute 164

Twenty Years at Hull-House 191–192

Two Treatises on Government 20

U

U.S. Congress
  Clayton Antitrust Act 197